Architectural Systems

Architectural Systems

A Needs, Resources, and Design Approach

Ezra D. Ehrenkrantz

McGraw-Hill Publishing Company
New York St. Louis San Francisco Auckland Bogotá
Caracas Hamburg Lisbon London Madrid Mexico
Milan Montreal New Delhi Oklahoma City
Paris San Juan São Paulo Singapore
Sydney Tokyo Toronto

Library of Congress Cataloging in Publication Data

Ehrenkrantz, Ezra.
   Architectural systems.

   Includes index.
   1. Architecture—Information services.   2. Industrialized building.
3. Modular coordination (Architecture)   4. Information storage and
retrieval systems—Architecture.   5. Information storage and retrieval
systems—Building.   I. Title.
NA1995.E37   1989   720'.285   89-8161
ISBN 0-07-019100-X

ISBN 0-07-019100-X

The editors for this book were Joel Stein and Caroline Levine,
the designer was Naomi Auerbach, and the production supervisor
was Richard Ausburn. It was set in Auriga by Progressive Typographers.

Printed and bound by Halliday Lithograph Corporation

*For more information about other McGraw-Hill materials,
call 1-800-2-MCGRAW in the United States. In other
countries, call your nearest McGraw-Hill office.*

Contents

Part Four / Conclusion

Preface

The desire to write this book began over 10 years ago when the lessons learned in the process of developing a number of different building systems made it obvious that the building industry is not structured to provide an appropriate environment for society's needs and aspirations. The initial programs, which focused on housing, health, and education showed that when there was a common purpose, accepted goals could be achieved. However, it required a major innovative effort, propitious timing, and the ability to engage groups to work together who normally do not communicate with one another. Unfortunately, these projects were considered unique and special instead of part of a normal search to optimize the use of our resources on behalf of agreed-upon goals. In the process of initiating and learning from these research and development programs, it became obvious that our society is not structured to permit the building industry to do its best. Legislative and economic actions frequently undermine the ability of the industry to improve its productivity and responsiveness. The result is continued fragmentation, not only of the building industry, but of those who regulate, finance, and use it as well. We do not have a system which, upon identifying national goals and objectives, can work effectively to achieve those goals. The understanding of the building industry as a system and the way in which it works is critical to its effective orchestration.

The book attempts to provide a sense of the industry through discussion of principles and lessons derived from experience and by reviewing case studies of a number of projects. The industry is seen through the eyes of an architect who believes the ethics of our profession required that through design we must try to balance society's needs and aspirations for the physical environment with available resources. This belief has resulted in the articulation of a systems approach to design which is applicable at any level, i.e., the design of products, buildings, or whole neighborhoods.

The designer must establish an understanding of the context in which we work. However, the "designer" may also be the Congress, a bank, the product manufacturer, the developer, and many others, as well as the architect and the engineer. Design is therefore carried out by a combination of many different actors, most of whom do not even realize that they are playing a design role and most of whom certainly do not carry liability insurance. The framework they establish for design affects the work at least as much as the architect and the engineer. Within this industry framework, the larger building systems projects described in the book began to provide the basis for the development of a new design philosophy and a concern for outreach to the inadvertent designers. They must understand that their actions have a significant impact on our cities and affect our quality of life.

The philosophy once developed was used for the design of conventional projects. The principles developed as part of and as a result of the larger systems programs were directly applicable to the design of more conventional architectural projects. The realization that the design principles and the understanding of the building industry were widely applicable to conventional architectural practice prompted the desire to write the book for all those engaged in design, knowingly or not. The book itself draws most heavily on the early building systems programs and a few of the individual buildings designed during that period.

The ethics of architecture requires a stewardship with respect to the stage on which the play of life takes place. The ability to provide the stage requires an appropriate balance between society's needs and resources. This balance can only be achieved through the design process when permeated with an understanding of the societal context in which we work. This is the primary focus of the book. The building industry with its many fragmented interests may be viewed by many as a "black box" with little idea as to how the input of needs, aspirations, and dollars relates to the output of completed buildings and coherent communities. We are experiencing major gaps between our ability to perform and society's needs. The industry itself is consistently undermined by volatile legislative, regulatory, and economic policies that have conspired to make a coherent program of establishing goals and then achieving them very difficult. The situation is reaching crisis proportions today, as, for example, only 20 percent of American families can now afford to buy a new house at market rate compared to 50 percent in the late 60s.

The building industry is the vehicle through which any response to the requirement for housing our population must be made, and understanding the system is necessary if we are to make it work. All participants in the process, and, most importantly, the designers who are not design professionals, must have an understanding of the building industry so that it does not act as a "black box" and can be directed to achieve specific objectives. An improved understanding of the industry will hopefully provide greater opportunities to shape and manage it.

The ideas expressed herein were developed as a result of working on many projects and interacting with many people. Some deserve special mention including William Allen, for whom I worked at the Building Research Establishment in England, and Jonathan King, of the Educational Facilities Laboratories, Inc., a division of the Ford Foundation. Both of them played a significant role in my early professional development and work. Over the years, I have worked with many sponsors, clients, partners, and fellow professionals who contributed to the formulation of the concepts presented in the book. Christopher Arnold, Peter Kastl, and Carl Meinhardt, in particular, worked with me on a number of the projects cited in this book. I would also like to acknowledge an initial grant which was received from the National Endowment for the Arts which enabled me to obtain assistance from Susan Brabrook to begin the effort. Many people have helped by reviewing the work at various times, including Tom Page, Jeanne Parker, Andrew Rabenek, and, most significantly and frequently, my wife, Cynthia.

Ezra D. Ehrenkrantz

Introduction

How I Came to a Systems Approach

In the mid-1950s I spent about 2 years working at the Building Research Establishment (BRE) in England, an organization analogous to, but more comprehensive than, the Center for Building Technology at our National Bureau of Standards. While working there as a Fulbright Fellow, I had the opportunity to observe how resources were allocated to rebuild the country after World War II. The conventional building industry was targeted to address the first priority, housing. Nontraditional approaches were sought to fulfill second priority needs such as educational facilities. Housing construction was putting tremendous demands on traditional materials, and thus educational facilities became the arena for significant innovation in industrialized building.

The work began in Hertfordshire, where a team of architects was employed by the county council to develop a system which could accommodate the projected need for 175 new schools in 15 years. The HCC architects resolved to overcome materials shortages by devising a factory-made system using average-size components which would allow the development of a grid dimension related specifically to educational functions and which was small enough to permit considerable flexibility. The building of these schools, first in Hertfordshire and then through analogous programs in a number of other counties, was the first successful, concerted effort to use nonconventional resources to build high-quality facilities in less time and with a smaller labor force than would have been required for conventional construction. Later, these school building systems were exported from England to the continent, where a significant number of architectural design awards was won by architects using these prefabricated systems. In time, a variety of continental educational building systems were developed in addition to the housing systems which had been given priority throughout the rest of Europe.

There were a number of basic conditions that made it possible for this program to succeed. The counties in England had their own school districts, each with a construction program equivalent in size to that of a small state in the United States. The county councils were, therefore, able to present a significant market for innovation. Each county council had its own architectural staff which could, and in many cases did, design its own unique building system which would be used to build a significant number of schools. By developing its own vocabulary for a given group of projects, the architectural design team could induce industry to make whatever it desired. Because single bids were taken for multiple projects, the architects were required to design the individual buildings within their predetermined vocabulary. But the vocabulary could be changed for the next significant group of schools. The results were good. Basic user needs were met, buildings were put up within a time and cost framework otherwise impossible to achieve, and the resources employed were not those committed for the reconstruction of housing.

In viewing this experience, a number of questions occurred to me. How could analogous procedures be established in the United States, where school districts hired individual architects to design each specific building, where there was no shortage of conventional building products, and where, if new products were developed for a specific school, there were no incentives to use the same products on subsequent projects? In effect, the industry would make any product that an architect wanted but at a price which school districts could not afford. For this reason, very little real product innovation to meet educational needs had been developed in the United States. On the other hand, sufficient money was allocated occasionally to individual office building projects to permit and, in specific cases, require building product development. If you wanted demountable partitions for a new school, partitions developed for office buildings would be the only available resource. Since they were not designed as chalk- or tackboards, a school program concerned with work surfaces as well as acoustic separation could not take advantage of the functional or cost benefits of integrating these different requirements. The school architect was in the position of having to specify on a hand-me-down basis products developed for other building types since individual school design projects could not underwrite the cost of product development. Innovative responses to educational needs required a cost and time framework that would combine a number of projects as in the case of the British work.

There was at that time an enormous need in the United States to "break out of the box" in school design. Changing educational philosophies and techniques were hampered by obsolete facilities, and frequently new schools were already obsolete at the time of first occupancy. Yet, school boards lacked the means to build new schools which could keep pace with changing teaching patterns. Although not dictated by war shortages, the American need for innovative construction techniques in this area was almost as pressing as in Europe.

Given this background, I worked from 1958 to 1961 to try to generate interest on the part of American school districts and other institutions which might give support to such a program. These efforts centered on trying to persuade Educational Facilities Laboratories, Inc., a subsidiary of the Ford Foundation, to support this approach. But in architectural circles there was considerable concern that the development of a systems approach to building schools would limit architectural freedom and that the development of "closed systems" of prefabricated parts would inhibit aesthetic and functional flexibility. A "closed system" may be defined as one in which all of the component systems (i.e., structures, air conditioning, partitions, etc.) are predetermined and the designer is committed to work with this specific vocabulary. In the case of the British county councils, the county architectural offices actually determined their own palette, which made the process acceptable. The possibility of having to work with a predetermined vocabulary obviously concerned many architects. They did not contemplate the possibility of open-ended systems, where components could be compatible with a variety of other systems and with the products of conventional construction, as there were no precedents for such an approach. There was also fear that legislation might be invoked to require continued use of the system once it was developed.

In 1960 Governor Rockefeller initiated a program in New York State for the design of three stock plans each for elementary, junior high, and senior high schools. In reaction to this even more undesirable approach, sufficient support was obtained from the profession to provide the necessary impetus to pursue the systems approach. A conference sponsored in 1961 by the magazine *Architectural Forum* and Educational Facilities Laboratories, Inc., was the turning point. The use of coordinated components developed to meet educational requirements was identified as a far better alternative than the use of stock plans. Key officials from California who attended the conference were also concerned that specific educational needs for flexibility, i.e., meeting changing school requirements, could not be met by available products while working within the cost context of the state-aided school construction program. In addition, newly mandated qualitative lighting requirements were very difficult to meet within typical budgetary constraints. The coincidence of these interests provided the background which made possible EFL's support of the program.

As a result of this conference and the active support of EFL and various California officials, I was finally able to begin the job of assembling 13 California school districts committed to working together, which formed an aggregate market of sufficient size to interest industry in developing a school building system. In this program the school districts joined forces as a new entity known as the "First California Commission on School Construction Systems" and the project was called the "School Construction Systems Development" (SCSD) project. I determined, through much discussion with manufacturers and through the analysis of the British experience, that 1.4 million square feet of building would constitute the minimum acceptable market for the purpose of inducing the anticipated levels of development. In order to allow for the possibility of secession along the way, we aggregated a potential market of 2.4 million feet. We actually built 1.9 million square feet. The school districts agreed to use products still to be developed for the design of at least 13 schools that would be built 3 to 5 years in the future. These products would be designed to meet a set of performance specifications that would be written once the user requirements of the school districts were spelled out. The fact that 13 separate school districts were willing to work together for this kind of program gives some indication of how constrained they felt by their inability to meet their basic educational requirements within the limits of available construction budgets. In order to proceed with the program, we had to satisfy the school districts that they would not be sticking their necks out too far, and so we developed a procedure that allowed any of them to drop out at several stages in the program.

1. If the user requirement statements did not include the requirements of their individual school project.
2. If the performance specifications did not in fact translate the user requirements into a form in which they could be properly realized.
3. If, at the design review stage in the bidding process, which was held

before price bids were taken, it was found that the product design did not meet the performance criteria.

4. If the bids did not come within the financial framework of the state aid budget.

5. If demographic conditions changed so that they didn't have to build a school at all.

With this kind of staged, conditional acceptance program, we were able to obtain the participation of the school districts. The design review process included the school districts' own architects who had been selected in advance so that it was possible to obtain reactions to the aesthetic implications of the products being developed. This allowed for good feedback to guide the industry in the design of the building components.

In general, we have found that valid exit opportunities are essential in getting people to commit themselves to unknowns. Staged commitment is a critical factor in aggregating a market. At each stage in the SCSD project, the school districts could show cause for exiting, but they were committed to building a systems school if none of the exit clauses were found to apply. Thus, it was up to us to keep them in the program.

In England, the individual county school districts had their own county architectural offices which made it easy to aggregate a market. Here we had to work with many school districts, each choosing its own architect. It was questionable whether building components could be designed which would satisfy all the independent parties. We, therefore, developed the concept of using performance standards, coupled with the commitment to accept the low bid price in meeting the specifications, to establish the "best value" that would in fact satisfy the educational requirements of the participating school districts and their architects. This performance approach combined with a design review stage in the bidding process provided a basis upon which we could aggregate the needs of the separate participating school districts and charge the building industry with a well-defined set of particulars. In essence then, the use of performance specifications became a normalizing factor that made it possible to translate the European experience into American terms. In developing the program, the performance specifications had to respond to the generic needs of all the districts rather than the specific requirements of any single group, thus providing a system with wide applicability. The performance standards were actually representative of hundreds of school districts throughout the country, as well as our 13 participants. They provided a basis upon which industry could gear itself to develop new products for educational needs.

Our concern was to create responsive schools within a controlled budget by taking advantage of the industry's latent potential for innovation. It was only after we were deeply involved in the work that a philosophy began to evolve that could be called "a systems approach to design."

The need to develop such an approach has become increasingly evident as we as a society discover our resource limitations. A systems approach must be concerned not only with the cost-effective deployment of technology and labor in the construction process but also with functional and operating efficiency and maintenance costs. The successful use of any technology or process must be predicated on the provision of a design vocabulary which will enable the architect to interpret and express the client's or the user's aspirations, as well as on the ability of the technology or process to meet the functions and economics of the situation.

As we consider the question of relating available resources to user needs, it is important to remember that one person's system is another's component. As architects, we might look upon the individual school building as a system, but to the superintendent, that facility is just one of a number of components used to educate the community. The mayor, on the other hand, might well regard the entire school system as a component in the social life of the city. And so, if, as architects, we are to design a building effectively, we must understand the context in which our system is reviewed as a component by the school superintendent, and as an even smaller component by the total community from its more distant perspective. The architect looking at a design situation views the total building as the system and the lighting and power system as a component. However, we must recognize that electrical engineers view the lighting and power system as their system and the lighting fixtures or controls as components. A sense of hierarchy and a realistic awareness of the impact of decisions made at the microlevel is extremely important. For example, we have found that a decision about school lighting made solely on the aesthetic merits of available fixtures and their application can carry an annual energy cost penalty equal to as much as 6 percent of the salaries of the teaching staff in an average size high school. This has a dramatic impact on the student-teacher ratio, the superintendent, the whole community, and the allocation of our national resources.

The dynamic nature of our society and the building industry calls for flexible mechanisms to relate to national requirements drawn up for the built environment which reflects needs, lifestyles, and resources. Good rules of thumb cannot be drawn up where conditions are constantly changing. Therefore we must develop methodologies that let us learn from experience, take account of different variables, assess their impact on the planning and design process, and translate specific experiences into a rational basis for projecting future programs. Without such a program we cannot gather appropriate and sufficient information for decision making at any point in the design process.

How this book is perceived may vary with the interest of the reader, but the main objective is to explain how the design process must work in a dynamic society, where the rules of the game, as well as the design vocabulary, are constantly changing. The designer's mission to meet the client's needs with the available resources remains the prime element of stability. Determining the way in which the design process must change in order to meet this key objective becomes the purpose of the systems approach.

As a result of the rate of change within our society, the traditional design process must undergo some considerable revision if we are to continue to perform our historic role. One of the prime functions of this book is to explain how one can compensate for the high level of contingencies and unknowns that now exists. This cannot be done in a workbook format, since the need for a systems approach would not exist if a workbook could supply the answer. Rather, this book is an attempt to describe a philosophical approach and process which may be developed within the context of the architect or designer's own office and which will provide information for organizing the variables which may be faced.

At no point in the process do we imply that good design is a result of the systems approach. Instead, we propose that good design begin with an achievable program, the analysis of the context, and the development of appropriate options. A systems approach offers a key to responsiveness and responsibility that enables the designer to equate resources and needs. For those who are not directly involved in the building process, the book should give some insight into the interplay among the wide range of different groups within our society whose needs and aspirations must be met by our buildings or who have a part in realizing them. When the industry is understood as a system, it becomes possible for experts in otherwise unrelated disciplines, such as economics, social sciences, and management, to bring their capabilities to the total process, focusing all appropriate skills on the problem of response of the built environment to human needs. But as long as the building industry remains a ''black box'' shrouded in secrecy, the industry excludes other disciplines from making valid contributions.

The existing processes in the building industry deal with problems of change in a way that is quite unlike most other industries, but they provide an insight into the process of industrialization that has transformed most of our society. In the building industry we still have an immense variety of different interests — the craft-based labor unions, the professional architects and engineers, the contractors and subcontractors who put the products together, as well as the manufacturers who make the basic products — all of whom must work together with checks and balances, peer group pressures, and social status governing their interactions. Although, over the years, this system has become fine-tuned and quite efficient, it functions in a way that complicates efforts to change any part of the process. Changes in any single element affect the overall balance of the system and, as a result, change is difficult. It may in fact be easier to make systemic changes in the roles of the participants while retaining their status than to reduce the status of a single but essential interest group.

The building industry is, in fact, of considerable academic interest to philosophers, sociologists, and psychologists in their research into the dynamics of change. But understanding the interactions of the total system is of even greater concern to the practicing design professional who must evaluate, within the context of the total building industry, the implications of any new development and determine what should be done and how.

The hope for this book is that it can make a contribution toward an improved environment by providing the designer with new insights into how to work within the framework of existing resources as well as into how and when to manipulate the system so that new problems can be met within a different, more appropriate context. The systems approach expands and makes the designer's work more scientific by giving other disciplines a basis for interface with design and by developing knowledge within the building industry according to organized procedures for its continued accumulation, testing, and evaluation.

It may be worth mentioning here that in today's climate of distrust of technology, with the current emphasis on self-help and ''small is beautiful,'' the systems approach to design is sometimes viewed negatively as identified with computers, controlled processes, and ''high-tech'' procedures. But, in fact, an essential precept of the systems approach is that the appropriate technology should be related to the task to be performed within the context of the industry as a whole. Each of the arts is founded on a well-organized vocabulary that provides ample opportunity for innovation, composition, and expression, but these vocabularies, when examined, are invariably found to derive from systematic efforts on the part of those who established the keyboard. In the design field, as we move from a vocabulary established by the individual craftsperson at the building site to one which calls upon the expertise of the tool and die maker, it becomes imperative that a level of systematization be introduced into the vocabulary, but this does not mean that ''high-tech'' processes are introduced for their own sake or that they are appropriate problem-solving tools in every situation. New technology must take its place within the total process, and the vocabulary now, as ever, must be determined by the designer's mandate to optimize resources to meet the real needs of the client.

I have tried to begin with an understanding of the way in which the design process has worked historically and with an analysis of the relationship of the building program to the requirements of the users. The translation of those requirements into performance terms provides the link with the second part of the book, which deals with the organization and management of resources. From this, there emerge basic concepts to feed back into the design process. The third part consists of case studies of a number of different projects which deal with buildings of widely varied types, scales, and opportunities for innovation, which demonstrate the application of the systems process in a number of different programs, and which actually provided the author with the basis for the formulation of the concepts themselves. The conclusion, Part Four, describes some recent applications of the systems approach.

Part One

Needs

Chapter One

The Case for a Systems Approach

Introduction

The primary reason for a systems approach to design is to better meet society's needs for a responsive environment. This means that we have to begin by understanding needs and developing a rational method of organizing the available resources to meet those needs on schedule and within budget through buildings that exhibit an appropriate level of performance.

If we look at the evolution of the construction industry over the last 100 years, we find that it lacks an organized basis for controlling the total delivery process. Before World War II, the development of new building materials was relatively slow as was cost escalation. In fact, as recently as 1961–1962, when we were developing the SCSD program, we were dealing with cost escalations of about 2 percent per year. Today, it is quite obvious that we are dealing with annual cost escalations many times that number and with a rapidly changing design vocabulary — as evidenced by the fact that 35 percent of the items in Sweets Catalog are new every 5 years. In such a context, it becomes extremely difficult for the architect to keep control of the design palette and to know how various products will perform, what they will cost, and what maintenance they will require. As a result, we find ourselves dealing with an industry that is dynamic, that fluctuates rapidly, and is not susceptible to the rule-of-thumb programming and planning that was part of the traditional design process. In days gone by, the architect would have an accurate picture of the building options that were affordable at a given price per square foot. The vocabulary of materials was known, and a 20-year maintenance and performance record could be established by going into the field and looking at buildings that had used the same palette of materials 20 years before.

In these circumstances, it was possible to go through the design process with the inherent concerns of the architect focused directly on the properties of the design. Architects could plan with the knowledge that, as long as ‘hey worked within the simple parameters of square feet and materials, the rules of thumb would apply and the project would be within budget. They would have to determine whether to place more emphasis on image or function, but the nature of the materials with which they had to work and their attendant costs were known factors.

Today, we are dealing with a better-educated client, an interested public, and a profession which itself recognizes its obligation to meet the needs and aspirations of a complex society. To meet these more sophisticated demands, we must work with a dynamic design vocabulary in which relatively few building components have been tested for as long as 20 years in the way that one would use them in a building and where costs are escalating significantly and often erratically. Architects, thus, find themselves responding to heightened pressure for responsive design in a climate which contains more unknowns in terms of costs and performance. Invariably, these unknowns curtail their ability to do the work in a timely manner. When a design goes over the budget and has to be redesigned, a series of inevitable problems related to scheduling work arise. This problem becomes exacerbated when a large and complex facility comes in over the budget. In the time devoted to the redesign process, the amount of money taken out of the building may be consumed by further cost escalations. This means that even though the architect may cut significant portions from the building program, when the time comes for the rebidding, little or no money has been saved.

When we consider progress within the building industry, we find a productivity increase of about 1 percent per year, as opposed to 3 percent or more in most sectors of the economy that have industrialized, including agriculture, automobile manufacture, and the chemical industry. Unfortunately, we find that as the average productivity of the country goes up those sectors of the economy whose increases in productivity are below average have higher than average price rises. When I began practice in 1960, one could install a window and a sliding door in a house for the price of a refrigerator. Today, we cannot install either one.

Another way to grasp the implication of this is to realize that as productivity in the industrialized sector of the economy rises, the cost of social services goes up as well. William Baumol, an economist from Princeton, has studied a variety of industries and found that the very efficiency developed within our society in relation to industrialization has increased the cost of service-based industries. While the value of the automobile has improved as a result of increased productivity of the individual worker through industrialization, this improved productivity has also resulted in higher salaries. The school teacher, then, will also obtain salary increases, even if less than those of the auto worker, or else the teachers would become auto workers or take some other high-paying job. The financial implications of this increase are quite significant for society since the teacher's quantitative productivity is essentially the same as it was 30 years ago. He or she may have had 30 students in a class then and may still have 30 today.

The costs of all our social services tend to go up in relation to the products we obtain from the industrialized sector of our economy. The lack of understanding that surrounds this condition causes much pain in our society when we try to obtain funds for social services and do not understand why previous allocations are no longer sufficient. Unfortunately, although the building industry has the low productivity characteristics of a social service, the public regards it as if it were an industrialized activity. As a result, society, understandably, views with a jaundiced eye the value of new building projects. Thus the problems of getting bond issues passed for new facilities must be seen within a context in which the relative dollar-for-dollar value of buildings compared with mass-produced artifacts is quite unfavorable. When Henry Ford first made his Model-T, the car cost one-third or one-quarter as much as a house. Today, if we consider $100,000 the cost of an average house, the $10,000 automobile costs only one-tenth as much. The relative cost of a house has increased about 300 percent.

We must understand that unless productivity in the construction industry improves at a rate that approaches the characteristics of other industrialized sectors of the economy, this industry is going to face persistent problems from a society which is not receiving what it expects in terms of value.

User Requirements

The simplest explanation of a systems approach is that it enables the designer to make the best possible use of available resources to meet the user's requirements. If you do not meet the needs of the user, your building must be considered sculpture. If you meet the user's requirements, this does not in itself guarantee good architecture but rather qualifies the work to be considered as architecture. Good design still requires a talented designer.

In fact, when we talk of user requirements, we are describing a combination of needs and aspirations. In physical terms, "needs" describes the demand for space, services, environment, and furnishings, while "aspirations" may cover a wide variety of the modes by which those needs and a variety of aesthetic and contextual concerns are met. At one level, they may include an extra bathroom, a basement, a 10-foot ceiling, or wall-to-wall carpeting. At another, there are requirements relating to security, image, privacy, or location, which can be correlated to needs or aspirations.

In designing a building, we must recognize that if all we do is meet user needs, the chances of our designs being approved are limited. But if, on the other hand, we relate only to aspirations, then it may well be unpleasant or even dangerous to visit the project after occupancy! Our concern must be to organize resources to meet a combination of the two.

Resources

There are five basic resources involved in the realization of a building project — land, finance, management, technology, and labor. The resources for any project must begin with some combination of land and finance. Without these two, no matter how good your management capabilities or design talents, a building will not result. Once you have those resources, however, you are in a position to make decisions about how to use them, and it is at this point that the third resource — management — comes into play. Management capability can be broken down into a number of separate components. But it must begin with the ability to manage the decision-making process from the establishment of the building program right up to completion of the project. Within the building industry, this management capability must provide a creative vocabulary for design and must be able to predict the performance characteristics of the constituent products and the cost effects of the different products and components on the project budget. Management is also concerned with getting materials and labor onto the site at the right time and with organizing the myriad contractual relationships that are part and parcel of getting a building built. Management is vitally important in controlling the design of the project in relation to the program at one end of the spectrum and the ability to build, maintain, and operate it at the other.

As we develop strategies for the optimum use of our resources in a building program, it is clear that we must rely on two further resources to get the building constructed: technology and labor. Although the decision about whether to use factory-made components or on-site fabrication for a particular job will depend on an analysis of the specific circumstances, certain levels of technology, and the attendant labor capabilities to put those technologies in place will be required for every job. Our concern is how best to deploy the five resources on any specific job to ensure the best results possible. To do this, one must be dedicated to careful analysis of the various applicable design options and to consideration of the implications of each for the eventual design direction.

In determining how to apply available resources to meet that combination of user needs and aspirations which results in the highest possible degree of satisfaction, we must have at our disposal a body of soundly documented information that allows us to make an objective evaluation of the various alternatives. We must know when space is a more important commodity than sophisticated services and when the quality of the environment will matter more than spatial volume. How should a building relate to its community and neighborhood? We must also recognize the effects of operating costs on a building's use, and determine how much should be spent in first cost with a view to the impact on long-term operating costs. The cost of energy with its unprecedented price variations is an increasingly confounding factor requiring normalization. Such trade-offs must be made within the context of knowledge and experience, which provide the systematic basis for decision making.

Although a systems approach provides no magic for getting something for nothing, it should allow us to analyze and organize the available options to ensure the highest possible level of user satisfaction. If we accept a systems approach to design, we imply that there is a significantly more scientific basis for projecting the impact of our design decisions on cost, time, quality, and enjoyment. Meeting these objectives demands the development of a rational methodology for more accurately matching resources with priorities, which will give the designer much more clearly defined parameters within which to exercise his or her talents.

National Policy

Matching needs and resources on a national basis demands a hierarchy of activities, each of which is vital to overall success. If we set new national goals without using new procedures to meet them, the results may very well be the opposite of those expected. A public housing policy, for example, which calls for diffusion of low-income housing into the suburbs but has the built-in disincentive of increased taxes for the related and required services carries with it the seeds of its own failure.

As we take a look at what has transpired in our cities, there is reason for concern over their accelerating deterioration, despite the substantial resources that have been spent on housing, redevelopment, and planned communities over many years. It is almost as though a process had been set in motion by a foreign power determined to weaken the United States from within.

An Apocryphal Tale

Let us accept this view for a moment and review the following scenario. In the late 1940s, when the Chinese communists first came into power, they were very much concerned with their effectiveness on a worldwide basis. Suppose they hired appropriate consultants to analyze each of the major powers with which China must contend, to see if it would be possible to weaken those countries at the same time as China built itself up. The consultant hired for the United States was particularly effective. After much study, he reported that, with their very limited resources, if the Chinese wished to weaken the United States from within, it could be done only by infiltrating and taking control of a U.S. government agency. Since the resources and ability for taking over the Department of Defense or Department of State were lacking, the consultant found that there was only one agency they could aspire to which had sufficient leverage to weaken the United States from within. From what has happened, one must assume that not only was their determination correct, but that they indeed took complete control. The agency was the Federal Housing Administration (FHA).

It was decided that, with this agency, they could begin a program to promote class warfare in true Marxist fashion. The first step was to develop a basis for class warfare, and they decided to inaugurate programs to move the bourgeoisie out of the city and into the suburbs, leaving the poor and the workers behind. The housing programs of the late 1940s and early 1950s provided mortgages with little or no down payment on suburban houses, but, at the same time, the monthly payment was high enough to keep the poor out. As a result, masses of the urban population were drawn to the suburbs. Schools, shopping centers, roadways, and necessary services were built, and much of the infrastructure was also subsidized. By the mid-1950s, we had a new demographic distribution. It was as though a giant cream separator had churned through our major cities.

In the meantime, the consultant was summoned again in the late 1950s because there was still an environment of peace, harmony, and good relationships within our urban population. The client was very much concerned that the conditions for class warfare had not yet been produced and asked the consultant to go back and find out why. He found that the bonds tying the communities together were still unbroken; families had lived in the same areas of the city for many generations; they knew the corner storekeepers; credit networks were established; and many of the essential fibers binding the society together into a working whole were unbroken.

The consultant determined that the only way to break these bonds and "liberate" the population for warfare was to move the people around and so the *urban renewal* program was invented. Its main concern was to tear down the existing housing in the poorer sections of our major cities and use the land for other purposes. To conceal the full intent of the strategy, the project had to build some housing as well, but the rules demanded that when low-income housing was removed, the poor could not be rehoused in the newly built facilities. In at least one out of every five cases, after the housing was torn down, nothing at all was built in its place. Most important of all, if there was the slightest chance that the poor had moved as a group to another district and were reforming their community, that district was the place to run the next urban renewal program to ensure that those community bonds would surely and finally be broken. By the middle 1960s we finally began to have riots within our cities.

The consultant was called back by the client, congratulated, and given a bonus. He went back to take a last look at our cities to make sure that no revitalization was possible from within. He saw at once that it would not be possible to regenerate communities by tearing down additional housing of the urban poor — even if you intended to replace it with good new housing for them to live in — for, at the first movement of the bulldozers, you would have an instant riot. To start a fix-up process, some degree of free land was necessary. If you built new housing on free land, you could presumably induce people who lived in poor housing to move into it and then rebuild where they had been. Thus, through a game of musical chairs, you could rebuild a city.

To ensure that this never happened, the most important step was to take the free land out of use, and what better way of doing it than by building low-density low-income housing. Thus, the *221, 235, 236 turn-key public housing programs* were born. These programs were so successfully employed to build a modest amount of low-income housing in a wide variety of urban communities that by the time Secretary Romney left HUD, he was able to declare that there was a shortage of land available for low-income housing within our major cities. New programs would have to be put forward, such as family assistance or subsidies, to enable low-income families to compete in the open housing market with blue-collar workers and lower-middle-income families. At about the same time, the Chinese were finally willing to meet the President of the United States. They would be on an equal footing! Then they left HUD, and little has been done since.

The illustration is apocryphal, but it serves its purpose. And when we examine the way in which our urban legislation has been written, frequently in contradiction to our national goals, we begin to understand the need for a systematic approach to the organization of our resources to respond to the environmental needs of society. If we are anxious to reduce the concentrations of the poor within our central cities, efforts to move people from the cities by introducing some low-income housing in the suburbs must have an incentive program to overcome existing resistance. Those few communities which have done so have found that the construction of public housing forces the more affluent within the community to pay more taxes for schools and other services. Thus, those with good will are hurt financially by relating positively to our national goals, and this pattern reinforces the position of the disinclined.

With respect to the early low- and moderate-income housing programs, the decision to finance these projects privately without setting criteria that take normal operating costs into account has caused a new round of failures or potential failures. The problems arising from emphasis on first cost and lack of proper consideration of the operating costs of these projects have been exacerbated by the energy crisis. Use of electric appliances for both space heating and hot water, poor insulation, and materials which require high levels of maintenance were used to reduce first cost. However, today's operating costs are moving out of reach. Deferred maintenance and eviction of tenants who can't pay are inevitable. The end result is bankruptcy of many projects and further urban blight.

It is obvious that our urban failure is not a result of Congress being peopled by individuals of ill will or of low intelligence. However, our modus operandi has remained relatively unchanged from an earlier and simpler era where issues could be tackled independently. Today, the context in which we work is usually more important than the issue at hand, and we cannot improve a component without affecting the system of which it is a part. It is this problem which must be addressed at every level of the hierarchy relating to design, energy, and environmental issues whether one is designing a lighting fixture, a school, or legislation.

Organizing the Building Industry _____

A systems approach demands that the interlocking hierarchy of needs, goals, policies, and means of production be seen as a unit that functions to produce a responsive environment. The building industry is a vital tool in this effort, but to understand both its problems and its potential, we must study its past evolution.

To understand the nature, size, and variety of building materials and products in use today, we should start in the Elizabethan era when the United States was first settled. It was at that time that lath and plaster techniques and half-timbered construction began to compete effectively with brick construction. During that era, the 9-inch module was basic to most construction. The dimensions of common brick were based on the measure of a man's hand span, which is approximately 4½ inches in width. The length was twice the width, 9 inches, to permit the coursing of brick — i.e., the proper construction of right angles and corners. The small houses of the day had fireplaces of two brick lengths — 18 inches wide — cordwood was therefore cut to 16-inch lengths. Since the lath was cut from cordwood, a 16-inch module evolved as lath and plaster construction techniques developed, while 9 inches continued to be the module for masonry.

When larger building products were developed, they invariably related to one of these modules. Plywood automatically followed the 16-inch wood and plaster dimension. However, a 32-inch door was not wide enough and a 64-inch panel was too wide to be held by a single individual. Thus the standard 48-inch plywood sheet evolved along with a whole family of products developed to this dimension. The basic cordwood module is still in use today, and the old 9-inch module still makes its appearance in many other product lines such as floor tile. Thus, many building products derive their dimensions from the size of the standard fireplace in Elizabethan times, rather than from anthropometric measurements, modern manufacturing techniques, or twentieth century functional requirements. The craft traditions of the sixteenth century continue to dominate a supposedly industrialized industry of the twentieth century.

In the sixteenth century, the carpenter would cut window frames to size on the job, but today standard windows must go into standard openings. We cannot afford custom-made products. The building industry was able to function effectively with the discrepancy of product sizes for a long time because the building products were basic materials which were patterned or made by craftspeople into more sophisticated components or which were placed directly into the new structure at the building site. We are now long past the time where our design vocabulary consists of undifferentiated products, and we cannot shave 3 inches from a prefabricated aluminum window. We must therefore develop our products to preset dimensions, which will assure not only that they will fit together effectively on site, but that they will be responsive to user requirements and provide the designer with an acceptable design keyboard. We must always be sure that the standards we apply meet the basic spatial requirements for the building type and use. It is not possible to impose the same modules on a hospital, a house, and a school. We have to relate specifically to the kinds of spaces and activities that are part of daily life in today's world.

This simplified review of some of the issues relating to product sizes should emphasize that regardless of the level we are working on, be it national policy, design of large-scale building components, or the size of a brick, we need a systems approach to design. Each step in the hierarchy, from individual product design to their coordination as a series of compatible components working together to form a total building, must be viewed and evaluated systematically as related activities in a carefully orchestrated, national endeavor.

Evolution of a Systems Philosophy

Once the reasons for developing a systematic approach to design are accepted, the application of the systems approach will vary according to the specific job situation. The philosophy described in this book evolved as a result of working on many projects, each of which required a different route for meeting a specific set of client – user requirements, and site and budget constraints. But the evolving procedures and processes eventually took on a recognizable organizational structure that served as the basis of a systems approach to design.

Initially, as indicated in the introduction, I was impressed with processes used in the United Kingdom that made good use of resources to build better schools in a postwar economy. When I returned to the United States from the British Building Research Establishment, I began to see how these procedures might be applied to the American situation, where we seemed unable to design and build the schools that were needed to respond to changing educational philosophies. This process, described briefly in the Introduction and in full detail in Case Study 1, took 5 years from initiation of the program to completion of the first round of schools.

The School Construction Systems Development (SCSD) project was very successful. Literally thousands of buildings now standing use components that were first developed as part of this program or that were designed by other manufacturers to compete with those of the successful bidders. As a result of the concerns of the University of California about the cost and quality of student housing, we began a second project — the development of a system for residential facilities for the statewide university system. A similar time frame was used, but by the time we had gone through the entire planning process, we found that our aggregated market on a number of University of California campuses had begun to evaporate. The program coincided with a period of dramatic and largely unanticipated changes in American campus lifestyles. During the time span of our project, the pattern of dormitory living had changed and the demand for traditional student residences had eroded. In the period between developing the first conceptual program of student numbers and needs and completing the system and building designs, the requirements changed. The market, therefore, had to be scaled down, and as a result, although a number of buildings were completed, the University Residential Building System (URBS) program never had the same kind of impact as SCSD.

We then became involved, as part of a large team, in a most interesting project for the city of Pittsburgh, which was planning to build a totally new secondary school system. When we began work, the school system's newest high school was built before 1920; the city sought to move into the future by integrating the school system by creating five educational parks to be served by the main transportation arteries leading to the center of the city. Each park was to include the equivalent of four small high schools, and together they would house the secondary school population for the entire city.

During the time of the selection of land to build on, the completion of the system, and the preparation of working drawings, the nature and attitude of the population of the city of Pittsburgh was changing dramatically. They no longer wanted, or were willing to support, integrated schools. The long response time of the planning efforts contributed to a feeling of despair and inaction on the part of many of the inhabitants of the city; that despair itself helped change their entire attitude, as militant leaders became more interested in promoting segregated communities than integrating the educational facilities. So, the response time itself became one of the factors in the defeat of a systems program, whose objectives I continue to believe were correct and appropriate.

As a result of these lessons, we began to be very much concerned with the time element. It was clear that the ability to react within the user's time frame was an essential ingredient of success. Innovations do not come quickly and it becomes necessary to distinguish whether a given project has the time and financial resources required for developing new technologies. If not, the designer must use materials already developed by previous systems programs or by industry's conventional procedures.

Another program for the state of Alaska overlapped our efforts for Pittsburgh and provided an interesting contrast. The task was to erect a group of eight buildings within a very short period of time. In this case, we used the components previously developed for the SCSD program, and by applying them to the requirements of the University of Alaska's higher education program, we were able to get eight facilities — on seven different sites 1200 miles apart — programmed and built in a period of 20 months. This was appreciably less time than would normally have been expected — probably some 2 years faster than the norm for the state of Alaska. At the same time, the use of the systems components made it possible to come up with significant financial benefits as well.

It was through this project that the importance of working with the results of previous innovative programs was driven home. The development of coordinated vocabularies of building components to do specific jobs makes it possible for future projects to be done more quickly and efficiently. This made us search for procedures by which we could assess exactly what could and could not be accomplished in the context of any single project. The kind of development that could be attempted varied with the availability of time and money. If much time and sufficient financial support were available, programs such as SCSD could be attempted. If very little time but appropriate resources were available, as in the Alaska project, already developed system components could be successfully applied.

From groups of projects and experiences, we began to understand that the first and common requirement for all projects was to determine the user's needs, the resources that would be devoted to the job, and the time in which it could be done. From this, we recognized that major innovation called for a lot of time and money, and that these innovations could be used for future jobs that did not have significant extra time or money; technical innovation would not be possible on jobs where time and/or money were severely limited. We then began to look for specific opportunities for organizing major innovative programs and saw other projects as opportunities for implementing the newest and best developments. A single project (for example, an elementary school) might well be a candidate for applying some innovative techniques, but only large-scale programs which offered the opportunity for sufficient market aggregation within an extended time-frame were appropriate for major product innovations. As we go through the various case studies within this book, it is important to recognize which projects were organized for innovation and which projects were part of an application program. The procedures used in a systems approach to design do not change inherently, but how they are applied is determined in the context of the specific objectives of the project. It should also be pointed out that the conventional building industry has survived to this date only because it is very adaptable. Any new developments made in systems programs are immediately embraced within conventional construction if they have a market.

When we began to work on the Academic Building System (ABS) for the state university systems of Indiana and California, it was evident that the clients were unable to guarantee a specific market volume in advance. As a result, the procedures that we had used previously to develop performance specifications that translate user requirements into an understandable form for industry to bid on were no longer appropriate. Industry would not do the research and development work unless the incentive was large enough. We, therefore, adopted the approach of developing the performance specifications with the knowledge that we would have to design the systems ourselves. This limited the opportunity for new product development and required a rational use of existing materials and components, although some requirements were set for modest product development. This response was used again for our program for the Veterans Administration in the hospital field because, again, we were unable to get sufficient market commitments for bidding on performance. In both cases, we had enough time to design the building system, and we took longer than an architect normally would to design a building. In fact, in both cases, we worked for 2 to 3 years before we began to design the prototype buildings using the systems. It is interesting to note that even though we did not have the kind of hardware approach which was part of SCSD, these system designs are now being used by others.

In 1969, HUD began its Operation Breakthrough program, and we became involved in the development of a new technology for housing known as Fibershell. In this case, the performance specifications were developed by HUD, and we were on the other side of the fence working with TRW to design a system that would meet HUD's criteria. (Many of the criteria actually originated in another study program in which we were involved called the In-Cities Experimental Housing Program.) The market size once again played a major role in the design. We began with the concept of making tubes which would contain a house by winding a glass fabric on a mandel using a technique developed by the aerospace industry. But when the approach was analyzed, it was found that tooling costs were so high that they could only be justified by a very large market committed over a long time period. Unfortunately, a major failing of Operation Breakthrough was its very inability to guarantee a long-range housing market big enough to warrant significant innovation and investment. Because of this, we modified our approach to a much less costly, smaller-scale fabrication effort, which could be rather easily located close to the building site. This process was used, and the housing which was developed had a fairly active market beyond the Operation Breakthrough program. Its use, however, fell off as a result of the general malaise in the housing industry in the early- to mid-1970s.

The Breakthrough situation was such that industry had to respond to what were essentially pump-priming commitments, but if we are looking for effective large-scale development which will be applicable over long time periods, it is essential that aggregated markets and policies be established which can sustain both innovation and application. If such a market is not sustained, even the best systems will inevitably fall by the wayside.

In 1973, we became involved in a large-scale program for the General Services Administration (GSA) where we had sufficient time and money to develop new systems and to ensure a high level of technical innovation. But, at the same time, one of GSA's major requirements was that the system, once developed, should be amenable to a very rapid construction process using a construction manager working on a phased construction schedule. The program sought to obtain major savings through a development process akin to that used in SCSD and URBS as well as to optimize life-cycle and particularly energy costs. This was one of the first times that a large-scale public project was bid on the basis of a comprehensive life-cycle cost program, as opposed to first cost. It was also the first new systems project we had undertaken since the energy crisis was formally recognized. In SCSD and URBS, we were trying to coordinate a group of separate component manufacturers who were trying to develop a coordinated building system and simultaneously align themselves in different ways over a longer period on a very simple open-market basis. The life-cycle analysis incorporated into these programs was related to single-component subsystems and not total-system interaction. Our concern in SCSD was not to reduce construction time but to get better value for the school building dollar. Time was, however, one of GSA's major concerns, since increasing escalation of building costs during the conventional term over which buildings are built frequently rendered the money allocated by Congress at the start of the project inadequate. As a result, GSA was anxious to coordinate all the component manufacturers into a single, controlled building system that could meet a faster time schedule.

Competition in this situation would thus be at the level of coordinated building systems, rather than at the level of the individual component subsystem. This approach has provided better coordination for accelerating the construction process, but has sacrificed, in the process, some of the flexibility achieved in SCSD, where the best subsystems were all compatible with one another. GSA is an example of a closed-systems approach, in contrast to the open-systems procedure adopted in SCSD. But the objectives in each case called for a different application of the basic systems approach in order to organize resources in an appropriate response to two different hierarchies of client priorities.

In any case, as we now look at the results of the GSA work, it is the better component subsystems that are being integrated within conventional construction and once again are being used widely.

Chapter Two

Evolution Toward Responsive Design

Architectural development over the centuries has been heavily affected by the nature of the available technologies and the cultural role of architectural monuments within the existing society. Today, our societal perspective requires that a building be evaluated from four different points of view, as in the film "Rashomon" where a single event was seen from different vantage points. These views relate to the various functions of a building, which differ with the perspectives of the observer, client, or user. Perhaps the most basic function is *economic,* which in its broadest view must be considered to represent all resources: land, water, energy, etc., as well as dollars. But we are also very much concerned that a building provide a good working environment, termed herein, the *climate* function; that it relate to the way individuals and groups will use it, the *behavior* function; and last, but certainly not least, that it reflect the aspirations of society, its *image* or aesthetic function. From an historical point of view, we find that buildings that have been accorded architectural importance are not necessarily those responsive to all four functions. In fact, from the perspective of today's architectural historians, the image function outweighs all others in selecting the works by which architectural history is traced. Steen Eiler Rasmussen once said "Architectural historians may be compared with little boys picking the cherries out of the Christmas cake without regard for the cake which surrounds them." While this may be only partially true, it is important to recognize the way in which the four-function model has become increasingly significant in direct relation to the growth and complexity of society and the designed environment.

If we consider the design of the temples of ancient Greece, we find that the technology was essentially that of the stone mason's craft, but this was coupled with great sophistication on the part of architects, who produced highly developed proportional systems which dictated how the stone was to be crafted to create a building. The structures that were built responded primarily to the image function, and this was enhanced by proportional

Figure 2.1 View of Parthenon.

Figure 2.2 Nave at Ste. Chapelle.

conventions perfected over the years. The Greeks were not concerned with exploiting the fullest structural potential of stone to achieve the greatest possible span. In those buildings which we consider their architectural monuments, they did not try to create internal spaces where large numbers of people could congregate and communicate in the course of daily business; they were more concerned with placing the buildings to obtain the most commanding exterior view as a symbol or backdrop to human activity. This aesthetic concern dictated the placement, proportion, and subtle shaping of the columns to create the optical perception of rectilinear design. In the same way, the pediment of a building was rounded slightly so that it would appear straight when viewed from a distance. The Greek approach to architecture is an example of sophisticated use of a simple technology to provide an appropriate aesthetic context for its culture. The image function reigns supreme (see Figure 2.1).

By the time the cathedrals of the Gothic period were built, many changes had taken place. The basic structural material was still stone, and the stone cutters who put the structure together had many of the same skills. The designer was concerned with not only external composition but with the creation of interior spaces which could house much more complex and large-scale human gatherings. The spiritual inspiration generated by these lofty structures stimulated designers to explore and extend the structural capabilities of stone, while developing new proportional systems for visual harmony. The technology of the Gothic period was more sophisticated than that of the Greek, and the behavioral function became more important along with image in influencing building design (see Figure 2.2).

If we move to a completely different era, and a much more personal scale, we can see that Jefferson's home, Monticello, provides an excellent example of sophisticated design combined with a creative response to climate and behavioral considerations. Designed and oriented to take full advantage of the views and breezes, the house has a small foyer between the drawing room and the reception hall. Jefferson placed his bed in this foyer. In conjunction with very large, triple-hung windows which admitted as much air as possible in the summertime, this design encouraged a venturi action of air moving from the windows and through the constricted space in which the bed was placed—the equivalent of a strong fan blowing over the bed which kept its occupant cool in the warm, humid Virginia evenings.

In Jefferson's house we see classical motifs and proportional systems

Figure 2.3 Monticello.

expressing image, the scale and placement of the rooms responding to behavioral needs of the residents, and great attention paid to environment and climate. The emphasis on all three functions integrated in the design indicates a project of uncommon sensitivity (see Figures 2.3 and 2.4).

Jefferson's house was obviously not the first such example. The Roman baths of Caracalla with an underground floor heating system, or hypercost, integrated into the design of a major public building was a much earlier example of a design solution which paid attention to image, climate, and behavior. However, long periods followed where the concern with the climatic function was negligible in the monuments of architectural history.

As we move from the concept of building as a purely craft-based industry toward that of industrial prefabrication, the Crystal Palace represents the first great use of industrialized technology in building. This building marked a major change in architectural history because the proportional disciplines and the component shapes and sizes were determined off-site. The tool and die makers became craftspeople as well. Using the available technologies—in this case, cast iron structural members and glass— Paxton developed even longer spans and evoked a completely different spirit than that produced by the Gothic cathedral. He explored the potential of structure and materials and pushed the technology of the time to its functional limits in order to respond to an unprecedented demand for vast and flexible exhibition space (see Figure 2.5).

The same kind of aesthetic is seen at a simpler, more workaday level in the cast iron commercial and industrial buildings of James Bogardus in late nineteenth-century America. In these buildings a relatively limited vocabulary of stock parts was assembled in a wide variety of configurations, creating a commercial aesthetic which, through the use of pattern books, came to be widely applied in the United States (see Figure 2.6).

When steel replaced cast iron, the technology was extended to permit longer span structures, while the introduction of the elevator permitted much greater building heights. With increasing population and developing technologies, a larger proportion of our built environment had to be consciously designed and, with the coming of the industrial revolution, cost and efficiency assumed a more important role.

Economic factors were a primary concern for much of the design work of the nineteenth century, which largely ignored the sophisticated environmental considerations that characterized Jefferson's buildings a century or

Figure 2.4 Jefferson's bed in foyer between large rooms.

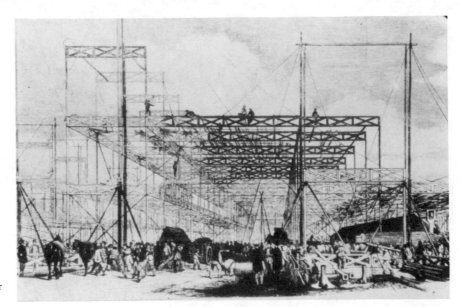

Figure 2.5 Crystal Palace under construction.

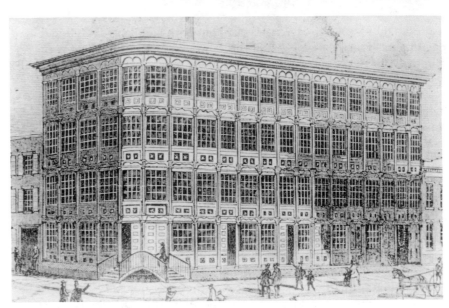

Figure 2.6 Cast-iron building (1851) by Bogardus.

so before. But the commercial buildings of the nineteenth century did push forward the frontiers of building technology. In the same era, however, there were also splendid examples of four-function buildings which paid equal regard to aesthetic, economic, behavioral, and climatic considerations as may be found in the work of Louis Sullivan. His Chicago Auditorium is an aesthetic and engineering masterpiece and one of the most spectacularly successful theatres ever built. However, the increase of knowledge about materials with respect to their structural capability culminated in a technological aesthetic, in which image overrode and included both behavioral and environmental considerations. The Eiffel Tower, the quintessential example of this approach, has something in common with the pyramids, in that both are single-function buildings and technical tours de force.

While "sophisticated" Western architects were preoccupied with developing the full structural capacity of "modern" materials, more primitive societies were working to modify the effects of climate — a concern of much greater importance in their daily lives. During periods when single-function image-oriented buildings typified monumental architecture, indigenous work related more particularly to the other three functions. In the regional

Figure 2.7 Troglodyte dwellings, each with its own courtyard.

architecture of less developed areas, we find sophisticated work which responds to behavioral, climatic, and economic functions. Technological developments have made it possible in advanced society to integrate all four functions in the design of workaday buildings.

In the troglodyte dwellings of Tunisia, people dig their homes deep into the ground and are able to reverse the thermal heat pattern of summer and winter, i.e., to be cool in summer and warm in winter. The depth of the room within the soil determines the degree of mass insulation. These houses are approached by means of ramps and courtyards (see Figure 2.7). The mud structures of the Cameroons show a more sophisticated way of using earth to provide an insulated environment. They are designed so that the stepped building forms provide footfalls for the construction process — as the building proceeds, the workers climb the structure and have a place to put their feet. This process permits unusually tall mud construction in the shape of an upturned ice cream cone with a narrow ventilation hole at the top. The corrugated building surface, which has double the skin area of a conventional building, reradiates heat at night at twice the normal rate, which enables it to equal the daytime solar absorption, thus providing a balance between solar intake during the day and heat outgo at night. The small opening at the top of the constantly reducing diameter of the building can take advantage of passing breezes to suck the hot air out — much as air passing over the nozzle pulls the mixture out of a spray-gun jar — in addition to the venturi action created by the building form. This may represent the limits of sophistication using earth as a building material (see Figure 2.8).

The buildings just discussed derive their form almost exclusively from climatic considerations. In nontemperate zones, the prime function of a building must be to protect its inhabitants from extreme weather conditions. The same principle used in the Cameroons is found from the Isfahan bazaars to the Australian aboriginal straw mat (which is large enough to act as a roof). All have a roof with an opening at the top and sides that stops short of the ground or is vented to promote air circulation (see Figures 2.9 and 2.10). These areas all have a hot, dry climate with considerable diurnal temperature variation. In other hot, dry climates of the world, evaporative cooling has been introduced. Wind scoops are used on houses in Hyderabad to create a kind of cooling chimney which draws air into the house where,

Figure 2.8 Clustered earth structures as built in the dry areas of the Cameroons and Chad.

Figure 2.9 Metal-working street in the bazaar in Isfahan.

Figure 2.10 Portable self-venting aboriginal mat.

before it enters the room, it is cooled by passage through a screen of wet rush matting, thus providing the cooling counterpart to our fireplace (see Figure 2.11).

In hot, wet climates we see forms, such as those of typical Indonesian housing, which create increased air motion to provide comfort through venturi action, much as in the case of Jefferson's home (Figure 2.12). This type of design, which looks to catch and increase air motion through the house, differs from those in hot, dry climates, where the idea is to expel smaller amounts of hot air which rise naturally to the top of the dwelling unit. These are only a few examples of our ingenuity in adapting our living quarters to inhospitable climates.

At the same time, many of the forms of these indigenous buildings are related to specific behavioral functions of the society. The single-room buildings of the Cameroons are clustered in circles with interior courtyards for family privacy and for defense; however, each wife has her own house.

Figure 2.11 Wind scoops in Hyderabad.

Figure 2.12 Indonesian houses oriented to catch the prevailing breezes.

The verandah in India, the bazaar in Iran, and the cliff dwellings of Mesa Verde all relate to more than just the climate function.

Although throughout history society has always been concerned with the four-function model when considering the built environment, the resources have not always been available with which to satisfy all functions in all buildings. Architecture became associated with the monuments that relate to image or aspirations, and the other three functions were handled more frequently, with many obvious and notable exceptions, by what we call indigenous architecture.

The exceptions to this tendency are numerous. The example of the Roman hypercost has already been mentioned, but the Mogul City of Fatehpur Sikri offers an example of a whole city designed for climate and behavioral functions. Its desert location called for evaporative cooling, which was used to such an extent that 12 years after its occupancy it had to be abandoned because the wells ran dry. This lesson should not be lost on us today as we continue to support the building of houses on the basis of two-acre, or I should say two-car, zoning. To continue this policy in light of the worldwide energy situation is absurd.

Even though many exceptions can be found to the thesis that we have been moving from a single function to the four-function model of architecture, the trend appears to hold. The development of our technical resources has made it possible, and perhaps even necessary, to view any and all buildings in terms of conscious design. As the appropriateness of indigenous solutions gives way to conscious design, we must retain the elements of climate control and awareness of behavior as we try to incorporate image within the framework of the economic function. Energy conservation has become a necessity, however, and we must ensure that the use of our resources is not distorted by the attention given to this factor. In many circles the attention given to energy and the thermal environment supersedes all other issues, including the efficient functioning of a building and those who use it. The next focus will be productivity and the balanced use of all our resources. Climate, economics, behavior, and image are no longer independent variables, and a responsive architecture must be an appropriate amalgam of these four functions.

Chapter Three

User Requirements

Today, it is no longer appropriate to concentrate all our energies on finding a solution to a single function of the built environment. Climate, which can now be controlled mechanically, economics, behavior, and image all vie for attention in the context of limited resources and sophisticated and articulated user requirements. The satisfaction of these needs, the establishment of priorities, and the allocation of resources to achieve the best possible solutions demand a systems approach to design.

Analyzing what the built environment requires to meet the needs and aspirations of the people it houses is a complex procedure. Although it is relatively easy to determine the space required to house a specific activity, such as six people eating at a table, the range of other activities which may also occur at the same table is a function of the family's lifestyle and will be heavily affected by the type of house, other available spaces, and the economic situation of the inhabitants. The table may be used for sewing, homework, food preparation, formal dining, or many other sets of activities. It may therefore be placed in the kitchen, multipurpose room, breakfast room, or separate dining room. The space required for these ancillary functions and the setting may be subject to considerable variation.

In order to deal with these complexities, we must recognize that user requirements have to be considered from many points of view and that the four-function model described in the previous chapter is both appropriate and necessary. In looking at the criteria which must be met in the design of any building, we must evaluate the results in terms of image, behavior, climate, and economics.

Image Function

If we define user requirements as a combination of needs and aspirations, the image function is found to deal more directly with aspirations than needs. The design of a building, a car, or a piece of furniture has always carried with it the onus of doing the job with style. Although relating to specific functions is the reason for the project, we must accomplish this task in such a manner that the design enhances the environment where the various activities will take place. The emphasis on image may be quite different in the design of a town hall as compared with low cost housing, but we must recognize that the requirements in both cases are quite specific. Housing project designs which provide for all physical needs but ignore image have frequently contributed to costly failures — even bankruptcy. The design of vandal-proof schools has simply trained a more sophisticated generation of vandals. In the workplace, the sense of being valued may contribute to a person's productivity as much as any other factor. An architect must design to meet needs, but if this is done at the expense of image, the project will not be successful.

Behavior Function

The behavior function deals with the full range of human activities and the way we relate to one another. The social sciences are interested in this function in all of its ramifications, but the definition of user requirements in the context of this book requires us to separate out those activities which are not building-related. Winston Churchill's often quoted, ''We shape our buildings and then they shape us,'' cannot be taken quite literally, or a Bachelor of Architecture degree would be a prerequisite for obtaining a masters degree in sociology or psychology. There is, however, a loose fit between these disciplines, and we need to be aware of the appropriate criteria in the social sciences that have a direct bearing on the design and use of buildings. Low-income housing regulations requiring small, enclosed, galley-type kitchens deny single working parents the opportunity to spend time with their children after work. This is obviously a misguided policy. There have been studies of how buildings should be clustered to provide for security, there is a National Bureau of Standards research program designed to reduce deaths by fire in half, and there are efforts to analyze the implications of urban homesteading on stabilizing communities. But we are a long way from knowing a tenth as much about the effects of hospital room design on medical care and the healing process as we know about how advertising will sell cars.

In any study of the behavioral function, we can begin with the definition of simple activities performed by a single person or a group of people intent on the same thing — such as watching a film. The needs generated by these activities may be expressed in terms of space, service, furnishings, and the environment necessary for accomplishing the task. For the moment we will deal only with space. To design a house, we need to know what activities will take place within the house and in which rooms. Each activity then needs specific space, services, and furnishings, and they can then be determined for each activity or task. If we then look at all the tasks that will be performed in a given room, we find that they will need a monumental amount of space, unless the various activities can overlap and use the same space and facilities. This is in fact what happens, but, while it is easy to determine how much space is required for personal hygiene, it is more difficult to know at what point a household needs more than one space for certain activities or to what extent the resources required for a second bathroom would be better spent on some other feature in the house. The design of a studio apartment for a single person is easier to resolve than finding an appropriate solution relating to the interactions of a larger family. The implications of designing a neighborhood are even more complicated. It is unfortunate, therefore, that little attention is being given to the organized development of this type of information for specific building types.

_____

The climate function relates to the provision of an appropriate environment for the performance of various tasks. Thermal, luminous, and acoustical requirements tend to be more universal in their application than the other functions. We find that while the thermal comfort zone for a lightly clad individual might appear to be universal, in fact it shifts up or down some 5 to 8 degrees for people from warmer or colder climates according to physical adaptation and actual physical, metabolic, or dietary changes. Similar variations take place in dry or wet climates. However, immediate environments can be modified by selection of clothing or by thermal control of inhabited spaces.

Consideration of the luminous environment must begin with knowledge of how people see and the amount and quality of light required for a given task. We are all aware that in an appropriate setting the light of a single candle does little to impair the quality of conversation and discussion and may in fact enhance it. However, in a seminar discussion where notes are to be taken, a low light level would be a major constraint, and in a situation where written material must be referred to, one candle would not support the activity. The quality and quantity of the light, the direction from which it comes, and the glare across the viewing surface all affect how we see. At night the lights of an oncoming car are blinding because of the contrast between the brightness of the lights and the relatively low illumination levels on the road. During the day, the light differentiation would be relatively minor indeed. However, the eye adapts to the brightest source of light within its vision and has difficulty discerning detail if the contrast is too great. In daylight hours, the use of glare-reducing glass for school windows to lessen the contrast between the daylight and the light on the desk or chalkboard is quite necessary in bright environments. Work done at the Building Research Establishment in England has shown that in hospitals, daytime lighting of the inside of outside walls pierced by windows is a factor in patient recovery because it reduces the glare or contrast between the window and the surrounding wall. Each task or activity has its appropriate level of illumination, contrast, and glare, which may be called "sparkle" when its effect is positive.

The acoustic environment probably has a greater impact on privacy than any other environmental factor. Noise which impinges on our sleep, concentration, or relaxation, may come from within our own house, through a party wall, or from an outside source. While learning our neighbor's business may be of some interest to us, the realization that this is a two-way street turns curiosity into dismay! Conflicts occur as soon as we open the window to let in the fresh spring breezes and the sound of a motorcycle comes in as well. Today's living styles frequently call for large, interconnected spaces without full partitions. While the functional flexibility they provide is most beneficial, the potential for acoustical conflict increases. The ability to control the acoustical environment depends on (1) the tightness and mass of the separating walls or floors, (2) the ability of surfaces to absorb airborne sounds, and (3) the ability of walls or floors to absorb noises which impact them directly.

That students of these environmental disciplines think of themselves as studying architectural physics is indicative of the universal nature of these factors. That the greatest proportion of consumed energy is spent to provide appropriate environments gives special emphasis to the importance of this area of study. Our current concern with energy conservation has given a considerable boost to the field of building climatology, or the study of building design and orientation to take maximum advantage of the natural thermal and luminous environment. Indigenous design has been rediscovered and legitimized.

There was a period in the twentieth century when building designers went about their work focusing on a single function rather than on the four functions described here. The designs of some glass curtain walls, for example, challenged the mechanical engineer to make the buildings habitable. In many cases the challenge could not be met. The human body gains or loses heat almost equally through radiation and convection; unfortunately this means that if large surfaces of the building are much too hot or too cold, little can be done to provide optimum conditions through air-temperature control alone. On the other hand, the totally enclosed and sealed building, which can be well insulated for thermal purposes, may face greater problems in providing fresh air, and there are potentially serious implications in relation to natural illumination, natural ventilation, and outside visual contact.

Economic Function

Needs and aspirations must all be measured against the economic function — the reality of what can be afforded. Thermal control, natural ventilation, day lighting, and a good acoustic environment all have major cost implications. When we consider the relative merits of, say, extra storage space versus air conditioning, a common playground versus larger lots, the clustering of houses versus the elimination of basements we see that there are thousands of possibilities. Any building program that responds to the needs and aspirations of both user and client (if these are not the same) but does not subject the inevitable three-function wish list to the discipline of the fourth is outrageous and unprincipled. It leads to expectations that cannot be achieved, and the resulting compromises are inevitably made in such a manner that the resources are not effectively used to provide a balanced facility. Failure to consider the implications of the economic function at the outset of the design process will lead to a disappointing final result.

The ability to consider the various trade-offs in the right context depends on the ability to develop the cost implications of the different options. Then the combinations can be tested by any number of different techniques — from gaming to professionally oriented decision making, where sufficient information exists for such actions.

The cornerstone of the building process, then, is understanding the client and user requirements and allocating available resources to meet the appropriate combination of needs and aspirations to achieve the best possible solution. In the design of any facility, the available resources must provide for more than just the basic needs. They must also relate to image, lifestyle, and aesthetics, and provide a level of performance which goes beyond the physical demands for shelter and safety in the daily tasks of life. The ability to perceive the right mix for any client requires communication, understanding, and the willingness to say early enough in the dialogue that they can't have both this and that. By recognizing that most professionals are sincerely trying to do a good job but are hampered by a process which frequently separates program definition from design, the systems approach is dedicated to helping the architect work in a more organized, systematic, and efficient way. Today, despite increased user participation, architects cannot, in the name of community or client involvement, abdicate their professional responsibility of identifying and specifying what is necessary to meet user needs. At the other end of the spectrum, they cannot assume that their professionalism enables them to know, as a matter of experience, the user's aspirations, or, worse still, to be a judge of what is good for the client. It is therefore necessary to apportion the budget correctly between needs and aspirations. The resources needed to meet needs must be professionally determined, but this can only be done if a sufficient proportion of the budget is available for discretionary purposes determined by the user.

Analysis of Needs

In developing a user requirement statement, we must first deal with the behavior and climate functions to determine exactly what is needed to meet basic needs. Once this part of the statement has been developed, we must see how well it fits within the budget; we must then recognize that, in this analysis, in addition to meeting needs, we must also cater to aspirations. A proper analysis of the economic function, therefore, will include the allowance of sufficient financial resources to respond to the image function.

Once needs and essential aspirations have been met, we can make a decision about how to use additional or discretionary resources. Should they be introduced in the form of additional space, or should the equivalent cost be translated into other services to improve the building environment?

Obviously, if we find that we have embarked on a project whose budget precludes meeting even the minimum space requirements, it is essential that we return to first base and assess the desirability of building at all, or look for other resources to support the necessary increase in space. Whether these resources come from restructuring the financial basis of the project or from reducing some of the services or environmental qualities called for in the program has to be determined by the client and the designer.

Any project begins with an analysis of needs, which can be subdivided into four major areas: space, environment, service, and furnishings.

Space

Space requirements must be set forth for all tasks that will be performed within a building at the individual and group level. This may be done on a room-by-room basis (see Figure 3.1) or by a series of diagrams which de-

Figure 3.1 Each activity has its own specific space requirements.

SLEEPING

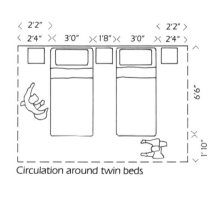

EATING

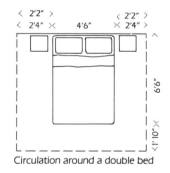

Making a bed

Circulation around twin beds

Circulation around a double bed

Sitting at a work table with a person passing

Sitting at a table for four and moving around

Sitting at a table for six and moving around

scribe the different activities and their space requirements. Once the activities are identified, the space needed for each of those activities must be determined. There may be many ways by which the space can be laid out (see Figure 3.3). To determine the *minimum* space required, all activities which take place within a given space must be scheduled to make sure that the same space is not allocated for objects and activities that take place simultaneously and that the space may be shared (see Figure 3.3). The actual space required may be made up of space used by a desk and chair, for example, together with space for someone to sit down or get in or out of the chair. The normal amount of space that can be justified for a room is one in which there is no overlap of use space among all the different tasks to be performed (see Figure 3.4). (If resources are available one may enhance the activities by adding space for aesthetic reasons. Unless one is designing for a wealthy client, that opportunity simply does not exist!) For most projects, somewhere in between the normal and minimum space requirements, a determination has to be made as to how much space is needed for an effi-

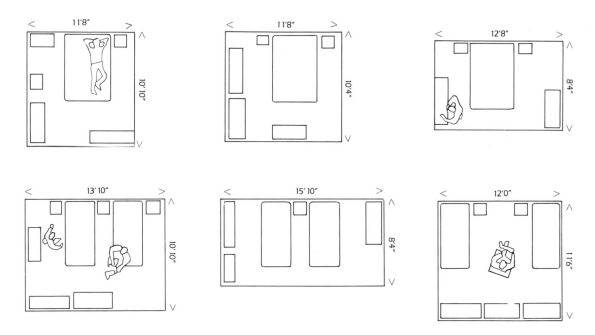

Figure 3.2 Generic layouts of minimum bedrooms.

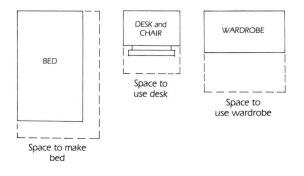

Figure 3.4 Typical furniture for student's room shown with its use space, i.e., the space required to make a bed or sit at a desk. Minimum design requires that the use space of various activities overlap one another but that sufficient space still be available for each activity.

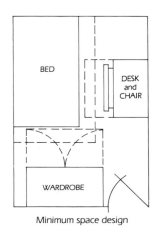

Minimum space design

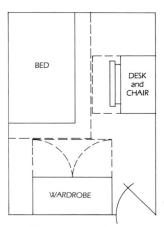

More gracious design with no overlapping-use space

Left section

	Living Room	Dining Room	Bedroom	Kitchen	Bathroom	Foyer	Utility Area	Private Garden
RECEPTION								
Activities								
Entry and exit				•		•		
Visiting						•		
Delivery				•		•		
Collection						•		
Servicing				•				
Furniture, appliances, and equipment								
Telephone				•		•		
Storage								
Closet						•	•	
SLEEPING AND DRESSING								
Activities								
Sleeping			•					
Making love			•					
Dressing			•					
Undressing			•					
Storing clothes			•					
Studying	•	•	•					
Furniture, appliances, and equipment								
Beds	•		•					
Chairs	•		•					
Table								
Dressing table			•	•				
Mirror			•	•				
Storage								
Closet			•					
Drawers			•					
Shelves			•	•				
PERSONAL CARE								
Activities								
Washing				•	•			
Bathing					•			
Excreting					•			
Making up			•		•			
Brushing hair			•		•			
Setting hair			•		•			
Cleaning teeth					•			
Taking medicine			•		•			
Manicuring			•		•			
Exercising	•		•		•			•
Cleaning shoes				•		•	•	
Brushing clothes			•	•		•	•	
Pressing clothes				•			•	
Washing clothes				•			•	
Furniture, appliances, and equipment								
Toilet					•			
Lavatory					•			
Bathtub					•			
Shower					•		•	
Urinal								
Bidet					•			
Exhaust fan					•		•	
Water heater				•	•		•	
Storage								
Medicine cabinet				•	•		•	
Towel racks					•			
Coat hooks					•	•	•	
SERVICE AND UTILITIES								
Activities								
Washing things				•			•	
Drying				•			•	•
Ironing	•		•				•	
Mending	•		•				•	
Cleaning	•	•	•	•	•	•	•	
Collecting rubbish				•			•	

Right section

	Living Room	Dining Room	Bedroom	Kitchen	Bathroom	Foyer	Utility Area	Private Garden
SERVICE AND UTILITIES *(cont.)*								
Collecting dirty clothes			•		•			
Sorting							•	
Storing linen			•				•	
Storing clothes			•			•		
Maintaining appliances				•	•		•	
Arranging flowers	•	•					•	
Repairs and renovations	•	•	•	•	•	•	•	
Disposing of garbage				•			•	
Furniture, appliances, and equipment								
Garbage disposal				•				
Dishwasher				•				
Washing machine				•	•		•	
Dryer				•	•		•	
Laundry tray				•	•		•	
Floor drain				•	•		•	
Furnace				•			•	
A/C filter							•	
H. V. C. terminal						•	•	
Fuse box				•		•	•	
Ironing board							•	
Sink				•			•	
Storage								
Linen closet				•		•	•	
Tool closet				•		•	•	•
Broom closet				•		•	•	
Shelves				•			•	
Drawers				•		•	•	
FOOD PREPARATION								
Activities								
Preparing food and drink	•	•		•				•
Cooking				•				•
Washing up				•			•	
Storing food				•				
Storing drink	•	•		•				
Refuse disposal				•			•	
Supervising kids	•	•		•		•	•	•
Furniture, appliances, and equipment								
Range				•				
Hood fans				•				
Refrigerator				•			•	
Kitchen sink				•				
Garbage disposal				•				
Exhaust fan				•				
Work top		•		•			•	
Chair or stool		•		•			•	
Telephone				•				
Storage								
Food closets				•				
Shelves				•				
Garbage bin				•		•		
Utensil closet		•		•				
EATING AND DRINKING								
Activities								
Eating	•	•		•				•
Drinking	•	•						•
Laying table		•						
Serving	•	•						•
Clearing away	•	•						•
Socializing	•	•						•
Parties	•	•						•
Furniture, appliances, and equipment								
Table	•	•		•				•
Chairs	•	•		•				•
Storage								
Drawers	•	•		•				
Closet	•	•	•					

Figure 3.3 Activities location chart, which acts as a checklist to determine which activities should be planned in each room. Specific lifestyles may thus be accommodated.

(continued)

ACTIVITIES LOCATION CHART

GENERAL LIVING	Living Room	Dining Room	Bedroom	Kitchen	Bathroom	Foyer	Utility Area	Private Garden
Activities								
Conversation	•	•						
Television	•							
Listening — radio, etc.	•			•				
Resting	•		•					•
Reading	•		•					•
Playing instruments	•							
Tape recording	•							
Studying	•	•	•					
Writing	•	•	•					
Entertaining	•							•
Playing games	•							•
Telephoning	•							
Growing plants	•							•
Making things	•							•
Sewing	•							
Collecting things	•							
Picture display	•	•	•					
Keeping pets	•			•				•
Showing films	•							
Storing equipment							•	
Supervising kids	•	•		•		•	•	•
Furniture, appliances, and equipment								
Tables	•			•			•	
Chairs	•			•			•	
Television	•	•	•	•			•	
Radio, etc.	•	•	•	•			•	
Desk	•	•	•	•			•	
Storage								
Closet	•	•	•	•		•	•	
Shelves	•	•	•	•		•	•	
Drawers	•	•	•	•		•	•	

PRIVATE OUTDOOR	Living Room	Dining Room	Bedroom	Kitchen	Bathroom	Foyer	Utility Area	Private Garden
Activities								
Gardening								•
Sun bathing								•
Eating barbecue								•
Drying washing							•	•
Stoop watching								•
Housing pets	•			•				
Supervising kids	•	•		•		•	•	•
Entertaining	•	•						•
Playing games	•							•
Washing car								•
Socializing	•	•						•
Putting baby out								•
Storage overflow								•
Furniture, appliances, and equipment								
Table								•
Chairs								•
Washing line								•
Hard standing								•
Faucet							•	•
Lawn mower							•	•
Gardening tools							•	•
Storage								
Shed or closet							•	•

Figure 3.3 (Continued)

cient facility. Once this threshold is established for space, financial allocations may be made for environment, service, and furnishings. One may have to recycle these allocations a number of times before it is possible to determine if the job can be done within the budget and then how it should be done.

Environment

Once the space requirements for the different activities have been determined, the necessary environmental conditions have to be established. Do they require enough light to thread a needle or work at a drafting board, or would a single footcandle be sufficient to encourage conversation and camaraderie? Is a temperature of 60 degrees appropriate for athletic activities, or is a minimum of 68 degrees needed for the comfort of sedentary workers? If one mandates too low a temperature for sedentary activities, productivity will go down and more people, space, and energy will be required to do the same job. The thermal-luminous-acoustical environments must all be specified in relation to the projected tasks. In complex buildings, once the basic environmental needs are defined, it becomes important to group activities that require similar environmental conditions so that they share spaces or adjacent spaces in the same control zone.

For an example of grouping similar activities in a single control zone, we can look at the case of a group of chemistry laboratories clustered together rather than dispersed throughout a variety of other classrooms within a school. The chemistry labs may need to be completely vented to the outside because of the potential for noxious odors. Clustering the labs allows this to be easily achieved without risking the return of foul air to the central equipment. But if the chemistry rooms are dispersed throughout the school, the duct arrangements and the attendant mechanical control zones become much more complex. In this case, if extreme care is not taken, the environment within the other classrooms may well be polluted.

The exact methods for meeting environmental requirements will be determined at a later point. But unless the designer is aware of the full spectrum of requirements at the beginning of the job, he or she may well provide for a juxtaposition of spaces which cannot respond to specific needs, or can only do so at increased cost. As specialized needs become more sophisticated, as in a hospital where positive and negative air pressures may be fixed for purpose of asepsis control, lack of clarity in the building organization can result in exorbitant costs or in an ineffective facility.

Services

In laying out the service pattern for a building, flexibility is the first priority, since the occupants' needs may change dramatically with the introduction of new kinds of equipment and new ways of working, or subsequent tenants may use the facility quite differently. In developing the building's service requirements for power, water, and waste disposal, we must once again set specific standards. A secretary performing normal office duties with a conventional electric typewriter may require 5 watts of power per square foot. If a microfilm reader is used, the power requirements may go up to 16 watts per square foot, but the space required may actually go down from 70 to 50 square feet. If a computer terminal is installed later on, the power requirements may go down to 7 watts per square foot, but the space requirements would probably jump to approximately 120 square feet per person. In determining the service requirements for a building, then, it is essential to account for potential changes in the power, water, and waste removal requirements of succeeding generations of occupants and design the building so that it can accommodate such changes without major structural or mechanical modification.

Furnishings

Guidelines for furniture and casework embrace a variety of fixed and movable elements placed within the space to meet basic user requirements. The bed, desk, dresser, and chair of a student's room, for example, all have their own space and design demands. In the past, student housing programs often called for fixing as many elements as possible, since funding was often tied to the amount of built-in equipment provided. But today, the program is more likely to specify a design which gives the student as many options as possible for organizing the furnishings to suit the idiosyncrasies of his or her lifestyle.

Discretionary Resources

Only when we have reached the point of establishing the relationship among these four major areas of concern and evaluating the cost implications of different levels of performance in each one can we determine what is actually needed for the job. We must establish thresholds of performance in terms of space, environment, service, and furnishings. At the same time, we must determine how much of our budget remains to be applied in a discretionary manner for either improving these levels of performance or providing other outside or common facilities such as landscaping the site. In designing a housing project, for example, we may have to choose between providing a swimming pool and community facilities, or allocating additional square footage to each of the dwelling units. Once the basic requirements within each dwelling unit are met, it is essential to take the specific character of the client or user into account to determine what use of these discretionary resources will provide the most satisfactory solution in terms of needs and aspirations.

Today, the user is becoming more sophisticated, more involved, and more active in participating in the formation of his or her own environment. This is an undeniable and, on the whole, positive trend in the design process. But it is of paramount importance that this user input be correctly interpreted in relation to the long-term satisfaction of the greatest number of users. In order to solicit and encourage this kind of constructive participation, many firms have developed techniques to clarify and focus the input of the user on realistic options. This can be done through mockups, models, intensive on-site planning sessions, specially designed questionnaires, and gaming exercises, where people assume different roles and juxtapose their space and environmental needs within a projected new facility.

Once we try to organize the occupants' activities within the building environment, the simple analysis of tasks, space, and support requirements gives way to a whole set of new criteria relating to the interaction of individuals with each other and with the physical environment. It is here that the designer must draw upon the knowledge and insights developed within the appropriate social science discipline. So far, communication between the designer and the social scientist has been disappointing. Social scientists have not yet seen sufficient evidence that their work has been effectively translated into a more responsive built environment to attract them in any significant way into this field. On the other hand, designers cannot be blamed for ignoring material presented in such a way that it is only of academic interest to the social scientists themselves and of no practical value in the context of the building process. What we need, therefore, is the equivalent of a technology transfer from the social science disciplines to the building industry, so that behavioral research has some chance of generating practical results. This demands structuring data so that they produce generic information. It is not the minutiae of individual reactions to a specific kitchen arrangement in a particular housing project that is of concern to the designer, but rather the kind of kitchen – living room relationship appropriate to the needs of the single working parent with family or to the traditional, two-parent nuclear family. The designer is asking the social scientist to provide information that can help understand this kind of generic situation.

In the absence of a well-documented body of knowledge in this area, our firm has developed our own — somewhat amateur — approach to obtaining this kind of behavioral insight into specific client groups and building types. Having seen sufficient evidence of failure, even where good planners and social scientists have worked together to project the behavioral results of a new facility, we realized that it was essential to conduct field studies. In the 1960s one well-known midwestern university undertook to build a new dormitory for first-year students. The campus officials analyzed what was taking place elsewhere and came to the conclusion that they would try to improve on the trends. First there was a general recognition that double rooms on a double loaded corridor with a large shared bathroom down at the end of the hall did not relate to changing student living patterns. Some institutions had been more successful in setting up alternate living patterns. One developed a small-house plan with approximately 25 students sharing common facilities. Later, other institutions successively reduced the student-group size for specific projects to 16, 13, 12, 10, and then 8. At each reduction, enthusiastic reports resulted, and the smaller numbers became associated with suites of rooms that usually had a shared living room and bathroom. The midwestern university in question thought that it would make the next advance with a suite for six students, each having a single room with common living room and bath facilities. The high hopes became a disaster when the project was completed and the highest freshman academic failure rate to that date was reported. It took 2 years to unravel the problem.

When students were studying at night and one of them wanted to take a break, he would invariably ask someone to accompany him. Since there were no snack facilities in the residence hall, they would have to go somewhere by car. The two students in turn would prevail on a third, the third on a fourth, and so on, until all six would go, since they could all fit into one car. This problem had not surfaced in the eight-student suites. It was only identified because it was found that the first-year students who lived in the same residence hall but did not suffer academically were strong individualists or loners who essentially did not participate very much, if at all, in student life. The solution was to convert a few student suites into an evening snack bar; grades then went back to normal. The key point of the story, however, is that behavior cannot be projected with any degree of certainty. You must build, test, and then learn the behavioral implications of specific human relationships.

Special caution is needed where government regulations exist or where the availability of funds is dependent on specific design initiatives. There is a tendency for Congress or administering agencies to intuit from separate precedents what would result from a new situation. As in the case of the galley kitchens mentioned earlier, unfortunately, it is difficult at best to project what will happen as a result of interactions between the built environment and behavioral patterns. Prototype projects that explore new directions before large-scale programs are entered into are a prerequisite of progress.

The tendency to look for a one-to-one relationship between needs and a specific design for other than mechanical tasks creates very serious potential problems. Changes in lifestyle, personnel, or task definitions could mean that a building will become prematurely obsolete. In the medical field, the great length of time from the start of programming a facility to its completion frequently renders some departments obsolete by opening day. Developing a set of user requirements should therefore take into account a variety of possible future uses to which the space might be put, with the opening configuration reflecting the clients' current wishes. This concept of analyzing the alternative futures while programming and designing a specific building is of paramount importance in a dynamic society. The tendency to design a school or hospital as a tailor-made suit is not only ridiculous, but it will cause significant failure that will discredit what was otherwise a logical approach.

Victorian houses were frequently designed with an excess of space which was very flexible in terms of how the space could be used. Today, the higher levels of performance required for services and environmental control, when coupled with increasing costs for energy and operations, require that we economize on space. For the overwhelming majority of the built environment, flexibility must be provided by design and not by an abundance of extra space.

Chapter Four

The Performance Concept

Introduction

The concept of *performance specifications* relates to what products must do rather than what they must be. The use of performance as a basic method of specifying building products is relatively new to the industry. Traditionally, specifications were prescriptive, calling for specific products or materials, although in some cases performance attributes were added to ensure that, subject to correct installation, the products would function at the required level. When you use a prescriptive specification, the opportunity to have new products developed to do the job more effectively disappears, as do the opportunities to use existing alternate products. The concept of specifying by performance provides for new ways to meet a given set of criteria, and opens new opportunities for ingenuity and innovation in the development of new methods and technology, and potentially for new ways to meet the basic user requirements.

Criteria can be set for reflectivity, abrasion resistance, flame spread, and many other characteristics without determining a product's configuration, material, or design. It is equally possible to determine performance so completely that only one product will meet the requirements. This is obviously counterproductive because if you know exactly what you want to do on a job you should ask for it outright. The use of performance specifications may limit bidding to more sophisticated contractors and thus reduce competition. However, when the desired results are known, but there is no specific way to achieve them, the use of performance opens the competition to a larger variety of these sophisticated bidders. When product or material specifications are used to determine product selection, performance specifications may still be used for quality control purposes in certain cases to set forth the in-place expectations of performance.

The performance concept takes on much more significance when seen in the context of the existing communications gap between the social scientists concerned with user requirements and the manufacturers concerned with marketing or selling products. The performance concept is the building industry's Rosetta stone through which the findings of social scientists and observers of human behavior can be translated into measurable standards that manufacturers of building materials, designers, and contractors can understand and respond to with effective products.

The success or failure of a building is measured most simply in terms of cost, time, and performance. Did it meet budget, open on time, and meet the user requirements? The measure of those requirements includes all aspects of the image, behavioral, and climate functions. The climate functions are easiest to measure in performance terms. The properties of the components which enclose the appropriate spaces contribute to the behavioral function, for example, chalkboards or tackboards on school partitions, or the organization and amount of residential storage space. The image function is most difficult to specify as it stems from the total synthesis of the project. It may be a property of how the job is done rather than of what is done.

In reviewing the various types of performance specifications, it becomes obvious that the precision with which specific requirements can be dealt varies according to the category being dealt with. When dealing with the fabric of the building itself, we can be very precise — whether it is acoustic separation, the fire protection properties of a partition, the thermal insulation or transparency of an exterior wall, the weatherproofing of a roof, or the extent of structural deflection.

Developing Performance Criteria

Performance may be determined in a variety of ways. In the area of environmental comfort, for example, we may specify performance by calling for temperatures to be within plus or minus 2 degrees of the thermostat setting at a given height within a room, for a certain number of footcandles to be provided at a desk or working surface, or for the extent of sound reduction between adjacent spaces that should be provided by a wall or door. In providing these criteria, we are not saying how the job is to be done but rather what the end result should be.

When we look at the properties of materials, we can evaluate the performance of a wall of masonry, Sheetrock, or wood paneling and develop levels of comparability. Once we have determined the required performance, we do not find ourselves asking for a higher level of performance because this would increase the cost without commensurate benefit to the user. We would not ask for a wood stud wall to be covered with sound insulation materials if that were irrelevant to the tasks being performed in the adjacent rooms. On the other hand, we would not permit standards to be lowered, which would be even worse.

In analyzing a variety of buildings at various times we found a number of anomalies. For example, when we were working with the University of California to develop performance specifications for acoustic separation between dormitory rooms, we found that — project by project — the acoustic standards and the thickness of the walls were being increased. This was primarily because students were complaining about lack of acoustic privacy, and the university responded by continually increasing the requirements for materials and/or the thickness of the walls. Unfortunately, we found that the typical residence hall had a double-loaded corridor, and that the return-air system used the corridor to draw air out of the rooms by undercutting the doors, thus there was a space between the bottom of the door and the floor covering. This was the path through which the sound entered. No additional thickness of the party wall would have any impact whatsoever on acoustic performance. Therefore, the establishment of the environmental criteria for the total room became the critical element of performance that made it possible to reduce the requirements for sound separation through the party walls and, at the same time, improve the acoustic privacy in the room by providing a better acoustic door. The acoustic criteria also required a more sophisticated air-conditioning system which reinforced the interdependence of all system components.

In developing performance criteria, our chief concern is to determine how well products will perform in the field as part of a coordinated working environment and not how well they perform in the laboratory. The development of performance criteria that apply in the field gives the architect a basis for rational decisions on all aspects of design that will add up to a properly coordinated result. It was obviously useless for the University of California, for example, to spend extra money thickening the dormitory walls while the doors were undercut. But as products are developed to meet specific performance criteria and as designers become familiar with performance data, it becomes easier to develop designs on a compatible basis so that the components can work together to achieve the required result.

To the extent that we can determine performance requirements, we can reduce uncertainties about what is needed. When we find that products do not exist to meet needs we must encourage their development. Gathering an aggregated construction market of sufficient size and providing appropriate incentives may be needed to stimulate the development work.

SCSD was the first development program to use performance specifications. The requirements for many school districts were defined in performance terms in a generic manner. Given specific performance targets, the industry developed new and responsive products which have been used in thousands of schools, but their specification today is invariably stated in prescriptive terms.

The purpose of pilot programs is to sponsor needed innovation. Once accomplished, it is appropriate that the results be folded back into conventional industry for widespread use. It is interesting to note that for the SCSD program, the labor unions understood this better than some of the professional and contracting groups involved.

When working for the various California school districts on the SCSD project, we found many instances of rooms that were too warm for the comfort of the average school child. Teachers had set the thermostats based on their own comfort. The average teacher, leading a relatively sedentary life, had a fairly poor metabolism and was prone to cold feet. In the winter, normal classrooms would have cold air coming off the window walls and lying along the floor, creating a type of air stratification that did not affect the thermostat, which was 4 to 5 feet above the floor. As a result, the teachers turned up the thermostats, put the kids to sleep, and, in the process, used sufficient energy to pay the salaries of a couple of teachers! Our innovation in this case was to set performance standards that required the room temperature to be within plus or minus 2 degrees of the thermostat setting at breathing level *and* at 6 inches above the floor. In this way, it was possible to provide an environmental climate acceptable to both students and teachers, and, at the same time, respond to life cycle costs, which were less critical in 1963 than they are today.

The examples so far have dealt with the type of criteria that may be established for environmental needs based on how the eye sees, on thermal comfort, or on acoustic privacy. But when we try to set performance standards for spatial requirements, we have quite another problem. It is more difficult to determine from a simple index how many square feet are needed in a dormitory room or the area a secretary needs to perform a given set of activities. We can certainly determine the space required for each piece of furniture, the apparatus required for the job, and the minimum amount of space needed to gain access to those facilities, but the way in which people will work within a space may well be affected by such factors as the overall square footage available, the perception of the pleasantness of the space, or how their specific area relates to others. No matter how adequate a space may be for a specific function, the policies set within an organizational framework will have a major impact on how well it works. In the development of performance requirements for space allocation, aspirations are difficult to pin down in performance terms, since they are affected by variables such as the amount of space provided for similar tasks by competing organizations. The performance concept can, however, be used to determine how much space is needed. The space needed for each piece of furniture or equipment, whether or not it overlaps its use space, as discussed previously, as well as the design of the objects themselves, provide a basis for determining adequacy for user needs if not aspirations. The use of space as a status symbol for an executive may have to give way in these days of concern about efficiency. Communications capability has become a new status symbol in an era when productivity and the sense of being "plugged in" is much more highly prized in the marketplace.

Performance will go a long way by itself, but it does not provide the ability to pin down every aspect of a job. The performance concept does not determine the total design of a building; it can only provide a limited framework for reducing the unknowns and providing a responsive design vocabulary. It should, however, take the designer as far as possible in developing a vocabulary of products so that he or she can satisfy aspirations as well as needs. How this is done is up to the individual designer. For example, in working on the URBS program, we found that small, shared bathrooms were both economical and necessary to meet the students' strongly expressed wishes.* In working with these shared facilities, we also found that students were reluctant to take baths rather than showers because of debris left by the previous bather. We are all aware of how difficult it is to clean a bathtub — the incoming water for cleaning pushes the debris upstream and when the water is let out, the debris stops in the same place. The first design alternative was to place the drain at the opposite end from the faucet, but obviously it would be very difficult to sit on a drain. The other immediate solution, placing the spigot behind the user's back, was equally unappealing because the user could be scalded when the hot water was turned on to top-up the temperature. Since a shower requires a greater width than a tub, it was possible to design a bath-shower combination with a work or reading counter alongside the tub section and with the drain located at the base of this counter. This made it possible to obtain a flushing action of water, which came in at one location and went out at another, while making good use of all the available space (see Figure 4.1).

Products developed in response to performance standards solve generic problems and provide components that can be used in different configurations and combinations. They are concerned not with meeting the specific needs of an individual vice president in the corner office on the tenth floor of the newest high rise building, but with the family of needs of senior executives in the modern office situation.

When we talk of performance requirements for services, we are frequently dealing with concerns about future, as well as present, use of space. For example, as we have said, a secretary performing a clerical task may use different types of equipment that require varying amounts of energy as well as different amounts of space. The decision may essentially be to reduce the number of people needed to perform a task by expending capital on more efficient tools. If you wish to create flexible use of space, you have to build in

* These user requirements are discussed in more detail in the URBS case study in Part 3.

Figure 4.1 Mock-up of bathtub design.

the possibilities for servicing blocks of space to meet viable options in the future. In evaluating service performance requirements, then, it is essential to take into account logical alternative futures for the building and the extent to which the increased services required to accommodate them can be amortized within the context of first cost. From this kind of analysis, the levels of performance appropriate to a specific building project can be determined. At the University of California, it was not the specific acoustical performance of the wall or ceiling that was our concern, but rather the acoustical relationship of one space to the next. If sound escapes between the wall and ceiling, the solution is unacceptable, no matter how good each of the products is independently.

Performance specifications must be used to provide a working integration of all products to meet the user requirements. If the user still finds the resulting environment unacceptable, then the performance concept provides measurable standards with which to specify improved performance levels on subsequent projects. Without the performance concept, we do not have a common language for learning. As soon as a feedback loop between acceptability and building performance is developed, we have the beginning of a scientific method for obtaining a proper fit between the building and the user—hypotheses that can be tested and retested so that we can alter building performance to achieve acceptability. For these reasons, we must move away from the concept of developing new materials on a prescriptive product basis and use performance specifications instead. It is only through the vehicle of performance that we can approach a responsible feedback loop through which to evaluate the success of a building.

Different levels of performance have different costs. Once it is possible to relate performance to user requirements and then to cost, we have the key elements for implementing a systems approach to design . . . the ability to determine how the available dollars can be applied to meet user requirements.

The architect working within a fixed budget is able to allocate dollar resources to provide for appropriate levels of performance for all the constituent elements of a building. There is a basis on which to decide, for example, between extra floor area or air conditioning.

The trade-offs required to achieve the best possible value for the money call for the development of an acceptable threshold of performance for meeting user requirements. Something above this threshold can perhaps be taken as a good average or desirable norm for most buildings. Levels above this norm must be considered discretionary. In certain cases, the aspirations of an individual client may suggest the allocation of all the discretionary funds into a single area or a few specific areas in order to achieve a building of unique character. But in other cases where funds are low or where the unique attributes desired are very costly, it may be necessary to go down to the threshold of acceptable performance in order to obtain the funds needed to meet the aspirations. A good designer, responsive to the client's actual as well as perceived needs, will never go below the minimum threshold. In many cases, codes and standards establish these thresholds by fiat.

The concept of performance thus provides an opportunity to organize the disposition of available resources in response to user requirements — seen as a combination of needs and aspirations. It permits interaction between designers and sociologists through the postulation of testable standards. We need this kind of tool in order to take an intelligent approach toward measuring the way in which resources are allocated. Once we do this, it begins to make sense to attempt to classify all the resources that can be used on a single building so that we can have sound cost-performance data on all our options, which will provide the basis for rational choice.

Performance in Use

When using the performance concept in an innovative program, we must begin with a knowledge of the user's requirements and the available budget. The size of the market and the time until occupancy will have a major impact on the process we select and on the level of innovation that will be possible. The essential reason for using performance specifications in an innovative program is to create new products that can better meet the user's requirements within the given economic context. The ability to engage the industry in this pursuit is dependent on the investment required for a market potential of appropriate size. If the required levels of innovation go beyond what the market will sustain, there will be no serious participants. If the budget is inappropriate for the levels of innovation, the most sophisticated companies will not participate in the program, while those that do will be frustrated when cost problems undercut the program. There must be a balance between expectation and cost, level of innovation and available time, and market size and investment required. Getting a better mousetrap just for the asking is not going to occur by magic because of the use of performance specifications. We must first determine how user requirements can be met, what level of research and development work will be required, what are the likely costs for component options which may meet the specifications, and whether the market size is appropriate for the required work. It is only when these studies have been carefully carried out that the performance specifications can be completed. (Figure 4.2 shows a prototype ceiling coffer that was designed and built while we were working to set the requirements in order to assure the working team that the performance standards could be met in an aesthetically acceptable manner and at an affordable price.)

When the performance specifications have been developed so that they translate the user's requirements into a form that can be bid within an appropriate working context, we can move on to study the procurement process. First we must determine which components of a building will be bid through performance, and which through prescription where no innovation is required. For example, the design requirements of exterior walls

Figure 4.2 Prototype ceiling coffer built to test practicality and acceptability of the design implications embodied in the performance specifications.

are so varied that the product performance for each building can best be determined by the design architect,* or the market size may be insufficient for a specific innovation such as a new size of fluorescent tube or a prefabricated kitchen-bathroom core unit. For those component categories where the level of innovation desired is appropriate to the job situation, it is still necessary to analyze the extent to which performance specifications can control all the required design implications.

The SCSD project, based on a performance concept, was begun in 1961, at about the same time that McNamara and the Defense Department were beginning to implement their systems building programs for defense procurement. SCSD was the first building project based on performance in the United States and perhaps the world. It is interesting to note that the low bidder in one of the component categories was disqualified because of failure to meet the specifications. The thirteen-school district client was sued, not because of claims that the performance could be or had been met, but because bidding on performance rather than on material or prescriptive specifications was claimed to provide an unfair basis for bidding.

In preparing for trial, our lawyers found only two precedents which had any bearing on the case: one was on bids taken on the lock for the Oakland, California, jail in 1928 and the other on bids for a chicken coop for a farmer in Vineland, New Jersey, in 1907. We were gratified that the First Superior Court of San Jose's findings were not only that the performance approach was vindicated but that performance bidding provided greater opportunities for competition than prescriptive specifications. It was an important victory for our approach.

If there is concern about the visual aspect of a performance bid, it may be necessary to have a design submission prior to the actual receipt of bids. This was done in the SCSD project, and in others which followed, to make sure that the design results were in accord with the intent of the specification. Bidders were required to obtain design approval before submitting prices. But if you try to specify the total appearance of all products you might as well prescribe products, since you cannot control design and cost, and then put the onus of performance on the manufacturer. However, one can set the limits so that the design framework is very carefully spelled out. For example, in SCSD, where it appeared that a post-and-panel approach was inappropriate for school partitions, the specifications read ". . . the partitions joint shall be seen as no more than two lines not more than an inch apart and there shall be no indentations or protrusions of the surface."

In addition to the design review, a performance review may well be appropriate. The basis of bidding is the ability of the various manufacturers' solutions to meet the specifications. It is easier to throw out or require modifications of a solution before it is bid in at the lowest price than afterward. The design and performance considerations create the rationale for a two-stage bidding process which provides a basis for determining the capacity and fitness of the proposed solution before final bids are permitted. On simple projects, however, or for components that do not have a significant visual impact, a single-stage bidding process may be acceptable. Once bids are received and the successful bidders designated, a development and testing program must be initiated to demonstrate that the products do in fact meet the requirements. The acceptance of the concepts in the two-stage bidding process attests to the reasonableness of the approaches, but in no way substitutes for the tests. As the testing program may require substantial

---

* As the interplay between components specified on a prescriptive and a performance basis affects total performance, it may well be necessary, for example, to state the permissible heat gain or loss through the exterior wall under which conditions thermal performance must be met. If the designer does not meet these requirements, the heating, ventilating, and cooling system is not responsible.

funds, it is not possible or advisable to require complete testing prior to selection of the successful bidder. Once selected, however, the testing program must be undertaken. Once certified, the products are ready for use.

Very early in our experience with the use of performance specifications, we found that prescribed products did not always meet the manufacturer's own criteria. In the SCSD program, we accepted that manufacturers' stated criteria for chalkboards were adequate. Five of the major companies said they all met the specifications, the criteria were stated in their own promotional literature, and the products were typically specified by many of our school districts. After adopting their specifications and taking bids, we were amazed to find that not one of the companies could meet its own advertised specifications. The use of performance specifications obviously protects the client.

In the URBS project we found that after occupancy the room-to-room acoustic separation on the top floor of the residence halls was not satisfactory. The performance was checked and found deficient. The responsible parties were called in, and they were requested to rectify the situation. Analysis showed that normal creep in the concrete floors caused some displacement of all the floor slabs, but as this was uniform throughout the building, the tolerance control that the partitions had to adapt to could compensate for this movement. On the top floor, however, the roof did not move so that there were cracks between the partitions and the roof slab which the partitions were unable to handle acoustically. In effect, the structural subsystem of the building did not perform according to specifications, and that subcontractor paid to modify the details of the joint between the partitions and roof slab.

It is essential that performance criteria for each of the building subsystems also include the requirements for compatibility with and responsibility for total building performance. If done well, this can pinpoint responsibility in a manner which removes any ambiguity. Single-source responsibility is an ideal toward which we must work; its achievement requires proper definition of the boundaries.

If the results of an innovative program provide good value, they will be used on subsequent projects and become integrated within the conventional building industry unless the manufacturer wishes to restrict their use to specific situations such as a closed system consisting of a totally predetermined group of products. In the first case, the new products will quickly be specified by prescription, and the net result of the process will be the enlargement of the design vocabulary for all to use. So enlarged, this vocabulary should be more responsive to evolving user needs within established cost expectations.

In the design of a single building where products are prescribed, the role of performance as a vehicle for quality control, as previously mentioned, ensures that the manufacture and installation of products meet performance levels on which tests can be run. Between these two extremes — large innovative projects and a single prescribed project — there are many variations on how the performance concept may be used.

Understanding how all products perform and their cost implications in response to user requirements is an essential skill which must be developed in applying the systems process to design. The mastery of this information allows use of the performance concept in the designer's decision-making process.

Part Two

Resources

Chapter Five

Resources Overview

In the preceding chapters, I have discussed the development and use of a process that makes it possible for the designer to identify and translate user requirements into an understandable form. The content and methodology of the building industry's response to this information will be the subject of Part 2, which deals with the correlation between desired and deliverable performance and what must be done to bring the two into mutually satisfactory alignment (see Figure 5.1).

The response to an expression of need is the complex generator of requirements for the built environment, but poor communication of needs may cause buildings to fail to meet user needs. The user and the industry are tied together in a synergistic relationship, but because they speak different languages and have different goals and motivations, industry's response has not necessarily been attuned to the real needs of the user. Incentives for success, on the one hand, do not correlate with satisfaction on the other. Yet, because the capacity to satisfy society's needs depends on interaction between user and industry, the prime focus for the systems approach is bridging this communications gap. Once communication is established, it becomes possible to deal with problem solving and to concentrate on the allocation of resources to meet specific needs.

Figure 5.1 In practice one must be able to determine the level of desired performance that can be delivered within the constraints of time, cost, and the various codes which regulate what can be built. This must be done before completing the program for any building so that the design process may be used for design and not for cost control.

Desired performance	Regulated performance	Deliverable performance
Predictive ability	*Interactive standards*	*Resource management*
"What *may* be asked for."	"What *shall* be asked for or provided."	"What *can* be provided."

We must deal with five resource categories: land, finance, management, technology, and labor. We must consider how they may best be used in the context of three main levels of problem solving: policy, program, and building design. Although we recognize that the individual architect or designer may not always be involved in policy or even program decisions, the success of his or her work is undeniably dependent on the successful resolutions of these considerations. For this reason, we will deal first with the policy level and then move from general to more specific considerations.

Levels of Problem Solving

The Policy Level

The policy level determines the context of societal goals and resource allocations at the federal, state, and local levels. Tax policy, zoning issues, mortgage insurance, etc., all tend to shape the framework within which the system works. When the user requirements of a large group of people are recognized in principle and resources have been allocated to meet them, the next step is to determine how these resources should be apportioned and to set priorities, such as housing, health care, or transportation. At this stage, we must establish a range of options that are attainable with the resources available for each area to be addressed, and we must determine how these alternatives relate to societal needs.

Priorities must then be set with an understanding of the initial and long-range implications of the choices. For example, if there are insufficient resources to meet the full range of community health needs, choices may have to be made between a new teaching hospital, scattered health clinics, a vaccination program, or environmental services relating to water and sewage. In such circumstances, it may not be appropriate or viable to build at all.

The Building Program Level

The building program level covers the stage at which general needs have been identified, but their full extent is still undetermined. You know the context you are working in; the site may or may not be selected; there are preliminary resource allocations, but their adequacy is not yet established. At this stage, the task is to determine whether a viable package can be assembled, and land, finances, technology, management and labor can be allocated so as to meet user requirements. The way resources are analyzed at this stage may well determine if individual projects can be realized.

At this level, before the program has been finalized, the kind of issues to be studied are those which balance user requirements on the one hand with dollars on the other. In this context, one must consider questions such as (1) the impact of the site selection on density, the community, and site services, (2) allocation of the available finances for land, infrastructure, and community amenities, and (3) the management process and the concomitant need for speed, cost control, and elimination of risk. Once defined needs have been translated into performance criteria and a reasonable allocation of resources has been made, design can begin. The parameters of the situation have been defined clearly enough to identify the problem as a design task. The design options and the building program should be developed concomitantly so that the image and contextual issues may be taken into account before the program is set.

The Building Design Level

The building design level begins when the site has been selected, the budget established, and user requirements embodied within a draft building program. At this point, the cost-performance trade-offs involving all of the aesthetic, behavioral, and environmental functions reviewed in Part 1 are the chief focus. When the requirements are known and adequate resources are shown to be available to implement an appropriate design direction, the designer's task is to design the best possible building.

Resource Allocation

The systems process is one which looks for optimization at every level. The trade-offs may be made at different levels: (1) first cost versus life costs, (2) construction acceleration versus cost overrun, (3) use of high technology versus generic products. There are literally dozens of trade-offs possible, but there are usually enough boundary conditions to prescribe a reasonable range of possible variations for a specific project. Shortages of labor, energy, or management skills, or specific project requirements for performance, time, or cost usually provide a series of givens which reduce the number of options to a manageable level and set up a ranking of key factors which determines priorities within those packages.

On one occasion, we were working on a public housing project which involved the construction of 1000 units per year on a turnkey basis. This assumed that approximately 80 units would be started every month. If the units took 6 months to complete, the developer's annual cash flow requirement would be $12.8 million. If they took 3 months to complete, the cash flow requirement was only $3 million. The search for a technology which would allow completion in 3 months thus became an essential part of the developer's game plan. The magnitude of the implications for cash flow, along with the interim financing costs, meant that the developer could afford to pay more for a faster way to build.

In dealing with any problem, you must first determine whether the user requirement and resource sides of the equation are in balance. If so, the task will be to allocate the resources among the different attributes in a manner appropriate to the client's needs and aspirations. If you fall short of meeting those requirements, you must restructure the context within which you are working in order to make the problem soluble.

The triad of cost, square feet, and quality of environment (QE) shown in Figure 5.2 may be used to represent the four-function model, which relates to the economic, behavioral, and climate functions. The image function is dependent on how the job is done and whether there is a modicum of surplus dollars once acceptable thresholds of economy, behavior, and climate have been met. The triad represents a group of static conditions with regard to interest rates, land availability, and technological approaches. Within this triad, if the dollars are constant and more space is needed, the quality of environment must go down and vice versa. If quality goes up and the square footage remains the same, then the cost must also go up. This is true in a context in which all the resources have fixed norms. But if you change the way the land is used, the interest rate, the speed with which the project is built (and, hence, interim financing), the application of technology or design innovation (which may affect both first and life costs, as well as the way in which labor puts the job together on the site) then you can change the situation significantly. You have, in effect, created a new context in which the problem can be reevaluated and, in some cases, potentially insoluble problems can be solved (Figure 5.3).

The task of the designer must be to solve problems, even if this requires changing the context within which he or she is working. We are no longer working in the era of the Medici, when the patron made these decisions on behalf of the population at large. In some cases it may be more important to

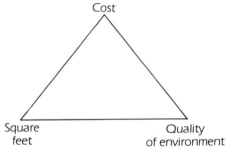

Figure 5.2 Triad of cost, square feet, and quality of environment.

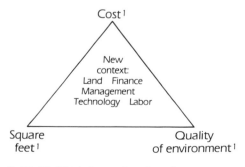

Figure 5.3 The balance of needs and resources may have many permutations. If a solution cannot be found within the conditions assumed for the triad initially, examine the context in which those conditions apply to find other possible solutions.

change the context in which we work than to increase the budget by 10 percent.

It is important for us to keep this problem-solving hierarchy in mind as we approach our work as architects and designers. Serious problems are created at any level of the hierarchy if we embark on the details of design without first defining the givens in terms of desired and deliverable performance. If we try to achieve a design solution without complete program information or before the budget allocation has been made, we run the risk of raising expectations that cannot be met or, conversely, of producing a building which is less than the best value for the money available. If people have been led to expect more than they actually get, even an otherwise acceptable solution may be rejected.

The review of resource areas which follows will relate to all three levels in the problem-solving hierarchy by identifying the issues most germane to each resource area and, where appropriate, by analyzing their impact on policy, program, or design decisions.

Chapter Six

Land

Selection Factors _____

The concept that land is a resource whose availability is a matter of critical concern seems unreasonable when we fly from coast to coast across the United States. But when we are faced with finding an appropriate parcel of land for a given use within an urban context, the competition among different uses and potential owners results in relatively high costs and in the need to use a very substantial portion of the building budget to procure the site. Location may be of prime importance and will very likely determine the value of a piece of land—whether it is the right location for a shopping center, a school, a one-acre home, or an industrial site with good access to workers and to transportation for materials and products. When a specific project site is selected, the project cost will determine the density at which such sites must be developed in order to justify the purchase price. The annual revenue required to make the project at that location economically viable and a variety of value judgments and market studies will contribute to this determination. In areas of high demand, the zoning designation is quickly translated into the asking price. If no one wishes to build a 40-story office building in a particular area, zoning parcels for this purpose will do little to enhance the value of the land.

Given the allowable zoning criteria, there are a number of trade-offs with respect to density which influence how a parcel of land may be developed. The lifestyle of people living in the suburbs may require the construction of single-family detached houses even though multiple dwelling units are allowed by code. In other cases, the cost of providing services for widely scattered units may create a pressure for clustering housing in planned unit developments. But as buildings are clustered, or as the number of stories increases, code requirements for fire protection and means of egress begin to offset the reduced costs of service. It is here that a variety of trade-offs may be made in respect to the density with which a piece of land is developed. The establishment of courtyards or recreational facilities without necessarily using the full potential for enclosing space may enhance the value of the buildings placed on a site. These trade-offs become important in the overall context in which the land costs, building costs, operations, maintenance, and finance charges are all taken together to establish a budget for construction and operation of the facilities.

Once location and density are determined, we have to examine more closely the nature of the site and services available to it in order to evaluate the way the building will sit on that site. The soil conditions may well dictate the use of piles as opposed to simpler spread footings. Construction on very rocky sites may require substantial outlays for blasting to allow for basements and the installation of underground utilities. All of these site-related factors have an impact on the cost of the building. The slope and orientation of the site are particularly important. A relatively inexpensive piece of land in a good location may well be available because it straddles an earthquake fault or has a 45° slope. Invariably, the cost of the property is inversely proportional to the cost of making it usable. The considerable engineering skills which must be employed in a difficult situation can cause nightmares for an unknowing client but it could be an area of opportunity for the creative architect and engineer. The orientation of the site and its access to transportation and services may well determine the building's configuration. A downhill slope facing north may raise considerable problems for providing appropriate orientation for living spaces with adequate privacy. The desire for sunlight may mandate large windows, but if these face the road and are exposed to view, a creative design approach is called for, which may be very effective architecturally but will undoubtedly add to the cost of the building and, in essence, increase the cost of the land.

The local climate or microclimate may also be an item of considerable concern when deciding where to build. The impact of conditions can be mitigated to a considerable extent if, like troglodyte dwellers, we can build at a sufficient depth so that the earth itself modifies the climate. This type of

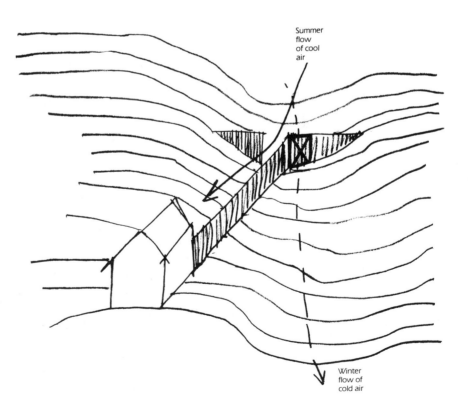

Figure 6.1 An understanding of microclimatology enables us to position buildings, fences, and landscape elements to modify the environment in favor of human comfort.

living may not suit our current tastes and in no case is appropriate to humid climates, but there are many ways in which we can build structures on a specific site so as to modify the environment for the user's benefit and take advantage of local variations in microclimate. Siting a house on top of a hill may cause it to be rather cool and windy in winter, but if it is placed in the bowl of a valley it will be quite cold at night when the cold, heavier air flows down the sides of the mountains and is, in effect, deposited in pockets within the valleys. The traditional location for sanatoria, two-thirds of the way up the side of a mountain facing south, typically provides the most beneficial climate.

Since the site location within a relatively small geographic area may well have a major impact on comfort, the microclimate can significantly affect the real value of a piece of land more than is normally recognized. Prior to the introduction of air conditioning, climatologists paid considerable attention to microclimate. Specific buildings were sited near natural drainage gullies coming off the sides of mountains and were designed so that in summer, when the cool evening air began to fall into those low points, dams could be used to channel cold air into the buildings (see Figure 6.1). In the wintertime, the dams could be opened, allowing the cold air to bypass buildings and go down into the valley. As we become increasingly concerned with the cost of energy conservation, we will have to consider how we place our buildings on a piece of land much more carefully. We will have to pay much greater attention to a building's configuration in relation to natural air movements and to the use of trees and landscaping to shade and protect, as well as to channel breezes into the buildings at the appropriate season. All of these factors affect the selection of any piece of land and the way in which it is used, and—considered in conjunction with other options—the amount of money available to put into the building itself.

Energy Costs

From time immemorial, until 1971, the cost of energy continuously declined. As firewood became scarce, a shift was made to coal, and then to oil and gas. But in 1971 the incremental costs of developing new sources of energy outweighed the unit costs of the developed energy resources, as shown in Figure 6.2.

During the time when energy costs were constantly declining, designing buildings to relate to the climate was of less significance in a technological society which could increase its discretionary financial resources through high levels of productivity. Many people thus designed buildings without regard to climate and, given the prevailing aspirations, those buildings made sense and were acclaimed.

Now we are faced with a situation in which energy costs are increasing, albeit with short term variations in price and will continue to do so for the predictable future. But, unfortunately, if we go back to earlier models of climate-related building designs, we find them inappropriate, since the densities and needs for which they were developed no longer relate to modern high-density urban patterns. New principles, processes, and applications of climate-related design, as well as new sources of energy, must therefore be developed.

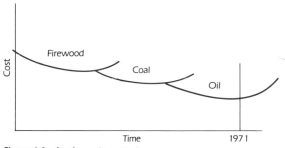

Figure 6.2 As the unit cost of energy increases, the need to conserve all our natural resources, including land, is emphasized.

Land Use

Assuming the appropriate selection of a land parcel for a given purpose, we must then consider the use of land for groups of buildings and for a variety of urban functions. The patterns developed in terms of street layout, pedestrian traffic, availability of services, and demand for school busing are all the result of a network of uses which have evolved over a considerable period of time. These patterns reflect the selection of various options available to society. There are not many American Greenbelts or Radburns with which to test the concept of shared communal lands and pedestrian pathways segregated from highways. If such planning options were offered to the population in general, we do not know whether people would choose them. The scale of development necessary to provide such options, as were provided at Reston and Columbia, makes it difficult for most developers to offer the choice. But the study of model super blocks that have more efficient use of roads and services and some level of internally developed community lands or that have the ribbon-type arrangement typical of much of the English new town planning should be undertaken. It is most important to consider the internal combustion engine as the basis for the form of current development. Just as we cannot look back to the seventeenth century for current climate models, we may soon not be able to look back at the twentieth century for applicable transportation models.

Energy concerns demand that we use space more intensively. The concept of denser urban communities makes sense when we combine living, working, and service areas with access to diverse activities in order to decrease reliance on the automobile. If current trends continue, the pressure for this combination of diversity and density will increase. This does not simply mean that houses will have to be closer together, but it means a mixed use of land which groups the functions of daily life so that they are accessible by foot, public transport, and bicycle as well as automobile. Such patterns are extremely difficult to develop because the options are currently considered in the context of the economic rationale of the moment. Economic planning which is based only on cash flow available at the time of move in must give way to a system which anticipates the realities of cash flow available 10 years later. Increasingly energy costs, with their implications for individual and national budgets, demand a tightening of community development. But this cannot be accomplished by moving a group of houses already on foundations closer together or by introducing a "mom and pop store" into a neighborhood with 4-acre zoning.

We therefore have to consider the development of other forms of urban clustering which make it possible to meet the economic requirements at the time of first occupancy as well as the costs of the amortization period. This calls for a completely new set of incentives in terms of allocation of federal resources for roads, sewer, and water grants and for a new review of the direction that our current zoning requirements are taking us. We cannot afford to ignore the dynamic situation in which we are living and to continue to build communities which our children will not be able to afford to operate. The very strength of any civilized nation relates to the capital plant which is set in place and on which succeeding generations can build. If we must start from scratch because our communities have developed in a way which is not viable within the context of any of the predictable energy and economic futures, then we must expend considerable national resources to bring future discrepancies back into balance. And if we continue to build as though that day of reckoning will never come, the shock will be so much the greater. The systems process, therefore, calls for an analysis of how to build on any piece of land, of how these units may be clustered together to provide multiple facilities to meet the full range of human needs within an economic context. In order to set these criteria, we must relate land use to master planning. Consideration of issues affecting the master plan in fact come first. Zoning decisions must precede land use patterns which, in turn, must precede decisions about how to build on ordinary sites.

Goals for land use, transportation, service infrastructure, and density are usually established by planners in the development of master plans which, if accepted, are implemented through zoning controls coupled with a combination of public and private expenditure for service infrastructure and buildings. Unfortunately, the master planning process all too often tends to regard the region or city in static terms. The allocation of land to different uses and the projection of transportation or other service facilities is based on the situation pertaining at a given time. By the time approvals are obtained and the multicolored plans produced in all their glory, the average community has issued sufficient variances to invalidate the published plan. If the plans do not fit the current situation, then further variances are granted. This is especially true when a system of economic incentives is in operation which works against the maintenance of the master plan. For example, when a piece of land is rezoned for a higher level of use, its value is increased. Such forces require that our cities change in response to the market place, even when the citizenry does not benefit. Since those who control the variances are not responsible for the overall management of the community, they do not have to provide money for school buses, water, or electricity. In the end, because of these actions, the entire master plan is invalidated.

A systems approach to planning accepts the fact that political decisions will be made which will affect any plan. The latitude for such decisions must be spelled out very carefully through development of an approved planning process with a decision-making model that permits the use of land to evolve in relation to specific sets of criteria — under the aegis of an approval hierarchy that determines what can or cannot be done. The decision on how land is to be allocated must be related to three factors: its public cost, its environmental impact, and its implications for future options. Constraints applied to the use of land for specific projects that do not impact any of these three factors should be most easily removed. Where a use decision incurs public costs, another level of decision-making machinery with greater constraints must be activated to deal with what has become a regional matter. Finally, changes in land use which limit or rule out specific alternative futures must have the toughest criteria for approval.

One might organize the decision-making hierarchy in the following ways.

Level 1. No measurable impact on the three factors — variances approved by administrative personnel.

Level 2. Impact on public costs — those responsible for overall budget implications must be involved in the decision process.

Level 3. Environmental impact — those affected at all levels must be heard.

Level 4. Impact on alternative futures — should require some sort of referendum or delaying mechanism so that spur-of-the-moment action based on today's whims cannot change the options of future generations.

A master plan which consists of effective machinery for articulating and organizing the decision-making process will be more effective and useful than any set of multicolored drawings.

If planning could take into account a whole series of alternative futures, the highest levels of constraint would be imposed when significant future options would be impaired as a result of exercising those options. Decisions should be made with fewer constraints when the perceived futures are not affected. At some point in the successive stages of development, a decision must be made with respect to choosing one direction or another after appropriate study. At this stage, it may be that all you can do is ensure that the options that are kept open — as against those eliminated — represent the most profound and far-reaching community interests. At a certain point, not choosing becomes a choice; but the time comes when decisions can no longer be delayed.

Rather than developing a static plan, the planning process should continue to produce new options for the development of a community while disposing of those which have become outdated because of the discovery of new information or considered community agreement. At present, we tend to lightly foreclose our children's and grandchildren's opportunities to make choices that will profoundly affect them in their adult lives. This is because the decisions we make today, which affect these future options so profoundly, may have relatively little impact on our own lives. The decision to concentrate health facilities, for example, in a self-contained Pill Hill may not affect the current population of a city of limited size in which the automobile is the viable form of transportation. But it may be disastrous for future generations whose health needs and access to transportation may demand a more flexible, decentralized approach. We must therefore adopt a dynamic approach to the use of land as a resource and establish an evolutionary pattern for its future development.

At the program stage, the planning process should be concerned with relating available resources to meet regional problems. Where land is in short supply, a land-gaining strategy can be employed so that when a new building complex is completed, a variety of existing functions can be moved to that location, thus opening up new sites for the next round of work. The proper scheduling of this work can add to the land available at each cycle and, over a period of time, open an otherwise constricted community.

When we were working on a transportation plan for the city and county of San Diego many years ago, we examined the desirability of developing population nodes through zoning controls with rights-of-way maintained between them. Any program dealing with transportation must recognize that the costs of obtaining rights-of-way are sufficiently high to price many rapid transit options out of existence. This approach would have provided incentives to cluster developments in relation to those nodes and reduce support for developments which would sprawl across the land. If rights-of-way were maintained, the higher density centers would then have the opportunity to install a rapid transit system. The decision makers of the 1990s or 2000s would thus have an option to implement rapid transit programs much more economically. (Figure 6.3 is a simple diagram of how this plan might look.)

Policy Decisions

In planning any type of development in the past, we have been concerned with the client's ability to afford the cost of owning and operating the facilities for the first year of occupancy. Afterward the cost of amortization represented a smaller portion of the money available because we were in a growth economy. If we planned a university campus for a 1965 date and were too optimistic, the facilities would not be fully occupied until 1968. If we were pessimistic, we would have to plan the next increment of work in 1963 or 1964. It was in fact a forgiving period in our planning history. Today, we face the fact that our economy will not necessarily grow each year, that we are subject to significant regional and demographic changes, and that because of the increase in energy costs, what we can afford on opening day

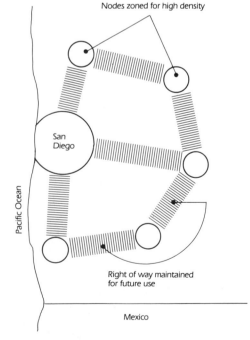

Figure 6.3 Zoning concept to permit future decisions on transportation options with respect to the city and county of San Diego.

might not be affordable 5 years later. It is not a forgiving environment. What are the implications for zoning?

As our communications and information systems advance to the year 2000, our energy use might go back to the 1960s. How we deal with these issues may determine our future viability as a nation. If our policies of dealing with our built environment are successively related to existing conditions which continually tighten, we will expend our national resources in a futile and wasteful manner.

It is possible to implement society's goals with more certainty than current procedures allow. There are a variety of tools which can be used to obtain specific objectives. The final report of the National Commission on Urban Problems, "Building the American City," suggests controlling land use by taxing zoned building capacity rather than existing structures. This produces an economic incentive *against* holding land for speculative reasons and *for* developing it quickly for its zoned use. Patterns of development could be significantly affected by such a tool. If there is a real concern to redirect our sprawl-oriented procedures, there are specific methods for inducing such changes.

A corollary might be the establishment of a land bank, as has been done in some areas of the country, to prevent agriculture or related uses from being squeezed out by high taxes. Such a system would permit undeveloped land to be land-banked and taxes to be lowered; however, if the owner changed his or her mind and wanted to sell at a later time, the increase in land value would be taxed as income in the year the sale is made. People who obtain tax advantages to hold land off the market should not also obtain tax advantages when they sell it later on. In this way, the zoning of agricultural land and the owner's option to join a green belt would carry with it some assurance that open space would remain.

The combination of denser communities with adjacent agriculture development on open land bespeaks a more self-sufficient type of community, less dependent on long-distance trucking and more energy conserving in itself. This pattern has some analogies to an earlier era in the United States when our per capita energy usage was much lower, but that does not mean that we should return to it. Our other organizing and information systems have changed to such an extent that we must look for new forms. However, as we begin our search to determine those forms, it is important not to perpetuate present practices which we know to be wrong: i.e., subsidizing or guaranteeing further urban sprawl at a time when we have few answers to the impact of energy costs on our future living patterns.

Chapter Seven

Finance

In an environment where physical resources are readily available, the scope of a project is determined by its financial situation. Although there are many ways that funds can be allocated for various aspects of a project, its feasibility depends on the availability of sufficient money at the project's outset. In the United States anything can be built if the money is available. However, where the budget is tight, if all the required resources are not used effectively, the project may not be feasible. It is no accident that we must satisfy image, climate, and behavioral requirements within the context of economics; the allocation of financial resources determines how much we can afford to spend on land, management, technology, and labor. In societies where other types of resources, such as land, water, skilled labor, or energy are in short supply despite the availability of money, then the central position of the economic function changes.

While it is true that the availability of investment capital will invariably determine the initial project scope, the effects of taxes, interim financing, and interest rates on the costs of owning a project are of major importance. Together with the cost of operating and maintaining a facility, they determine a project's affordability.

Building Costs

Cost of the Building Proper

The cost of buildings should be dealt with at three different levels. There is the cost of the building proper. How much does it cost to build the physical plant? How much should we allocate for space, environment, services, finishes, etc.? These factors determine how we should apportion the available funds for a particular project. Do we wish to have more space, or are we willing to sacrifice a number of square feet in order to improve the environment within the structure? Do we wish to have improved finishes and an extra bath, or would we like an unfinished basement to provide room for expansion? These kinds of trade-offs are part of the decision-making process. The project design derives directly from the user requirement studies, where evaluations are made with respect to the building's square footage; the luminous, thermal, and acoustic environment; the appearance of the exterior walls; the solidity of the interior partitions; and the nature of the casework, furnishings, and fittings that are used to complete the building.

Project Costs

An analysis of the project costs offers new opportunities for understanding how a project can be built. In addition to the building cost, we must take into account the cost of land and site development, administrative and design services, interim financing, and any other costs incurred to complete the project.

The number of units that share a given site and its infrastructure determines the unit cost and the context within which trade-offs are made. More units per acre may allow the addition of air conditioning without the sacrifice of floor area. However, increased density of use does not always result in lower costs. With higher densities, we may find that in addition to structural costs, there are limits on how space may be used. For example, fire and other building codes may require higher levels of protection, which in turn may raise the price or greater density may demand multilevel parking structures rather than ground-level parking, once again adding to the cost. Nevertheless, increasing the density usually lowers the unit cost because land and service costs can be amortized against greater built area.

Life-Cycle Costs

Life-cycle costs take into account the amortization of money borrowed to pay project costs, taxes, operations and maintenance, and, eventually, building alterations to meet changing user requirements. The allocation of limited funds to inexpensive finishes requiring high maintenance may make it possible to accommodate extra space initially. However, long-term physical deterioration may result because of deferred maintenance which costs more than the extra space could justify.

It is essential, therefore, that appropriate trade-offs be made at all three levels of planning to assure balance and responsiveness. The process used to allocate the available dollars in the design of a building is relatively simple and can easily be improved upon and systematized. The simple equation demonstrated by the triad in Chapter 5 (Figure 5.2) must give way to the listing of all the elements which make up the completed building. The desired performance must be determined for each of these components and the resultant cost ascertained. The sum of all of these expenses is the building cost. By adding the land, administrative, and financing costs, we get the total project cost, which must fit the budget. Trade-offs can be made within this framework to optimize the use of resources. The quality of the various components selected will all have their impact on the project's life-cycle costs. Cost-performance information for the various components must provide both initial and long-term cost factors which can be added to yield the total cost of ownership. The choices which establish the owner's operating costs for energy, maintenance, insurance, painting, etc., when taken together with amortization and taxes, determine whether the building is affordable. Determination of feasibility prior to design, termed "predictable performance" (see Figure 5.1) means that the building design is not established until an acceptable bottom line figure is obtained. This is analogous to a developer determining that the bottom line of a project is acceptable before exercising an option on a piece of land.

The Effect of National Policy-Making on Building Costs _____

In taking a rational approach to the allocation of resources, we must remember that the built environment takes shape as a result of planning, design, and construction decisions which are only partly influenced by a consideration of national priorities. Policies for taxation, interest rates, and service support, among other things, influence construction and frequently determine not only whether to build at all but what should be built.

The application of economic policies that exploit the countercyclical capacity of the building industry to act as a stabilizer for the nation's economy has caused many firms to lose their critical mass of people and skills or to go bankrupt. The construction industry has, in fact, provided the nation's economists with a vehicle through which they can heat up or cool off the economy. The size and nature of the industry uniquely qualifies it for this role. In the 1980s we have seen interest rates so high that the automobile industry was caught in the vise usually reserved for the building industry. A 4-year car loan is obviously less sensitive than a 25-year mortgage, but since the pressures of high interest rates have been felt by other industries, perhaps the building industry can look to some understanding and relief in the future.

During the 1979 to 1982 period, high interest rates reduced new housing starts from an average of just over 2 million per year to under a million. Development of newer, more capital-intensive industrial processes for the production of building products and maintenance of vertically integrated production-developer-construction firms require an even market. The strong influence on the construction market of policies not related to the market needs of the country can make any corporation or entrepreneur schizophrenic. The Kafka-esque impression of various firms and individuals about the condition of the building industry is appropriate, and there can be little wonder that the per capita investment per construction worker is much less than that per agricultural worker. The government's frustrating policy of intermittent support and withdrawal discourages those who look for opportunities for becoming more efficient through capital-intensive investments, which are frequently in line with stated national goals. Thus, the real effect of governmental policy is to support the status quo.

The building industry's tendency to follow the productivity pattern of a service-based rather than a manufacturing industry can be related directly to these fiscal policies. Today, we bemoan the fact that fewer than 20 percent of our nation's families can afford to buy a new home. If a series of deliberate policies makes it impractical for the building industry to invest in productivity, the economists cannot, at the same time, use the industry as a scapegoat for inefficiency. In treating the industry as a discretionary component of the nation's fiscal system, the economists are undermining those who would like to respond more effectively to our building needs.

In many respects these attitudes have produced an unholy alliance between the fiscal experts and the low-tech adherents in their contention that the development of technology has little importance in the cost of a house. They support this view by citing the relatively large amount of money spent on land, finance, and taxes, in relation to the relatively small amount spent on the cost of construction.

The cost of financing is, however, directly related to the first cost insofar as this is the basis for a mortgage. For an interest rate of 8 percent, more than $3000 in interest is paid for every $1000 borrowed; this number increases rapidly as the interest rate goes up. Moreover, local taxes are determined by the cost of the dwelling unit and the land on which it sits. A decrease of $1000 in construction costs may well result in a decrease of $1000 or more in taxes over the typical 25- to 30-year amortization period of the dwelling unit. Therefore, a construction cost saving of $1000 typically decreases a family's expenditure by $5000 during the mortgage period. Leverage on this scale indicates that we must look to technology to help keep our first costs down and achieve a significant saving over the life of the building. Concern over value of the construction dollar is fully justified, and we must move toward economic policies which reward, rather than punish, innovative approaches to increased productivity.

Life-Cycle Cost Considerations

Until relatively recent times, there was so much concern about first cost that little consideration was given to the life-cycle costs. Today, the rapid rise in energy costs has focused interest on operating expenses to such an extent that the entire area of life-cycle costs is viewed with equal interest by individual, corporate, or institutional builders. Studies of life-cycle costs in relation to different building types has provided enough background information to give us a reasonable picture of where we are heading.

The emphasis on first, as opposed to life, cost has been encouraged by a society concerned with building and selling with a short enough turnover time to ensure maximum profit in relation to tax laws. As a result, there is a failure to focus on life cost. But clients are becoming more interested in exploiting our existing building stock and are becoming more wary of increasing operating and maintenance costs. Therefore we must study life-cycle costing on projects in order to upgrade and use these buildings more effectively.

Residential Life-Cycle Costs

In the housing field we have gone through an era in which the gap between supply and demand has widened. Even with substantial subsidies to the homeowner through tax benefits and through matching grants on sewer, water, and road costs, the percentage of the population which can afford new housing has decreased. This is due to the building industry's low productivity rate and to the rapid increase in local taxes and land costs, which are climbing faster than any other component involved in home building. According to a report by the National Commission on Urban Problems, the cost of land rose almost seven times faster than wholesale commodity prices and almost four times faster than the consumer price index over the 10-year period from 1956 to 1966.

The rapid increase in energy rates has led to a significant series of failures in government-supported housing programs. Because feasibility was so difficult to establish, pro formas to obtain government support for low and moderate income housing were prepared without adequate allowance for operations and maintenance. The tax shelter opportunities provided incentives for establishing feasibility, even when the project was not feasible.

Many federally supported low- and moderate-income housing projects have failed because only 25 to 35 percent of the monthly rentals was allocated to operations and maintenance costs. Experience has shown that as much as 55 percent of the monthly rent was required for operating and maintenance. As a result, maintenance was deferred, the buildings ran down, and many of these projects were foreclosed. The incentive program which provided tax shelters for the development of low-income housing backfired when tight first-cost budgets led to low-quality construction, so the original estimates of low operating costs became unrealistic. Although a great deal of housing was built, the ensuing deterioration and bankruptcy in many cases cost much more than if the projects had been properly constructed in the first place.

The rising cost of housing is creating an even larger, unmet need. Minimum support programs for new housing in the recent past have resulted in deferred maintenance and frequent failure. However, substantial support programs can antagonize those who do not benefit from the support programs, but who are on the next rung of the economic ladder. There is no easy solution. Nevertheless, we must look for every possibility for savings, and none can be dismissed as inconsequential. The problem of providing affordable housing is increasing in scope annually.

In addition to the emphasis on first cost we must develop a better database of housing operations and maintenance costs so that the proper decisions can be made at the planning and design stages. Materials selection, layout, service system efficiency, and energy use are all of great significance in this regard. Our office gathered data for one program of steady-state housing maintenance; the results indicated that of the total maintenance costs 17 percent was related to exterior painting, while 27 percent was related to interior painting. Over the 40-year life of a building the cost of painting may well be close to three-quarters of the first cost. The decision to use materials that do not require painting can result in substantial savings.

Maintenance of the heating, ventilating, and air-conditioning systems accounted for an average of 10 to 13 percent of the total maintenance figures, and this figure becomes more significant when energy costs are taken into account. Energy-related operating costs tend to equal the total maintenance program and all other operating costs.

The costs of roof and site repairs account for a smaller percentage followed by the costs for plumbing and all the additional areas to which maintenance funds must be applied.

Mortgage lending institutions do not typically evaluate the cost of building operations which encourages a low–first-cost high–life-cycle-cost mentality. These institutions, therefore, contribute to conditions which increase the number of mortgage failures. An evaluation of the life-cycle implications of the design should affect the amount of money they lend for specific projects. The variations in the monthly cost of operations and maintenance are of such significance that they must be considered in any study of financial feasibility.

Nonresidential Building Life-Cycle Costs

In the nonresidential area, one of the earliest studies was done in the early 1960s by Benjamin Handler at the University of Michigan. He analyzed the cost of owning and operating some 250 Michigan schools that had been in use for 40 years. He found that, on average, the finance charges used to pay off the school bonds were equal to the first cost. (With today's interest rates, those charges would be much higher.) The operating and maintenance costs were some 2.5 to 3 times first cost, and the alteration costs were approximately twice first cost. Thus, about one-eighth of the cost of ownership represented the cost of building construction; the other seven-eighths was required over the years to keep the building functioning, to pay off the mortgage, and to relate to changing needs.

When we began to study life-cycle costs in the Academic Building Systems (ABS) project for the universities of California and Indiana, we found that the average university structure in use for 40-years had an alteration cost of 3.3 times first cost, a figure considerably in excess of Benjamin Handler's findings for public schools. We also found that 42 percent of the alteration costs in a science-laboratory type of building were related to gain-

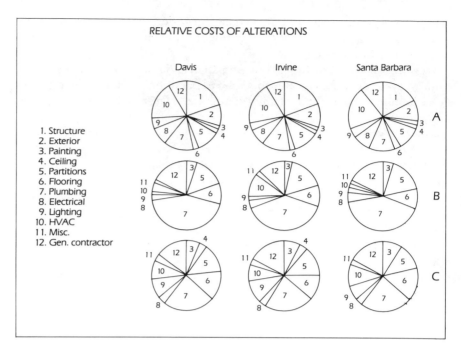

RELATIVE COSTS OF ALTERATIONS

Davis   Irvine   Santa Barbara

1. Structure
2. Exterior
3. Painting
4. Ceiling
5. Partitions
6. Flooring
7. Plumbing
8. Electrical
9. Lighting
10. HVAC
11. Misc.
12. Gen. contractor

Figure 7.1 Pie charts show different remodeling scenarios with their related costs as supplied to three specific buildings at the Davis, Irvine, and Santa Barbara campuses of the University of California.

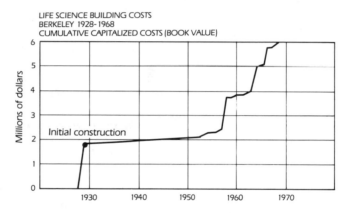

LIFE SCIENCE BUILDING COSTS
BERKELEY 1928-1968
CUMULATIVE CAPITALIZED COSTS (BOOK VALUE)

Initial construction

Figure 7.2 The initial construction cost of the Berkeley Life Science Building was approximately one-third its 40-year cost.

ing access to and to altering the plumbing system (see Figure 7.1). As a result we designed building components that would permit easy access to the plumbing system, since, in effect, this is where more than the initial cost of the building would be spent during its 40-year life.

Figure 7.2 shows a comparison of first cost versus 40-year cost of an average university building. Note that for the first 22 years, relatively little money was spent for alterations, but then costs began to accumulate. However it became apparent that for newer buildings (Figure 7.3) alteration costs began shortly after occupancy. Thus, instead of feeling confident that a building, once occupied, would actually suffice for a substantial period before changes had to be made, we found that our more dynamic society requires an ever-changing physical environment.

Extrapolating the costs of alteration for more recently erected buildings over a 40-year period, we could come up with a figure that averaged between 6 and 10 times first cost, rather than the 3.3 times. These findings emphasize the need to design buildings in such a way as to reduce the costs of future alterations so that it will be economically feasible to keep buildings current with the needs of the people who use them.

In a more recent study of office buildings for the General Services Administration (GSA), we found that for this building type, operations and maintenance costs run approximately 3 times first cost over a 40-year period, a figure which compares with Benjamin Handler's work on schools. But if we examine the 40-year cost of owning and using a government office building, we find that the first cost represents 2 percent of the total, operations and maintenance 6 percent, and staff salaries 92 percent. It becomes obvious, therefore, that if we design buildings which are expensive to change or are inflexible, the potential loss of productivity over the life span of the building is equal to more than 4½ times first cost if we assume a possible impact of 10 percent on productivity due to building obsolescence.

The GSA project, as described in Case Study 6, was bid on a life-cycle cost formula which included energy costs. Heavy emphasis was put on the design of energy-conserving building components which, at the same time, would provide for flexible use of space and good environmental conditions.

The University Residential Building Systems (URBS) for the University of California in 1966 was an early project organized on a life-cost basis. This project gave us an annual opportunity for checking the potential for reallocating resources within a life-cycle cost situation. In the state of California,

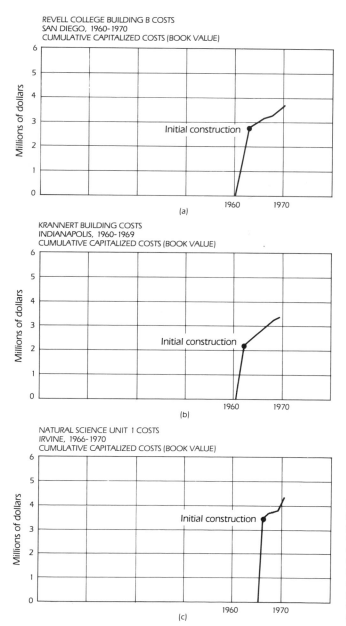

Figure 7.3 More recent buildings have required alterations at an accelerated rate, making it necessary to project 40-year construction costs in excess of 5 times first cost. It became obvious from these studies that designs which would facilitate the continued changing and up-grading of university laboratory buildings was essential to the long-term efficiency and usefulness of these buildings.

student housing was frequently financed with HUD – college housing loan funds or with Regent's bonds. There were already a substantial number of residence halls on the various campuses. With the addition of each new residence hall, the cost of amortizing the new facility was shared by all the others within the system, and consequently the cost of all residence halls went up. Because the overall housing program had to be self-supporting, we examined the various components that were used to build the residence halls and affected maintenance costs. There were a variety of recurrent material failures. For example, the angle arm door closers which hung out into the corridors were relatively cheap as compared with concealed closers. Wherever they were installed, it was just a matter of time until students recognized the potential for locking a fellow student in his or her room by chinning on the closer. This became a vogue within residence halls, and over the years, repairs averaged $1.00 per student per year just for maintenance of door closers. Similarly, Sheetrock walls would give way to basketballs or other kinds of student rough-housing and also required $1.00 per student per year for repair. Suspended ceilings with a soft tile surface were used for sound absorption and were easily damaged. The annual repair costs for a 180 – square-foot double room shared by two students averaged $5.50 per year. Regent bonds at that time were sold at interest rates of 3 percent per annum, so an annual payment of $1.00 would amortize $20 of first cost for the construction of these facilities. Therefore, the $5.50 spent on repairs could have amortized an initial expenditure of $110 per room, which amounted to 65 cents per square foot of ceiling area. At that time, many appropriate ceiling products cost about 33 cents per square foot, so a better ceiling could have been installed without raising student costs.

Gang bathrooms, which were shared by 20 or more students, inevitably experienced leakage through the floor after about 7 years of occupancy, which resulted in expensive repairs. The first cost for the bathrooms was about $300 per student. In contrast, if four students in a suite of double rooms shared a bathroom, the first cost would be about $450 per student. Thus, there seemed to be an apparent financial imperative to continue building double-loaded corridors with double rooms sharing gang bathrooms. This design approach was severely criticized by students because they felt it deprived them of privacy and the flexibility of a more informal lifestyle. But the authorities, whose overriding objective was the availability of higher education to all who qualified, considered it the most economical approach to student accommodation.

After reviewing student desires and lifestyles along with current operating procedures, we found that it was costing the student more to live in a less desirable manner. Our analysis was as follows. Custodial services were required to keep the gang bathrooms clean, since so many people used them that a self-policing system was infeasible. We compared this situation to that of bathrooms shared by four students who would keep them clean. The results of our findings (which are shown in Table 7.1) coupled with the very strong student desire for a different housing pattern made it possible to discard gang bathrooms in favor of a much more private, human, and less-expensive arrangement. The analysis showed that there were also many opportunities to save money on the ceiling, partitions, and hardware, while providing a much better total environment.

The substantial implications of life-cycle cost studies make it apparent that a significant body of information is needed if we are to make the appropriate trade-offs in meeting the client's needs and society's objectives. It is difficult to project the effects of first-cost decisions in a society where the rapid depreciation of buildings is rewarded by tax advantages — undermining the rationale for true life-cycle quality. But recently there has

Table 7.1 Annual Cost of Gang versus Shared Bathrooms

	Gang Bathroom		Four-Student Shared Bathroom	
Custodial cost		$ 30		$ 5
First cost		300		450
First cost amortized by custodial service	30 × 20 =	600	5 × 20 =	100
Total initial expense		$900		$550
Annual cost to student		$ 45		$ 27.50
Result of using a four-student shared bathroom: A per student annual saving of $17.50				

been a new conservation consciousness resulting from the energy crisis and the desire to save our heritage through preservation of significant historic buildings and precincts. This will, it is hoped, result in new policies that deal with our environment in the context of annual costs and provide a basis for the reevaluation of many of the givens which, at present, lead to marginal performance. Only when decisions are made that take life-cycle costs into account can we hope to obtain a level of quality in our urban environment that can enhance economic growth and improve the value of our cities on a sustained basis.

Chapter Eight

Management

Management of the building process calls for the organization of all activities and participants and of the supply of building products involved in a project from inception to completion, beginning with program definition and ending with occupancy. There is a sliding scale of project size, time, and available money that affects the opportunity for innovation. Different levels of innovation are possible in a single house, a school, a hospital, a group of schools, or a very large-scale development program.

In this chapter, many management-related factors are discussed with examples related to larger-scale projects; however the principles apply at all levels. These management activities occur in three separate segments of the industry, even though for certain types of design and contracting procedures, two or more of these segments are united within a single entity.

1. The *professional's* role is to determine what needs to be built, whether it can be built within the client's budget, and how it should be designed and constructed. This includes inspection of work at the building site.
2. The *contractor's* role is to translate the plans into the completed building. The flow of labor and building materials into the job is scheduled and controlled so as to produce the specified building at the agreed-upon cost.
3. The *industry's* role is to supply the products to the contractor and make performance information available to designers.

Responsibility for product performance is assumed by the manufacturer as long as the products are installed by the contractor in accordance with the manufacturer's instructions. The contractor's responsibility is to see that all the products are put in place in accordance with the construction documents. Professional responsibility *traditionally* includes inspection of the work and covers the overall performance of the completed job.

In developing a design, the professional, in consultation with the client, determines the specific roles and responsibilities which will apply to the project. If they are unacceptable to a contractor, he or she need not participate, and if a manufacturer's products do not meet the specifications, he or she need not, and should not, bid. But once the decision to participate is made, everyone has a job to do and responsibilities are delegated to the various parties. If a building does not perform in accordance with program requirements, the client's normal reaction is to call the architect, who will determine where the fault lies. Then, if appropriate, the architect will call the general contractor, who in turn will correct the fault or, if it is a case of a product breakdown, call the manufacturer.

The real problems occur when buildings are designed so that responsibility for a particular defect can be assigned to several parties. The client calls the architect and says, "My classrooms are too cold!" The architect calls the mechanical engineer and relays the problem with the admonition to take care of it quickly. The engineer says that the boiler is defective, the ducts are improperly installed, or the control system does not work. The control sub-contractor says it was installed according to instructions and pronounces other equipment defective or accuses the mechanical engineer of designing the system improperly. The other manufacturers say their equipment is fine and would work if properly installed within a well-designed system. The mechanical engineer is then on the defensive because every complex building has a unique mechanical system designed without the benefit of the kind of development and testing process normal to high-volume production. He or she tries to pin the specific fault onto other participants, who in turn say "Not me!" During this time, the architect is trying to explain to the client that everyone is working on the problem, but the client, who has just spent $12 million on the school building, is unimpressed.

These experiences are not uncommon and cause everyone in the industry to protect themselves. Redundancies and safety factors are built into a project to protect all the participants. It is possible for everyone to protect themselves so well that clients cannot afford to build anything at all.

The cost of architects' errors and omissions insurance has reached unprecedented heights today because of the difficulty of coordinating so much new and relatively untried material and at the same time trying to organize drawings and specifications to establish clean lines of responsibility. The impasse of the mechanical engineer blaming the equipment manufacturer, who in turn blames the control manufacturer who in turn comes back to blame the mechanical engineer illustrates why errors and omissions insurance has become so costly in our litigious society.

From the client's point of view, the building has to work. He or she is not really asking why it doesn't work, but simply saying that it must be made to work using low bidders for both the materials and their installation. If the architect cannot trace the direct path of responsibility and make the responsible party repair the problem, he or she is in trouble.

Given a modicum of professional and technical ability, the key element of management is the management of risk: that is, what safety factors should we work with and how can responsibilities be delegated so that contingencies are reduced? This kind of management is essential if the client is to obtain value for the money invested. Part of the management process is to have the client recognize and accept that varying degrees of risk are part of a large project. The elimination of health and safety risks is usually determined by code, but there are many performance options for temperature control, movability of partitions, and the acoustic separation between spaces.

In designing any project, it is a complicated matter to determine the occupancy date, the project cost, and the performance of the completed building. If a client wants to be sure that everything will work exactly, but cannot spend one-quarter of one percent of the project cost — either during or after construction — to fine tune the building and make certain that every detail meets the given standard, then an extra 10 percent or more of the project cost will probably have to be devoted to redundancies to guarantee against shortcomings. All parties are bound in this process with the client.

The roles of the professional, the contractor, and the industry are closely intertwined. Three separate factors determine whether the client's requirements can and will be met: (1) the professional's willingness to specify and use the products made available by industry; (2) the ease with which the products can be put together correctly on the building site; (3) the contractor's understanding of installation techniques, which affects the anticipated performance levels.

This organization of management resources assumes that financial feasibility has been previously determined on behalf of the client and that an acceptable budget has been set. If the financial picture is in line with reality, then these management activities can proceed. If not, the criteria for financial feasibility may have to be reset and the total process recycled.

The Architect's Role

Within the context of the overall mandate to design the best building that can be built with the available resources, the designer's management role deals with organizing the appropriate methodologies and vocabularies to control the construction process. This should obviously be done within the context of the four-function model. In this process, the architect must clearly determine the best ways of doing the job. But as professionals working on an individual project, we have to keep in mind that in order to design the building at a reasonable cost, we must work within the discipline of readily available products. Where necessary, we must also select those systems whose compatibility is demonstrated and whose suppliers have the ability to assume responsibility for performance in the building context.

In the management of the building process we must recognize that we are in essence designing for change. Our society is so dynamic that in the period between developing the program and undertaking the design and construction of a building, aspects of our client's needs change. Components of the built environment, however, last for many decades. The concept of the disposable building does not work in practice. While some portions of a building may rapidly become obsolete, a very large portion of the investment is for components that will have value over a much longer period. As architects we must consider the client's needs within the given time frame and the specific context of the project, but we must also try to understand developing trends in specific subject areas, such as health care or education, and the changing lifestyles or social customs which affect the functional life of a building. The most creative architects are those who develop an insight into the dynamic nature of society, can understand and interpret trends, and design to accommodate a reasonable range of alternative futures in buildings that capture the spirit of the age. The dynamic nature of society is such that unless we do this, we can expect some very considerable and costly failures. This projection must be done within an environment that is becoming increasingly less forgiving.

During the course of a project that we did for the Pittsburgh high school system, we learned that programs must be designed and managed for a moving target. When the educational parks program was originally developed to replace old and outmoded high schools, the mood of the country was in favor of integration and the development of the educational parks for that purpose. By the time the plans were completed, riots in Newark, Detroit, and Watts had occurred, and by the time we were ready to go out to bid for integrated schools, both the black and white populations of Pittsburgh wanted segregated facilities. And so, the bond issue failed. The lack of a quick response invariably reduces stability in such a situation. We require research and much developmental work to have well-thought-out and responsive vocabularies of products and design approaches available so that we can respond quickly to building problems related to social needs.

In the more typical case, we recognize that a client has a certain amount of money, a site, and a set of goals; our job is to organize the available resources into a handsome structure that will meet a specific set of user requirements, and there are many different paths by which the goals may be realized.

Knowing that everything must be defined and accounted for in the program and the resulting design, the architect is anxious to erect a building that will take advantage of the best that the industry can provide. How is this goal to be achieved? Should the design be prepared on a conventional basis with a full set of working drawings completed before going out to bid? Or should a contractor be selected early on with a negotiated price? Should the architect recommend that a construction manager be engaged to manage the project's cost and schedule the work? Should a phased or fast-track approach be tried, where in order to save time, construction is started before all the contract drawings are completed? Separate contracts are let for succeeding portions of the work as the drawings are completed and prerequisite work on the building site proceeds. Is it a situation where, to meet the client's exact requirements for cost control, it is beneficial to team up with a contractor and do the project on a turn-key basis? If a client with a very substantial wish list has an absolute and very tight price ceiling, he or she should not have the architect design a building, go out for bids, come in over the price, and become involved in a time-consuming redesign process. In this situation the architect may have to find a contractor to work with and say, "Okay, we'll form a design-build team. This is what I'll do with my specifications. This is what my details will call for. Here's a rough outline of the job. What can we provide for the price?"

If the client is absolutely determined that the job cost no more than $3 million and the architect really does not know if it can be brought in for this price, then a construction manager may be inappropriate and a turn-key process may make sense. In this situation, the client does not spend large sums of money until it is known that the design-build team can do the job for the price.

What also happens in the situation where cost accuracy is being pushed to the limit is that the contractor and the architect sit on the other side of the table from the client. As a result, the selection of materials and substitutes may not always be to the client's advantage or preference. But if he or she cannot take risks or provide contingencies on cost, the client may have to settle for some performance risks.

Clients are often anxious to get a building put up fast — it may be because they need to save on cost or avoid escalation; or the school is needed for next September, but it took too long to get the bond issue passed; or the institution will qualify for a National Science Foundation research grant if the laboratory is completed by such-and-such a date. There are many reasons for phasing the work by using a fast-track process which will invariably involve the participation of a construction manager or an architect who has these management capabilities. This process involves commitment in concrete to a specific building configuration before the working drawings are completed and before it is known that the total project can be built for the available funds. That takes enormous amount of sophisticated management because a good deal of responsibility is involved. We can find ourselves with 65 percent of the money spent and only 50 percent of the building up; it is extremely difficult to get the next 50 percent built for 35 percent of the money. At this stage we cannot cut enough and an almost insurmountable problem exists. Some of the risk can be alleviated by using performance specifications to take early bids on components worth about 50 percent of the job, which are relatively easy to define. Another 10 or 12 percent of the job may be bid in demolition, site work, and foundations. In this case, by the time the go-ahead is given to start the site work, 60 percent of the job may be pinned down, while bids are being let for the site work, which comprises the first 10 percent of the work. This greatly reduces the risk. If, on the average job, you have a 10 percent contingency and 60 percent of the job is fixed by bid so that it requires little or no contingency, then the 10 percent contingency becomes a 25 percent contingency for the remaining 40 percent. In most cases where our firm has gone into phased construction, we have sought to reduce our risks by using this kind of technique.

There are trade-offs to be considered between the various construction procedures, each of which has its advantages and disadvantages. In phased construction, it is difficult to design everything as accurately as if you had completed a set of working drawings on a conventional basis. In that case you have everything on paper so that you can closely coordinate every aspect of the job. Service systems can be coordinated with one another, and they can be fitted to the passageways allowed for them in the structure. The heights of the windows and the doors can be checked along with the dimensions of related design elements. You have much more control. However full working drawings take more time, and there is the potential for greater cost escalation. One of your most important responsibilities when orchestrating a project is to be aware of the available permutations and to have the courage to use the appropriate ones. You cannot say "I only use conventional methods" because there are times when no change involves substantial risk. If you have a fixed price and you are designing a job so as to exploit all the available resources during a period of high cost escalation, you run a tremendous risk that if you go over the budget, you will never be able to bring the price back down. When you try to reduce the project scope, you waste time in the process, and in this way the savings are offset by further escalation! Such situations are not at all uncommon, and are in fact a major occupational hazard of the industry, where under certain circumstances "playing it safe" and designing a project conventionally may turn out to be very disadvantageous.

In the practice of architecture, it has not yet been fully recognized that control of the total building process should fall within the designer's decision-making function. It used to be taken for granted that everything would be bid competitively based on full working drawings, as this was the standard way of doing business. But since there is no standard way of doing business today, the industry's resources must be carefully assessed in relation to the specific demands of each project. On really big projects, it may be necessary to divide the job into a number of separate bid packages in order to get good competition. In upstate New York, for example, there may not be many local firms who can bid on a $100 million job. The possibility of such variations must become a familiar part of the architect's background, experience, and knowledge. The architect has to know if the specified designs can be made efficiently and whether the building trades can install them. He or she must establish the right division of responsibility with the related consultants; delegate responsibility among contractors, subcontractors, and manufacturers; and project an accurate picture of how that responsibility will flow. This ability is an essential ingredient of successful practice; if you do not pinpoint responsibility so that everyone knows the boundaries of his or her own sphere of activity, then complicated problems are almost certain to arise.

None of this eliminates the need for good designers. If we examine a number of architectural offices in some detail, we find that they are repositories of a tremendously varied amount of experience and expertise garnered over long periods of time. As a result, some offices develop a kind of synergism that enables them to function as a whole at a level of quality considerably above the talent of any one individual in the group. In this kind of office, there is inevitably someone who really knows construction and others who are "crackerjack" specification writers. There will be some good designers who may not know much about costs, but they can rely on the estimators to take care of that side of the work. In this way, over a period of time, a team is developed which depends on the group of people working together and communicating through their own kind of shorthand. One of the worst things that can happen to such a team is to interject it into a dynamic situation where things do not work in predictable patterns, for when the work is shared by many different people, each fulfilling a closely defined role, their ability to respond effectively to a new situation may be dissipated very quickly. That kind of office has a critical size beyond which it cannot function effectively, nor can it be permitted to shrink below its critical mass, since its expertise has been developed by a group of people, each of whom has a particular role. Since it is not geared to analyze new procedures, the group is likely to break down under the pressure of rapid change. When the team depends on too many people that are locked into specific tasks, it becomes too cumbersome to adapt easily to new situations that demand changes in the work roles themselves.

Today's problems and pressures are likely to produce new models for working teams in architectural offices. Volvo has made a major impact on automobile manufacture with their small teams that have a high proportion of senior people who have an overview of the project's total scope and have decision-making capabilities. These kinds of teams will be a key ingredient in making large architectural firms into effective organizations, while the pyramidal organizational pattern will become less and less able to design creatively. If a firm is perceived as being founded by a group of people concerned with perpetuating their own imprint, then as the size of the organization increases, the firm will tend to become weighed down and static. But if a firm maintains continuous management activity and looks to seed innovative teams that become generative forces on their own account, then the firm is likely to grow and stay creatively alive and in touch with new developments. We do not yet have a defined model of this type of firm operating successfully in an architectural context, although there are some precedents of which our firm is one. But if architecture is to develop as a knowledge-based profession capable of making a significant contribution to the future of the environment, it will have to be concerned with consciously organizing its professional framework in this direction. The organization of responsive practice is essential to the future role of the designer, although organization is not in itself a substitute for talent. Group practice does not mean decision by committee, but it implies a structure which can focus talent on the problem to be solved.

The Contractor's Role

When we examine the nature of the contracting industry today, we find that the nation's real entrepreneurs are the contractors, who, in effect, put their houses on the line every day when they bid a job. Theirs is a genuine risk operation. Their bids are based on sets of drawings and on their past knowledge of how particular architects will enforce those drawings. Since their bids are based on a number of factors that cannot be precisely pinned down, they must compensate for this uncertainty by providing for contingencies that they will also claim as "extras." They are competing with each other on their wits and on their knowledge. If they know that they can get less expensive substitute products accepted as "equals," then when they are trying hard to get a job, they take advantage of such knowledge and perhaps come in with a lower price. But if they know that they are dealing with an architect whose specifications may be slightly vague but who will enforce everything to the letter of the law and beyond the point of reason, then the contractors will bid high on this person's work because they have to put in a contingency to solve problems on the job. The cost of doing business — of having estimators and assembling bids — is substantial. They are in a situation where, in order to stay in business, they have to bid, they have to put money on the line, and they have to be accurate every time they bid. If they cannot do this, they are going to be out of business fast. If their price is too low, they lose money. If it is too high, they get no work. They are a group at constant risk. They cannot make money without winning bids, and they cannot win bids without taking risks.

A significant percentage of contractors in this country go out of business every year. Sometimes this is a result of poor general economic conditions, but often it is a result of misjudgments on the contractor's part. Many contractors start as building tradespeople, or in some related job, and begin to contract for work. Certainly the percentage of failures is swelled by a fringe of fly-by-night firms which go in and out of the field with great rapidity. But all this aside, it is genuinely so tough a field that today many major contractors are looking to play a professional role, where possible, as construction managers. They prefer to give up the risky bidding process and to provide a service by becoming construction managers, taking bids from subcontractors for distinct portions of the work, coordinating job progress, seeing that it gets done, and transferring the risk of bidding to the various subcontractors. Some place down the line someone has to take risks, however, if we are to keep efficiency up and pricing honest.

In a bid situation, contractors, of course, always try to share their risks with the subcontractors, by basing their prices on both their own estimates and on those of their subcontractors. Each general contractor establishes a set of work rules for the subcontractors. The subcontractors protect themselves by knowing the general contractors' previous work records and how hard they are to work for. Each subcontractor also makes agreements with his or her suppliers with regard to prices.

Contractors are also facing a situation in which the manufacturers are trying to maximize profits by making products for the least cost, in some cases disregarding quality where they think they can get away with it. In fact, quality erosion is frequently designed into products to keep the manufacturers in business. (The 2-year battery is not designed to have a 5-year life.) When performance specifications are introduced into the building process — for example, where our specifications say that materials installed according to the manufacturers' instruction should provide a specific acoustic rating in place — a high-risk environment is created for anyone substituting inferior materials. If we are doubtful about whether the criteria have been met, we can have an acoustical test performed. If the materials meet the performance criteria, all is well, except that the client has had to pay for the test. If the materials do not meet the criteria, then the contractor and/or the manufacturer have to expend their resources to solve the problem and, if the specifications are well written, run another test at their own expense to prove the results satisfactory. It should be noted, however, that this type of specification will not necessarily result in the lowest cost for a specific job.

The Subcontractor's Role

Subcontractors are faced with a different set of problems. They do not participate in the total bidding process but must perform their own trade within the context of the job as a whole. The scheduling of personnel, coordination with other trades, and access to the architect-engineer or client take place via the contractor. But while the general contractor has a sense of the job's scope, the subcontractor does not, so scheduling becomes more difficult. Just as a contractor must know the architect for the job being bid on, the subcontractor must know the general contractor as well.

Subcontractors know that if their part of the work is in question or if they have to wait for the completion of another task before performing their own, they run risks that require contingency provisions that are even greater than the general contractor's. The subcontractor's greatest risk relates to unmet building performance specifications. If there is a performance failure which grows out of a part of the project for which the subcontractor was not responsible, he or she may have to go to considerable trouble and expense as a result.

Subcontractors get the work done. They buy materials and supply labor. They frequently depend on credit from major manufacturers and distributors, even while they are having such companies bid against each other. They are invariably proud of their procurement skills, which may be affected as much by the time allowed for payment as by price. Moreover, they have a close relationship with the building trades. Masons, as well as masonry subcontractors, want buildings to be made of brick. If material costs rise too fast in those trades, other materials will be substituted, for example, concrete instead of brick.

On the other hand, the electrical or plumbing trades must work on every job, and these trades and subcontractors seem to have much more power to guard their prerogatives. It is precisely in those areas that the largest and strongest subcontracting organizations have been formed.

Changes in technology or in procedures through which building contracts are let have a much more radical impact on the subcontractor than on the general contractor. Not wanting to become labor brokers, subcontractors are concerned with technological changes by which they no longer have clear title to install specific products or with the substitution of systems which remove certain activities from their jurisdiction—such as pneumatic instead of electronic controls—and with the parceling out of some activities to others, such as the utility companies. The battle to protect territory and to reduce risk contributes to a general feeling of worry and concern over change. The risk of doing anything first is high. But once something is shown to be better, not getting on the bandwagon fast enough carries even greater risks. At the contractor and subcontractor level, the industry is slow to innovate but quick to imitate.

The Manufacturer's Role

The really large firms can be found in the industrial sector of the building industry. By their very nature, many industrial processes require substantial capital investment. Research divisions, surprisingly small or nonexistent in the rest of the building industry, may be substantial here, and a considerable proportion of the nation's knowledge about what can and cannot be built resides in these institutions. Since product literature is passed on to the professions for sales and information purposes, the profession's knowledge of these industrial capabilities is filtered through the companies' sales departments rather than through their research personnel. This filter makes it possible for a manufacturer to prolong sales of an already accepted line of products, providing better amortization of existing plant and lower costs for training sales and other personnel about new products. On the other hand, when innovation is required, the architect must frequently turn to small specialty companies. When good ideas emerge, the larger companies will pick them up. Prior development reduces the risk to the large manufacturers when they tool up for a new line. This generates the prevalent attitude that risk and cost are reduced by being second. Since most of the industry research force is at work for companies which would rather be second than first in a new field, many opportunities have opened for smart entrepreneurs and inventors, but no basis for ordered progress has been provided.

Creativity and new developments have to be pushed or enticed. The absence of an ordered vocabulary of building components and of a design tradition which specifies standard components makes slow response to new ideas a very logical mechanism for the industry. The expense of designing new products, of organizing their manufacture and distribution, and of training the installers is very high. If, at the end of the process, no one will specify the products, the company has sustained a major financial loss and the initiator has lost his or her job.

The Industry and the Development Hierarchy

The manufacturing industry is organized in some rather interesting ways. Each type of component manufacturer, e.g., structure, air conditioning, or partitions, works to a completely different kind of pattern. Some manufacturers regard the entire country, or perhaps even the world, as their market. This means that for certain classes of products, competition exists over a very wide geographic range. For others, such as concrete panels, the bidding becomes limited to companies that are sufficiently close to the building site that a round trip from the plant takes a day or less. If there are plants close enough that two loads can be delivered in a day, bidding may be further restricted.

On the SCSD project, described in Case Study 1, an interesting economy was achieved in regard to the air-conditioning equipment. The multizone units, which were developed by Lenox, were purchased in quantity for the 2 million square feet of schools built and put on standing order from the fabrication plant in Columbus, Ohio. The units were distributed in California from a central marshaling point in Los Angeles. An arrangement was made with Flying Tiger Airlines that whenever a plane was deadheading from the east to the west coast, it would pick up three multizone units in Columbus and deliver them at a price that was lower than truck or rail transportation. A regular pattern was thus developed relative to availability and convenience. If Tiger's deliveries fell behind a certain schedule, then Lenox would ship by truck or rail. When a project is large enough to develop its own logistics, opportunities for economy increase.

It is not easy to understand the kind of market stratification that exists within the industry. For example, although USX wants to sell steel, the corporation is not particularly interested in fabricating long span joists. This type of product is made by rolling sheet steel into a variety of simple, lightweight sections which are then joined with relatively simple and inexpensive tooling into the long-span joists. But there are many fabricators who supply this product, and, in fact, USX is very pleased by this because they can supply the sheet steel.

If one of the large steel manufacturers were to compete in this market, it would have difficulty in providing the required local service and would lose considerable business because the smaller fabricating companies would not buy their materials from a competitor. But if there is demand for a lot of massive sections — big, heavy, rolled members for which the cost of separate fabrication facilities is extremely high — then the large companies are interested and become suppliers. In this case USX's competition would be Bethlehem Steel and perhaps a few other major companies.

When you examine the nature of these large product companies—whether they be manufacturers of steel, cement, aluminum, or other commodity products—you find they are often not particularly interested in being saddled with on-site construction responsibilities. As discussed earlier in this chapter, the nature of the building industry is such that there exists a hierarchy for passing on responsibilities and large companies often hesitate to get involved in situations where back charges for delays in delivery may occur or where their products may be questioned. They know that if they have to sue for payment in a small subcontractor's home town the chances of winning are reduced. If anything goes wrong they will be regarded as the party with the deep pockets. These interrelationships make it difficult to streamline the industry. And so, as the products have less material content but require more fabrication in order to custom fit a specific situation, there arises a whole network of small fabricators who buy the basic materials, make up the product, and supply the small subcontractors because large companies won't.

We must find a way of establishing a large enough market so that the big companies have no choice but to become involved in innovation. When we look back at our firm's experience in the GSA project (see Case Study 6), where Armstrong and Bethlehem Steel competed against Owens Corning Fiberglas and U.S. Steel, we realize that large firms were induced to participate because the project was simply so large that they had to become involved and come up with new products. But, as soon as we developed a pattern which pinned responsibility on the prime companies, who were unaccustomed to it, the number of firms willing to participate and innovate was reduced. The major companies that participated in the project were designated as team leaders who would seek out subcontractors who would have to work for them. The manufacturers were reluctant to do this because normally the subcontractors were their customers. By reversing the normal process, however, we made sure that the newly developed products would be properly used.

At the time of the SCSD project, an unrelated experiment was being conducted in California. Westinghouse decided to develop a subcontracting arm. They would not only make the products, but they would install them. They started out in Los Angeles on a very big project where they acted as a subcontractor so that they could supply and install the products. They were boycotted by NECA (National Electrical Contractor's Association) throughout the state of California. About 2½ years later, the experiment was abandoned. A critical factor in that situation was that they bid on jobs with existing products, putting Westinghouse in direct competition with the subcontractors they normally supplied.

In trying to harness the skills of subcontractors as part of an innovative program, manufacturers may use a different process than they will use to market the products once they are developed. The subcontractors will accept a temporary dislocation on what is clearly a development project as long as normal working procedures are restored once the product is in common use. If manufacturers are to get involved in major innovative developments, they must determine just which segments of the industry are essential, what procedures are to be used, and what incentives are required to obtain genuine participation.

Big companies must be harnessed for major innovation, because they are the only ones who have sufficient resources. However, some of the smaller specialty companies can be amazingly inventive and skillful in putting their products together. In component areas, such as interior partitions or lighting, relatively small companies or creative people often come up with first-rate, innovative product concepts. But if, for example, you are looking for the development of a better acoustical environment which demands effective coordination of structure, lighting systems, air conditioning, and partitions, you need the support of considerable company resources.

Since there are many different interest groups within the building industry, it is important to recognize the many roles taken by the various companies, the influence of company size, and the major impact these factors have on the creation of a usable vocabulary. The people who have the greatest influence within most companies with respect to new product development are company sales managers. Frequently research is a service activity to help sales. Salespeople will ask for research to develop the kinds of products that they think are wanted and that will win bids. This means that there is a tendency to manufacture products that just meet the specification at the lowest possible price. Sales managers are not oriented primarily toward building quality. Their concern is winning jobs, and, in a competitive situation, that is done by being the cheapest. This either means cheapening products to a barely acceptable level, or to the point where it will not be found out; sometimes this is a level below technical acceptability. During the development of SCSD and a number of other systems projects, salespeople who were presented with performance specifications did not know if their products could meet them. If they did not have an appropriate product, instead of cheapening an existing product, they had to use their research people to develop products to meet the performance specifications and suddenly, the research person was on top.

In our own practice, we have found it beneficial to talk with people in research departments of major companies to find out if specific performance requirements can be met. If their response is uniformly negative, we inevitably reduce the requirement because it is economic suicide to take bids on specifications to which no one can respond. On the other hand, we often find that sometime later a researcher will call and say, "You know that specification we were talking about; we can do it now, ask for it." It is highly unlikely that a research department can get a product developed and marketed unless somebody outside specifies it. It is important when calling for new products to communicate directly with the research people. Large projects with high budgets have the great potential to stimulate innovation. We must rely on these projects to play a major role in expanding the building vocabulary.

Total Project Management

The construction industry has its balance of forces — interest and pressure groups analogous to those in the legislative, judicial, and executive branches of the federal government — which have to be kept in some kind of equilibrium. All the groups are sensitive to change, fearing its negative impact on their modus operandi. That is why precedents must be developed within a protected environment, where failure is possible without major negative impact. The place for federal or other support of building industry research is in the initiation and sponsorship of pilot development programs with a high level of controlled experimentation.

Although many in the industry are afraid of being the first to develop or use a new product or technique, once it has been proven they react quickly and positively. But in an industry whose members are prone to regard innovation and bankruptcy as natural partners, strong support and financial or market incentives must be provided for the initial development effort.

Our ability to meet evolving needs may well require studies of trends within the knowledge disciplines of each of the various building types: for example, determining the implications of population trends, mobility, the way in which people interact, and new developments being successfully tested within a field. When we try to meet present requirements, and also provide for evolution, we may need to develop new generations of building products. However, it is very difficult to get the industry to make new products for today's market, let alone tomorrow's. Often during periods of rapid change, a design team focuses on a specific facility, and it interprets needs in a new way or calls for a different mix of product types or sizes. If industry gears up too early to produce efficiently and in quantity before specific needs can be pinpointed, the manufacturers will go out of business.

Professionals, clients, or others who take responsibility for the delivery of a project must understand how the industry works if they are to deliver the best possible end result. Such understanding must be matched with user requirements and resources, but since the procurement and construction program affects so many parties whose own financing patterns, risks, and territory are involved, this group could be compared to the United Nations Security Council whose many members have the right of veto. Our biggest risk is becoming atrophied and unable to respond to national needs. We must, therefore, manage the experimental process intelligently and use the perceptions gained to obtain the best possible results for any client. Before anyone can manage the delivery of a completed project, they must understand the constraints and strengths of those who will be engaged in the process. Figure 8.1 illustrates how industry relationships are organized.

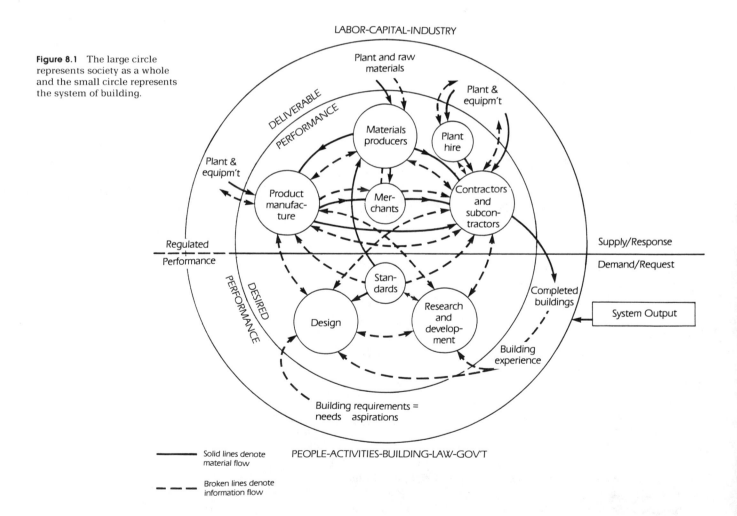

Figure 8.1 The large circle represents society as a whole and the small circle represents the system of building.

LABOR-CAPITAL-INDUSTRY

Plant and raw materials

Plant & equipm't

DELIVERABLE PERFORMANCE

Materials producers

Plant hire

Plant & equipm't

Product manufacture

Mer-chants

Contractors and subcontractors

Regulated Performance

Supply/Response

Demand/Request

DESIRED PERFORMANCE

Standards

Design

Research and development

Completed buildings

System Output

Building experience

Building requirements = needs aspirations

——— Solid lines denote material flow

– – – Broken lines denote information flow

PEOPLE-ACTIVITIES-BUILDING-LAW-GOV'T

The development of innovative programs requires testing and evaluation. When projects are completed, it is essential that they function well, that they be economical to maintain, and that they can be efficiently operated.

Program results must be tested against the initial goals and objectives. If we find that the building generally meets these goals, but that the users' satisfaction is still incomplete in certain areas, it becomes obvious that the goals must be modified to correspond with the users' actual needs. Or, if we find that in certain respects the building falls short of program goals, this tells us where we must change the process or the products. These changes may be in the design and manufacture of the products, the design of the building itself, or in control of the installation process. Our overall concern must be with the function of the building on a life-cycle basis. We must be able to test its ability to carry out all four functions — image, behavior, climate, and economics. If it falls short in one area or another, we must ask whether resources for analogous future projects should be redirected or whether an actual lack of resources caused the shortcomings. If the latter is the case, then we may well be doing the best possible job with the resources at our disposal.

Our knowledge is continually increased by our ability to organize information on programs where specific goals have been set, cost-performance trade-offs are made, and the impact of those decisions on the environment are measured. The objectives must be stated in sufficient detail to allow the completed building to be tested and to decide whether, in fact, the decisions were correct and the users are satisfied.

Any type of management within the building industry requires this feedback. Without it, we shall continue to design individual buildings relating to people's assumptions rather than to hard information, and to be unable to judge if these assumptions were appropriate. A database may be constructed from information on every job analyzed in this way. Such a database starts with conventional projects, for it is from this information that we can determine when unconventional approaches are appropriate or necessary. The understanding and related organization of the path by which a project is brought to fruition is common to every conventionally designed project. On the other hand, the experiences obtained in working on specific innovative and developmental programs provided insights which would not have been so clear on our normal design projects.

Chapter Nine

Technology

Buildings should be built to make the best possible use of the available resources. Management of the process will determine the specific approach. The criteria for selection of the approach will relate to time, cost, and quality. A systems approach does not call for the use of specific materials, methods of construction, or an a priori group of factory-made products. It is concerned rather with the logical selection of materials and methods in order to obtain optimum value in terms of the four-function model. The selection process begins, therefore, with knowing the cost and performance of all the alternative materials and methods by which the building can be constructed. Local conditions, the desire to build quickly, the availability of skilled labor, the client's emphasis on image, or concerns about energy conservation may all have their impact on the specific technology chosen. In order to understand how these factors are weighed, we must review some of the most frequently used approaches to the selection of building materials and existing product options.

Structure

Although in many modern buildings expenditures for the mechanical and electrical subsystems far exceeds those for structure, it is essential that we begin with structure when reviewing technologies. The structure forms the armature, or matrix, on or through which the other systems operate. It provides the framework for the building's enclosure, space division, and other major building subsystems. Historically, the importance of structure as a form-giving element helped to establish a special bond between the architect and the structural engineer that frequently exists to this day. The architect and structural engineer tend to concentrate attention on a building's layout, configuration, and appearance before giving any serious consideration to how these factors will affect the other service systems. The concept of the structural engineer as some type of grand vizier to the architect is no longer appropriate within today's society, where we need to coordinate all portions of the building's design within the context of the available budget. Architects, engineers, and contractors must work together as a

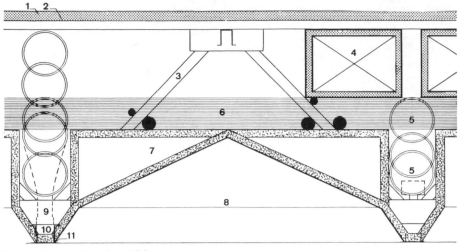

Detail section through roof sandwich

1 insulation
2 steel deck
3 lattice girder
4 rigid duct, 9in × 13½in
5 flexible duct, 9in dia.
6 service freeway
7 fireproofing insulation
8 lighting coffer
9 connector
10 air diffuser
11 ceiling runner

Electrical conduits rising from the service core into the service 'freeway' in the roof sandwich

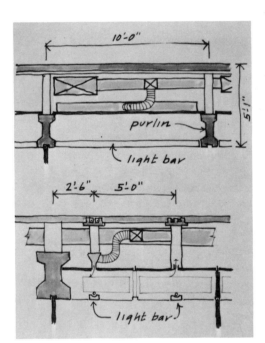

Figure 9.1 Two different approaches to meet the SCSD specifications.

team to coordinate structure, enclosure, services, environment, and furnishings within an acceptable building design that meets the basic user requirements.

In considering a building's function, we must set forth the requirements in such a way that we understand the users' total range of needs. There are many structural solutions to any given set of needs. The specific selection of span, material, and configuration provides a variety of alternatives for the passage of services. The expression or covering of the structure must be carried out in such a way that the full range of requirements—fire protection, acoustics, lighting and ceiling—is satisfactorily fulfilled. The structural approaches can be drawn up in relation to all other building services and subsystems with which they must be compatible, and the composite relationships of these subsystems must be compared with one another in terms of cost and performance. It is important to recognize that the simplest or cheapest way of meeting the full range of behavioral and climatic requirements may not represent an acceptable aesthetic solution. The design process must, therefore, be concerned with selecting an appropriate mix of building subsystems that meets basic needs and, at the same time, expresses the desired image.

Simultaneously, we must be concerned not only with the allocation of resources vis-à-vis the first cost of the building but with the implications of the design and system selection for life-cycle costs. Such a situation arises when ducts must be squeezed into the spaces provided by a given structural system with the result that there is a very considerable impact on the efficiency of the air-conditioning system and hence on its operating cost. Thus the compatibility of building subsystems, vis-à-vis both first cost and life cost, becomes a prime criterion for design acceptability. The available design keyboard provides for enough options for compatible performance that it is possible to assemble an array of acceptable solutions for any project. The final decision on the specific direction for meeting program requirements may then be made. Figures 9.1 and 9.2 give examples of different types of component compatibility, each of which can meet the same performance standards. The selection of a particular design approach must be predicated not only on the specific program for the opening configuration of that building but must also take into account the range of possible uses, at the very least over the amortization period.

The greater the amount of space allotted within a building for a specific job, the greater the building's capacity to accommodate change. Excess space creates flexibility. But as we plan for higher levels of service, additional area substantially increases both first and operating costs. There is a dichotomy, therefore, between flexibility through additional space and cost of higher levels of service needed for reduced but more efficient space. But this in turn gives us less *unplanned freedom* for future variation. The selection of compatible technologies must help us bridge this growing gap.

In developing a sequence for selecting specific structural approaches and for finding ways in which to relate the service systems to those approaches, we must focus all our efforts on the total mission of the building. The requirements for the acoustic environment provide us with a good example of how many different building subsystems must work together to perform a single function. The development of an appropriate acoustic environment

Figure 9.2 Early compatibility chart showing how different structural, HVAC, and lighting-ceiling products would work together to provide compatible performance.

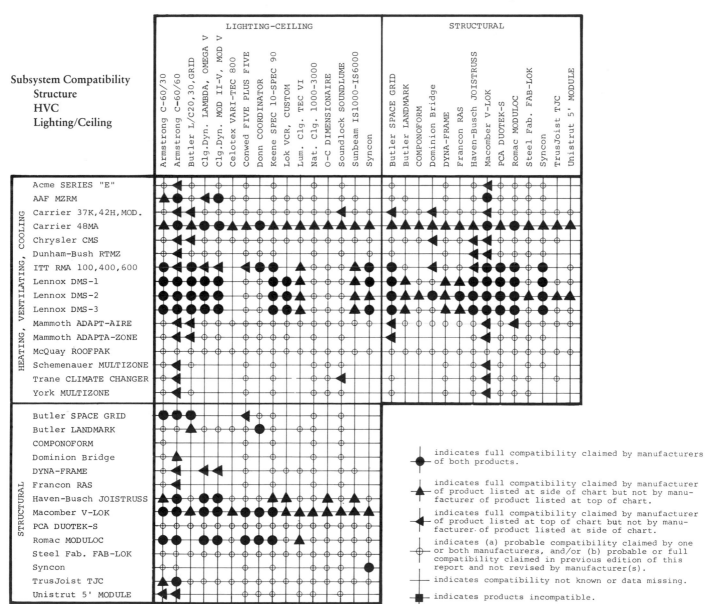

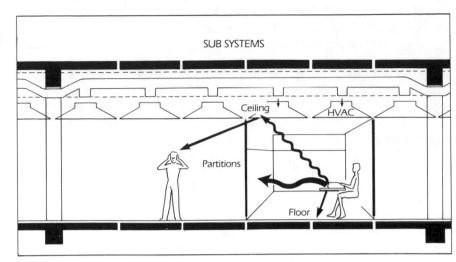

Ceiling HVAC

Partitions

Floor

Figure 9.3 Acoustic privacy is dependent on the compatible performance of many components which must work together to provide an appropriate office environment.

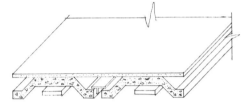

Figure 9.4 Concrete sections designed to act as lighting coffers and to define the route for the mechanical services.

must relate to the nature of the six separate sides of any space that is to be controlled. The impact noise from above, vibrations that might be generated within the building structure, transmission through walls, and appropriate absorption within the space all have considerable impact on total acoustic performance. Structural mass and vibration, ceiling absorption and reflection, sounds transmitted through the air-conditioning system, and the absorption properties of the walls and floors are all critical factors. If any one of these individual subsystems fails to meet its respective criteria, it becomes difficult to achieve the required level of overall performance. Figure 9.3, which is taken from the GSA office building program described in Case Study 6, shows how all the subsystems must work together to provide an appropriate acoustic environment. In this case it was extremely important to achieve speech privacy in a landscaped office environment, so that people working in adjacent spaces could hold meetings or telephone conversations without disturbing others or having private conversations overheard.

Similarly, in providing for fire safety, we are concerned with a variety of different subsystems within the building, each performing its function effectively in relation to the other components. The type of protection provided by a specific ceiling system when it is used with a concrete structure will not necessarily be acceptable when that ceiling is used in conjunction with a steel structure.

Building Subsystem Components

Building subsystems can be coordinated by articulating each of the subsystems separately, so that each stands alone and is totally accessible. In this situation, each function is handled by separate components. Alternatively, we may work to integrate a group of separate subsystems so that a single component performs many functions. A hollow-tube structural column may become an air duct, or a shaped floor deck structural member may function as a lighting coffer (see Figure 9.4). The flexibility which results from dealing with each subsystem separately is reduced by this integrated approach. However, when a single component does more than one job within the building, more resources can be devoted to its design. More money can be spent on a structural member which also performs as a lighting-ceiling or air-distribution member. There is, in fact, a continuum between an articulated and an integrated approach to design. Analyses of needs, accessibility, available resources, and methods for joining different building subsystems provide a substantial range of options for response to image, function, and future flexibility. Figures 9.5 and 9.6 give an example of a design approach which emphasizes articulation of the various subsystems as developed for The Great High School project in Pittsburgh. Integration of building subsystems is illustrated in the URBS case study where the structural subsystem forms a plenum for air return of the heating, ventilation, and air-conditioning (HVAC) system.

The key to proper development of any systems approach to design is the appropriate selection of building components, whatever their degree of site or factory fabrication. It is, however, essential to make certain that work done at the factory does not have to be redone at the building site. While a sheet of plywood can be cut to fit at the site, a sandwich panel with an aluminum edge that is 1¼ inches too long cannot be. For this reason, a range of tolerances for all building components must be specified. The individual responsibilities for the different component systems have to be established so that appropriate and normal tolerances are provided within a reasonable

Figure 9.5 Model of flexible structural system designed to permit HVAC ducts to run at the center of the span and to provide openings for the passage of other services.

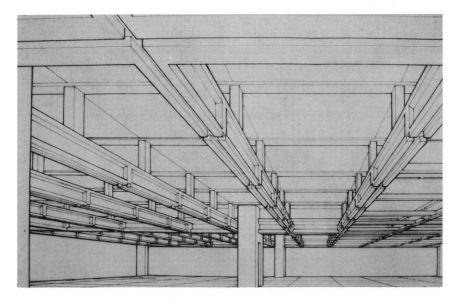

Figure 9.6 Drawing showing the structural system from eye level. Ceiling and lighting elements can be placed at many different levels, thus providing a variety of visual appearances to suit the various functions to be housed in different parts of a building.

price range. On any project it would be possible to demand that a slab on-grade be poured with an accuracy of ±½ inch. But to achieve that level of performance for a building area of 10,000 square feet or more might require the expenditure of more than twice the amount of money demanded by a tolerance level of ±1 inch. A normal 2-inch tolerance thus demands the development of details for the installation of interior partitions which have the capacity to compensate for such variations in floor level. This can be achieved, for example, by shimming at the base to compensate for unevenness in the slab and by having the base cover the varying distances between the partition panel and floor. Certain approaches to detailing are more successful than others in hiding variations in tolerance. If, for example, a shadow line reveal was desired instead of a covering base, it would still be essential that the partitions follow the curve of the floor. The variation of ±1 inch would be easily seen in the height of a 4-inch shadow line. Therefore, the individual partitions must be cut so that they do, in fact, fit, either at the base or at the top of the partition panels. Otherwise, the normal variation in building tolerance will be very obvious, making it appear poorly constructed. The cutting and fitting of each panel is costly and inflexible. The particular approach to detailing therefore, has a considerable impact on tolerance requirements and cost.

It must be recognized that as buildings age, they settle and move, and that provisions must be made for them to "breathe." When movement takes place, we must be sure that non-load-bearing members do not in fact become load-bearing. The following example demonstrates how this can happen. As a ceiling is installed and attached to the structure, it is leveled. But, as furniture is moved into a building and certain areas are heavily loaded, additional deflections are going to occur. Non-loading-bearing partitions are invariably attached to the ceiling for stability, and significant deflections can make them load-bearing. Eventually, damage to the ceiling, partition, or structure may result unless the building tolerance system has been designed to adapt to these changes. Buildings must therefore be designed so that overall performance can be maintained under varied loading conditions. Our present use of lighter building materials forces us to provide even greater opportunities for "breathing" than has previously been the case in building design.

Our firm worked a number of years ago on the Woolworth Building in New York, whose terra cotta skin was installed when the building was constructed in 1913. This building, for 21 years the tallest in the world, predates the development of the expansion joint, which was invented in 1920 and was in common use thereafter. As the tallest building ever designed without expansion joints, the building has been subject to a buildup of pressures that have caused or contributed to deterioration of the terra cotta facade. The necessity for designing buildings so that they can breathe and move is very poignantly demonstrated by the deterioration of the building's overstressed facing materials (see Figure 9.7).

The use of more and more sophisticated building components, along with appropriate site construction techniques, causes significant tolerance problems. These products must fit at the building site and accommodate to the tolerance needs of the neighboring components. The leeway that exists in cutting stone and other masonry products or in working with sheet materials such as plywood or gypsum board gives the designer considerable freedom in the size and shape of building designs. When working with vocabularies of factory-made components, building tolerances must be developed in the design of the jointing system itself. Any size and shape of precast concrete panel can be made, but 2 inches cannot be cut from each panel to fit actual site conditions. In some types of mass production, standard products must be produced to given sizes and shapes. Light fixtures

Figure 9.7 Areas in distress shown marked on a large portion of the facade.

designed to hold fluorescent tubes are one such example. It is essential that such standardized components relate to the basic functional and anthropometric requirements of the user. The development of product sizes for different components based on these "universal" anthropometric and functional requirements frequently calls for considerable dimensional variety; for example, a dimension of 4 feet will not do for all components. This increases the problems of joining different products as they must first mesh with one another before tolerance can be considered. A 5-foot square ceiling and lighting panel may be the most functionally appropriate for a given purpose because of room and furniture sizes and lighting levels. At the same time, 40-inch-wide partition panels may best meet user needs. At this dimension, a panel equals the width of a door and its frame, so panels and doors become interchangeable — a useful device for flexibility. It is necessary, therefore, to develop some form of dimensional coordination to maximize the opportunities for combining different products, each of which is designed to meet specific requirements. Such a discipline will call for groups of related products that can fit together simply and in a variety of ways.

Component Sizes

The variety of product sizes is also increased by virtue of the different handling characteristics and weights of the various materials involved. Weight and/or size may determine handling by one or two hands, one or two people, or a machine.

Another important factor in the design of building components is limiting waste when sheet materials are to be cut at the building site. For example, if a house is designed on a 28-inch module so that every 4-foot plywood or Sheetrock sheet has 20 inches cut off and thrown away, it would obviously be very expensive to build.

Building, as an additive process, calls for the placement of similar-sized products next to one another, whether they be bricks, blocks, windows, or spandrel panels. We must, therefore, be able to deliver products to the building site, stock them easily, and have appropriate sizes available to the installers. If a variety of different sizes have to fit together, the progress of construction will be much slower and the ability to control patterns will diminish. If bricks of random length, 8, 9, 10, 12, and 16 inches, were to be used to fill different distances, it would be much more difficult to incorporate them into a wall than to use a single size brick and cut the end one — if the dimensional variances could not be taken up in the mortar joints. We find, however, that the product sizes for different components, such as wall, ceiling, and floor panels, each march to a different drummer, and that these sizes need to be compatible in order to coordinate building components more effectively.

For this reason it is important to base our ranges of different product sizes on dimensions which have the greatest number of matching permutations. *The Modular Number Pattern* was devoted to this principle and called for the use of a range of basic product sizes based on the elimination of prime numbers and their multiples — starting with 7. The range of numbers available for use is shown in Figure 9.8. The number 72 is selected rather than 71 (which is a prime), for example, because a variety of different products can

| 1, 2, 3, 4, 5, 6, 8, 9, 10, 12, 15, 16, 18, 20, 24, 27, 30, 32, 36, 40, 45, 48, 54, 60, 64, 72, 80, 90, 96, 108, 120 |

Figure 9.8 Numbers contained in the modular number pattern up to 120.

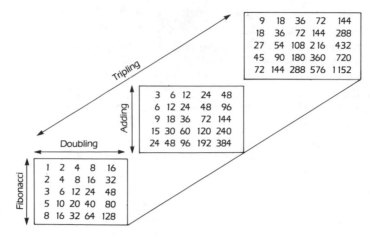

Figure 9.9 The three series — doubling along the *x* axis, tripling along the *z* axis, and adding $(1 + 2 = 3, 2 + 3 = 5, 3 + 5 = 8)$ along the *y* axis — provide the basis for the modular number pattern. An examination of this matrix shows many simple numerical relationships. It can, therefore, provide a base for coordinating different product sizes in a unified design.

be used to make up 72 inches, for example, nine 8-inch bricks, four 18-inch windows, three 24-inch panels, etc., while 71 inches has no similar analogy. The greater the number of factors, the greater the possibilities for interchange between components designed to meet the basic requirements of their discipline. This group of numbers, which has the greatest possible range of factors, can be arrayed in a doubling, tripling, and additive sequence, according to the Fibonacci series, to provide the full range of relationships between those dimensions (see Figure 9.9).

The development of number patterns provides a basis for determining the nominal sizes of compatible components to be used within a building. The actual dimensions call for tolerance control so that products designed to fit, will, in fact, do so within the framework of normal building conditions. The use of coordinated ranges of product sizes makes it possible to design the different component systems of a building according to basic anthropometric data and in sizes appropriate to weight and handling criteria so that workers can install them easily at the building site. The resultant vocabulary provides a wide range of proportional and spatial relationships. Such a keyboard provides the basis for design flexibility even while working with the controlled sizes and proportions inherent in the use of manufactured products. Where the manufacturing method allows products of any size to be produced — for example, with use of computer-aided machine tools — the designer is free to use random sizes. However, shipping may be very difficult and workers must be given very specific instructions about which products to install and in what sequence.

When prefabricated and site-fabricated materials are combined, one approach to tolerance control is to install the prefabricated products first and fit the site-fabricated products to them. It obviously makes little sense to build a brick wall without building in the window frames or providing details which have ample dimensional flexibility. Otherwise, installing the windows after the fact would call for extremely tight tolerances. The development of any design keyboard requires a wide range of different products which fit together at the appropriate junctures. In spite of the rich variety of products available to designers today, the fact is that there are relatively few differently sized components that will work together appropriately on the building site. For this reason, designers frequently work with a single module for all products used in a building because they know that the products will fit together, even if the product sizes are not expressive of the building's functions or its occupants. In tight planning situations this may also result in a waste of space as all functions may not be provided economically by a single module. It seems important that a discipline be developed which resolves this dichotomy between flexibility of use and specificity of function. The lack of such a keyboard induces designers to continually order special products even when there is a premium for doing so. When a company feels that too much of its product is ordered in special sizes, it will not produce and warehouse its standard products. The entire manufacturing and distribution system therefore becomes keyed to batch rather than mass production. There are potential gains to be made in cost and quality control if we can determine in which situations mass-produced products make sense. Mass production requires a sufficiently flexible dimensional system so that designers of most buildings have an appropriate means of expression within the standardized framework. The artist who does not have constant colors to work with would find it very difficult to paint a large mural and, indeed, most of the arts require a disciplined keyboard capable of great variation in composition. Architecture, I believe, is no exception, and the proportional systems of Alberti, Palladio, and other great theorists in history tend to bear this out. Today, however, in order to achieve this goal, architectural designers must work with the tool and die maker, the modern equivalent of Michelangelo's stone mason.

Factory Fabrication of Subsystems

Factory fabrication and assembly of compatible subsystems may result in the production of "super components," or of three-dimensional space modules. These modules may make up a small portion of the building, or may be fully serviced, such as a mobile home. Imagine several trailer units that are hooked together at a building site to create a large single space whose thermal environment is controlled by a single air-conditioning system located on the roof. Similarly, other subsystems may be made separately and then combined with a three-dimensional space module and installed at the building site. These complete or partially complete space modules can be used to form entire buildings that require varying degrees of on-site finish-

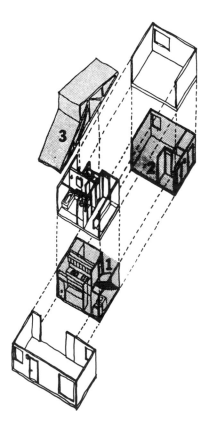

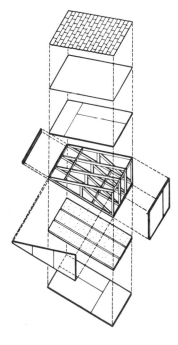

Figure 9.10 The Alodex system was based on the use of relatively small, 12-foot-wide boxes which could be grouped together to form a house.

Figure 9.11 These photographs depict the process of building a five-bedroom house. Work started on site in the morning, and at 11:15 a.m. the first roof unit is shown being set in place.

Figure 9.12 Bathroom-kitchen core unit being lowered into place attached to its prefabricated concrete floor panel.

ing. (See Figures 9.10 and 9.11 which show several three-dimensional box units developed for the Alodex Corporation placed together at the building site to form a complete dwelling unit.) For certain situations, it may be desirable to combine densely serviced and costly portions of a building, such as kitchens and bathrooms, into three-dimensional units with the larger space-enclosing components formed by panels or built more conventionally on site. This would reduce the need for shipping large volumes of air. This is the basis of the system developed by the Forest City Dillon Company — shown in Figures 9.12 and 9.13 — for whom we have designed a number of housing and hotel projects. It was also the basis on which we designed U.S. Embassy housing in Budapest and Libreville. An example of completed houses is shown in Figures 9.14 and 9.15.

One way of thinking of these "super components" is as a group of building subsystems fabricated so that site construction savings are greater than the transportation costs. The emphasis must be on value per cubic foot. One such super component is described in Figures 9.16 and 9.17. The total complement of products that may be shipped from factory to building site ranges from pieces and parts to total building units, such as a complete trailer. Within this continuum, appropriate selections must be made as to the level of technology appropriate for the specific job.

Figure 9.13 The bathroom units are shown in place on the concrete floor structure, and the wall panels were then set in place for the next floor.

Figure 9.14 Libreville housing.

Figure 9.15 The housing units in Libreville were designed to be built conventionally or using a system of prefabricated core units designed for the State Department.

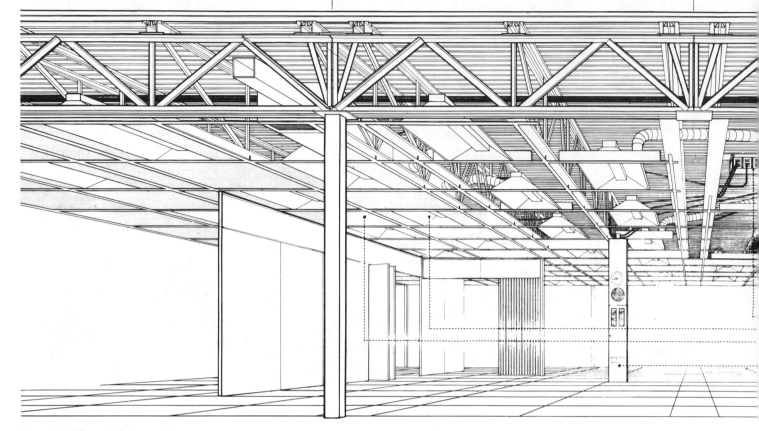

Basic Component Module

Figure 9.16 Completely integrated 10-foot-wide structural, mechanical, lighting roofed units with plug-in electric units, finished ceilings, etc., were fabricated in the factory for shipment to the site. Typical unit length was 60 feet.

Figure 9.17 Two units, which will be wrapped in a tarpaulin, on leaving the factory.

Development of Technology

The level of technology needed for any given project will depend on which methods are appropriate to it. A large, concentrated market may well make it feasible to provide more complex elements with high levels of prefabrication that are shipped to the site in the form of building units. A large but diverse market which is not properly aggregated for a massive program requires lower levels of sophistication and more effective distribution methods that can work over longer distances. Given the specific situation relating to a given project, the designer must determine the appropriate mix of available technologies. The conventional way of building has evolved over a long period, with a variety of new techniques being incorporated as they were developed. This makes it possible to build as economically as possible within the current system of financing and marketing.

The development of new multifamily housing systems involves considerable economic risk. It is difficult to aggregate markets sufficiently so as to guarantee continuing productivity for the more highly industrialized approaches, and thus capital investment in such plants becomes unwise. In addition, conventional materials are relatively cheap for certain tasks when compared with the cost of prefabricated components used for the same purpose. When we compare the cost of gypsum board installed on site with that of a prefabricated panel, we invariably find that for homes gypsum board is cheaper. In other types of buildings, such as schools, the kind of wear and tear involved makes feasible more sophisticated and expensive

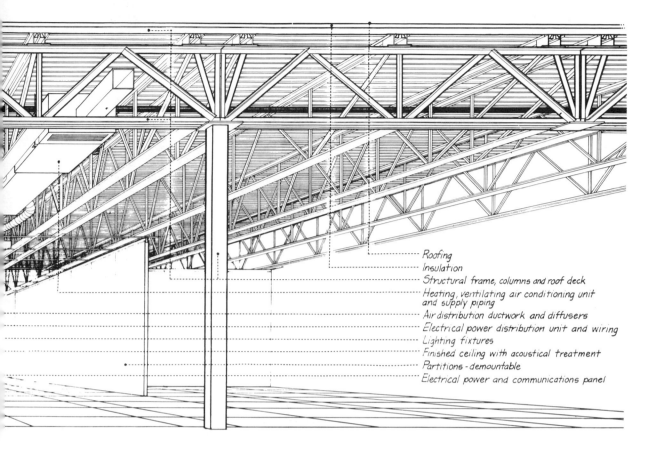

Roofing
Insulation
Structural frame, columns and roof deck
Heating, ventilating air conditioning unit and supply piping
Air distribution ductwork and diffusers
Electrical power distribution unit and wiring
Lighting fixtures
Finished ceiling with acoustical treatment
Partitions - demountable
Electrical power and communications panel

partitioning materials which can also be used as tack and chalkboards. Since considerable first cost is expended on the partitions and educationally oriented finishes that comprise the total school wall system, it is possible to develop prefabricated products at a competitive, or even lower, cost. Cost becomes the significant factor in determining the applicability of industrialized components. Although the requirements for a dwelling unit may be considered complex by many, there are already developed products that work quite simply and economically. It is for this reason that the evolution of new approaches to housing will occur more frequently for subsystems rather than for total building systems. Invariably, these developments will be incorporated within the vocabulary of conventional building. There has been limited success in the use of total boxes for housing, except for mobile homes. The use of panel construction for low-rise housing has had some regional success. In some parts of the country the sophisticated use of precut lumber and packaged components delivered to the site for the builders' installation has proven to be effective. At this point, however, any significant new developments will probably be dependent on material rather than design innovations as quality lumber becomes harder to obtain.

High-Rise Housing

When we search for techniques with which to organize the construction process more efficiently in order to meet the challenge of high-rise housing

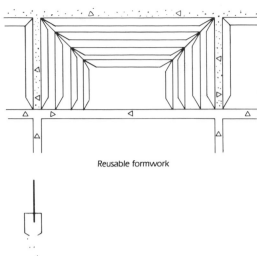

Reusable formwork

Slipforms

Figure 9.18 Reusable formwork has wall and/or ceiling forms which may be reused when the concrete has set up. The work is typically repetitive. Slipforms are usually moved vertically as the concrete sets up. Concrete is frequently poured continually to provide for a homogeneous structure.

in a systematic way, it makes sense to first investigate the various techniques that may help to order the building process.

The different approaches to the development of building systems for high-rise housing are inevitably described in terms of structure, even though it invariably represents less than 35 percent of the total building cost. This is because structure plays a major role in defining the individual dwelling units and as a byproduct, providing the ceiling, and frequently the exterior walls, as well as many of the interior partitions. All of the other systems (such as the mechanical, electrical, and plumbing) must fit within or be supported by the structural framework.

Site-Formed Systems

Reusable form work and slipform construction (see Figure 9.18) are two techniques that have been used successfully. The form work may be part of an existing standardized forming system or may be designed for a specific project, and the forms may or may not be used again. Amortization is most frequently considered in terms of the individual project. The relatively low cost of these forms makes it possible to use them on a project-by-project basis without regard to large-scale market aggregation. Other techniques have been developed to minimize the reuse of form work, such as the lift slab approach, where the previously poured slab itself becomes a main part of the form. Tunnel-forming techniques, where sophisticated forms are reused daily, are at the opposite end of the spectrum (see Figures 9.19 and 9.20). Since lift slab construction generally provides for slabs that have spans larger than those typically required for housing, this approach has not had any major impact on the housing industry.

Tunnel forming provides for cross-wall construction with relatively narrow spans and is one of the better approaches for low-income housing or housing for the elderly. The tunnel-forming system tends to be efficient in that there is a predetermined rhythm to construction of the structure, which is completed more quickly than structures formed by competitive techniques. In addition, the full structure does not have to be in place before the other trades can begin work, as is the case with lift slab. But the design constraints resulting from the short spans and relatively thick, dense, and heavy floor and walls make tunnel forming uneconomical for long-span buildings and for more luxurious housing.

The use of tunnel forming in this country has been limited because significantly large repetitive building projects are needed to justify the use of the forms. Wherever it is possible to build short span projects repetitively, tunnel forms provide an economical option. On the other hand, where longer span cross-wall construction might be appropriate, panel construction usually provides better design flexibility because it provides for a greater variety of configurations with the potential for longer spans.

Prefabricated Systems

There are a number of different ways that buildings can be prefabricated. The simplest uses prefabricated columns and beams with floors that are constructed entirely on site or that use factory-made components. The problem with the orderly use of this type of construction for low-cost housing is that the vertical supports are in addition to the cross walls, which must still be designed to provide for acoustic privacy. The provision of columns, beams, and an acoustic infill, which could also take part of the structural load, tends to be more expensive than construction of bearing walls. In higher cost housing, where greater flexibility for internal space planning and potential change is valued, column and beam construction may make sense. However, establishing a market for a specific range of column and beam sizes is difficult because it is just this market that does not want to be standardized. Column and beam construction is therefore applied more frequently on a custom basis.

There have been approaches to the use of building systems based upon three-dimensional structural members that include columns and beams within a single element (see Figure 9.21). Such systems deal directly with how the building is put together and make great structural sense, but their three-dimensional shapes make them relatively inefficient for shipping, and their very precision limits dimensional variation. All they are providing are the columns and beams typical of higher cost types of housing construction, where their inherent constraints are less acceptable. Thus the appropriate markets for this kind of approach are limited, but its structural validity keeps this kind of technique in contention for certain projects. A great benefit of this approach is that the members are joined to one another at the point of least stress.

Panel Systems

The next higher level of prefabrication is cross-wall systems erected on site with factory-made panels, the basis of most high-rise housing systems (see Figure 9.22). The development of factory-built panel systems requires adequate markets for continuity in production within a region appropriate to the shipment of large, heavy panels, since it is unreasonable to incur the excessive costs of shipping panels great distances. When panel systems are designed it is possible to use prestressed and/or voided planks which can be lighter and more effective than those formed with typical tunnel-forming techniques. The location of panels for bearing walls can vary, and mixed spans can be incorporated into the building design. This allows considerable flexibility within the framework of an economical building system where the wall panels themselves provide the structure as well as the closure between one apartment and the next. This system has greater economic benefits than typical column-and-beam systems that require infill.

The assembly of panel systems, however, depends on the development of good joint systems that permit the effective handling of the four-way connections of wall and floor panels. The structural redundancy occurring in site-poured buildings allows stresses to flow through secondary routes. This does not occur in a prefabricated building because its joints permit stresses to flow only in a predetermined manner. Greater care must, therefore, be taken in designing joints and in joining panels on site, because alternative paths for stresses have to be predesigned into panelized building systems.

As the cross-wall construction approach represents the largest proportion of systems-built high-rise housing, it is appropriate to analyze some of the joinery problems that have evolved over time. The original development of high-rise panel systems took place after World War II in France and then in Denmark. The two generic joinery systems had much in common, each

Floor slabs are poured one on top of the other on the ground floor slab.

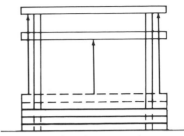

After floor slabs are cured, the top one is lifted into place, then the next, and so on.

Figure 9.19 Lift slab construction is most effective for midrise buildings of even spans and average bay sizes.

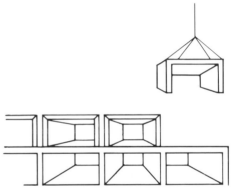

Tunnel forms are put in place, concrete poured, and forms removed as soon as the concrete sets up, then they are lifted to form the next floor.

Figure 9.20 The three-dimensional tunnel forms must collapse internally so that they can be extracted for reuse.

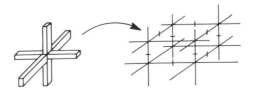

Figure 9.21 Three-dimensional column and beam components.

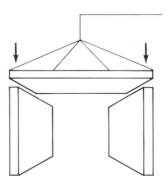

Figure 9.22 Cross-wall panel construction.

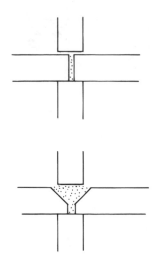

Figure 9.23 Typical design of four-way panel joints. Variations in slab edge details to accommodate site grouting are shown.

requiring a four-way panel joint (see Figure 9.23). In essence, wall panels of reasonably precise length and width could be made in a variety of molds. However, it was difficult to control floor-panel thickness, which is affected by how the concrete settles in the mold, which in turn is affected by the consistency of the concrete, i.e., the mix of sand and water, and by the amount of vibration occurring when the concrete is poured. (Anyone who has tried to use a cake mix with consistent results will understand the problem.)

The traditional panel systems were in effect all variations on a general theme: the wall panels for each new floor were raised above those of the floor below by means of steel rods with bolts set for leveling purposes (see Figure 9.24). When set in place, the panels were braced by steel angles and grout was shoved into the four-way joint to achieve structural continuity. This process has the disadvantage that inspection is required to ensure that all the appropriate reinforcing bars are set in place because failures have been noted where this was not done. Since the grouting process covered up the work done on the joint, the inspection had to be a continuous process if construction were to proceed at a reasonable rate.

There are, however, other, more effective approaches to joining panels: poured and dry joints. A successful use of the wet joint technique can be seen in the work of the Forest City Dillon Company in one of the original Operation Breakthrough systems that has proven most successful in the marketplace. This system uses hollow-core wall panels with half-thickness concrete floor slabs. When the panels are put in place, the remainder of the floor slab is poured with concrete filling the openings in the wall panels to create a three-dimensional homogeneous building structure (see Figure 9.25). This system provides considerably more quality control than any of

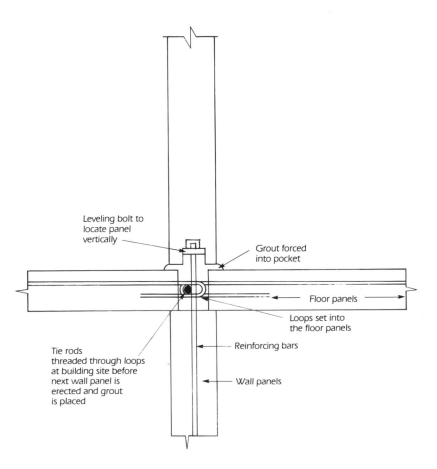

Leveling bolt to locate panel vertically

Grout forced into pocket

Floor panels

Loops set into the floor panels

Reinforcing bars

Tie rods threaded through loops at building site before next wall panel is erected and grout is placed

Wall panels

Figure 9.24 Detail of typical four-way panel joint.

the traditional European types of panel systems. In addition, the University Residential Building Systems (URBS), described in Case Study 2, used a similar approach to develop a structural system designed for mechanical as well as structural purposes. In the 1970s our London office worked on a number of dry joining systems, one of which is described below, in order to eliminate the on-site quality control problems of the four-way grouted joint.

The column-in-wall system (shown in Figure 9.26) has a wall configuration that permits one wall panel to rest on the wall panel below so that thickness variations in floor panels do not affect the building's tolerance control. The floor panels themselves rest on the wall panel in such a way that when the wall and floor panels are put together they lock into each other, allowing the transfer of lateral or sheer loads. The connections between wall and floor panels are made in an open pocket which could be grouted at any time; thus inspection could take place intermittently, allowing construction to proceed. This development permits the use of an effective detailing approach that can eliminate some of the quality control problems of the more conventional panel systems.

Figure 9.25 Forest City Dillon system detail. See photographs in Figures 9.13 and 9.14. The combination of the panel structure with kitchen and bathroom core units is shown.

Box Systems

The next level of prefabrication of high-rise housing is the box system, which works in one of two main ways—either with boxes that are (1) structurally self-supporting or (2) designed to rest on separate structural supports. The major advantage of box systems is that they permit the organized control of the entire building process in the factory and facilitate quick completion at the building site. Their major disadvantage is that they re-

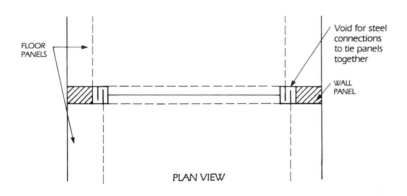

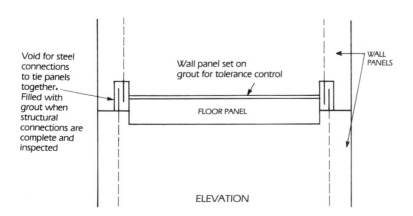

Figure 9.26 Column-in-wall system: Notched wall panels permit connections to be inspected for purposes of quality control after they are made.

quire a well-organized production line with relatively high capital investment. Because of high shipping costs, continuity of manufacture must be based on effective marketing in relatively small regions of the country. It is difficult to use prefabricated box methods for high-rise construction without market aggregation and a marketing approach that can supply the needed volume of projects in orderly succession. If the shipping radius has to be increased, the boxes become uneconomical, because a considerable amount of empty space must also be shipped, since with the exception of bathrooms and kitchens, the boxes are not densely filled. A number of different techniques have been developed to improve the economic viability of boxes where on-site construction time was a significant issue. A number of special conditions have provided opportunities for the effective use of box systems. The timing for construction of the San Antonio Hilton in time for the San Antonio World's Fair was particularly tight and provided an opportunity for the Zachary system, which stacks fully outfitted concrete boxes, to excel. Our own approach for an Alaskan student housing project, where wood panels were barged from Oregon and made into boxes in Alaska, is another example of where time was of the essence and the box approach was most appropriate. (see Figure 9.27).

Concrete boxes may be (1) poured three dimensionally or (2) made up of panels joined together in the factory and then properly finished and outfitted. The span and weight of these boxes must be carefully controlled for this method to be economical. As seen in Figure 9.28, the HABS system is used for housing and hotels. Another approach is represented by the Stressed Structures systems, which we refined at the time of Operation Breakthrough using expansive concrete to combat problems of weight. In this case, the reinforcing ribs of a thin-wall structure provided the form work in which columns would be poured for high-rise purposes (see Figure 9.29). But lack of a continuous market caused the company to go out of business. Other approaches have been developed for obtaining more value from prefabricated boxes: for example, using them in a checkerboard form to achieve single-walled rather than double-walled buildings, as in the case of the Shelley system, another of the Operation Breakthrough systems (see Figure 9.30).

In Case Study 5, which describes our Fiber-Shell housing system, the relative merits of these two approaches are discussed in greater detail. But it is appropriate here to state our conclusion that whole boxes are more eco-

Figure 9.27 University of Alaska dormitory units.

Figure 9.28 The HABS System using three-dimensional concrete boxes.

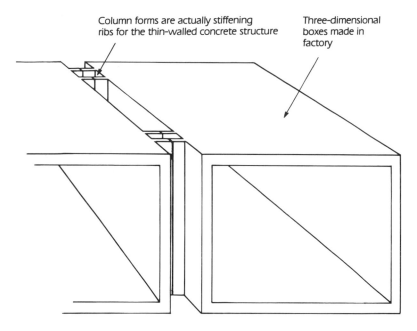

Column forms are actually stiffening ribs for the thin-walled concrete structure

Three-dimensional boxes made in factory

Figure 9.29 The Stressed Structures system featured the use of expansive concrete for a thinner and lighter structure.

nomical and effective than checkerboard approaches. The rationale behind the use of prefabricated box systems is to preempt on-site activities with factory production. The combination of factory fabrication and on-site infill of the checkerboard pattern creates logistical problems which we found to be more costly than the savings in building materials.

In looking at approaches to shipping boxes — given the generally low cubic foot value (vis-à-vis the shipment of air) — we recognize advantages in the combination of panels and service core boxes within an integrated building system. This has been done by Forest City Dillon as already mentioned, and we have used this approach as the basis for our design of U.S. Embassy housing in Budapest and Libreville (see Figure 9.31). The construction of the housing in Libreville, however, was done conventionally. It does appear that this combination provides the best of both worlds, coupling cross-wall construction with the use of highly serviced box units. Since the value of prefabricated core boxes stacked and shipped on a truck is analogous to the payload of an automobile carrier, there are more potential

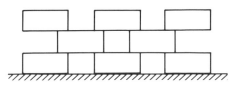

Figure 9.30 Shelley system – checkerboard arrangement of boxes.

Figure 9.31

markets within a larger shipping radius than would be possible when transporting box units alone.

There are obviously many nonconcrete alternatives to factory fabrication of panels or the use of site-forming techniques, but so far, costs, fire protection, acoustic separation, and tolerance control problems have generally rendered these nonconcrete directions less useful for high-rise housing construction. Unfortunately, some of the more interesting directions have not received sufficient market support. Moreover, the continued use of the housing and construction industry in general as a tool to correct economic problems makes it difficult to organize consistent markets for high-rise residential industrialization. The successful approach of the house trailer industry to offsetting, at least to some degree, the effect of market fluctuations, that is, the storage of a significant number of units by dealers, is unsuitable for high-rise off-site fabricated housing. High-rise construction invariably calls for a level of individual detailing in response to a specific project that cannot easily be translated into production for general market purposes and dealers are unable to store units. Success therefore is tied directly to a continuous market demand, which we have not been able to generate on any widespread basis.

Low-Rise Housing

The development of a systems approach to low-rise construction began early in this country's history with the development of the balloon frame. This approach enabled the designer, the contractor, and the worker to communicate with each other very efficiently and to put together a wide variety of different house plans that could be spelled out very simply on paper and were widely used. Given the nature of our housing market and the very effectiveness with which site construction techniques have evolved, opportunity for major cost savings through prefabrication is reduced. Conventional materials used for low-rise housing are as low in cost as any conceivable alternative method for providing acceptable or equivalent performance. In looking toward prefabrication of low-rise housing up to now, we have dealt primarily with efficiencies in labor rather than in labor *and* materials; this provided a relatively limited opportunity for making cost breakthroughs that are sufficient to amortize the capital costs of prefabrication. The conventional home builder has taken advantage of a wide variety of different developments made over the years—from the use of precut lumber, to trusses, prefabricated cabinetry, bath-shower units, and effective panel systems. In the future, changes in the availability and price of quality lumber may well alter the material composition and processes used for low-rise housing systems.

Specific design and building concepts may be developed that make economic sense for a period of time, such as Carl Koch's Tech-Built houses. But the need to maintain a continuous market invariably causes such systems to come up against hard times. Given an appropriate operating environment, however, their value has been demonstrated in various locations throughout the country. Because systems building is rational and makes sense inherently, it is tried repeatedly.

The greatest potential for savings occurs when the design and construction of the entire home takes place within the factory. The mobile home industry initially was able to change the code requirements for homes that were supposedly not permanent, which allowed them to reduce both material and labor costs and made them a significant factor within the housing industry. The most significant innovation, however, came from dealers who placed factory units on their sales lots, and then marketed them, thus allowing the factory production cycle to be evened out to a significant extent. Thus the mobile home industry can make boxes on a relatively economical and continuous basis, capturing a very significant proportion of all new housing starts across the country. Modular homes provided under the factory-built housing laws are increasing in use in various sections of the country. However, more sophisticated boxes, developed for the design of custom housing, have some of the traditional problems because they do not have the advantage of the sales lot for storage and need design and code approvals for each project.

As in the case of high-rise construction, there is much to be said for the use of prefabricated bathroom, kitchen, and service core units in low-rise housing. The opportunities in this direction have not yet been fully realized, but some of the more interesting developments, with potential for low-rise housing, are effective roof systems which can sit on a combination of core units and panels or other supports. In such cases, the major vertical interior and related services might best be built at the building site (see Figure 9.32). Just as the development of latex paint has provided building occupants the opportunity to contribute to the finishing and upkeep of their residences, it is conceivable that properly developed systems that provide service core, roof structure, and enclosure could be developed with "do-it-yourself" infill systems that make it possible for potential residents to make a significant, individual contribution to the construction of their homes.

Even in the absence of continuous markets, there is an opportunity to continue developing new materials and methods which will be absorbed within, and improve, the conventional building industry. This industry is most resilient and will very quickly incorporate new techniques (up to the factory construction of total houses) that pay off within the marketplace.

Nonresidential Building Systems

In the design of nonresidential projects, the development of building systems and the use of different types of building technologies call for a different type of organization of building subsystems than is typical for housing. The first, and greatest, difference is that in nonresidential buildings the role of the structural subsystem becomes much less important; the cost of the structure is typically less than 15 percent of the total cost. The longer spans between potential supporting walls or columns permit and demand a level of infill which — together with requirements for services and environmental needs — call for the development of more sophisticated subsystems for space enclosure, service, environment, and finishes. In addition to meeting a wider range of program requirements for a specific building, changes in use over time must also be allowed for.

This means developing more sophisticated mechanical and electrical services, together with a variety of ways in which space may be subdivided and enclosed. If we examine the design of a hospital, school, office building, or shopping center, we find that the structure acts as an armature or matrix that holds the service subsystems which penetrate it in appropriate patterns so that services are provided where needed within the building. The relative cost of the structure and structural work represents quite a small percentage of the building's total cost.

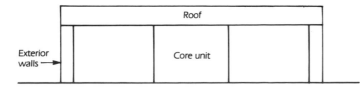

Figure 9.32 Roof supported on core unit and exterior walls. Prefabricated roof and core units can be combined with site construction. This approach should be considered particularly for those cases where some degree of self-help labor is desirable and available to complete the interior.

Current concerns with environmental performance may well be the driving factor in the development of design teams balanced to represent all the required specialties. If we think of a building as consisting of separate layers — with its structure, air conditioning, lighting, and ceiling providing a ceiling-to-floor sandwich — we find that the depth required for all these service systems will frequently be greater if they are totally layered than if they share the same space (see Figure 9.33). Performance may be reduced when, for cost-savings purposes, we are pressured to squeeze the service systems into less space than may be appropriate for their function. When designing any building, we must organize the flow of all the service systems into and out of the building in a manner analogous to the way that stresses flow through the structure, from beams and columns to the foundation. We can, in some cases, combine elements of the building so that they perform multiple functions as shown in Figure 9.4. We can integrate the service and structural systems so that they are tied very closely together, or we can separate and articulate them in such a way that they move independently but are compatible in their relationship within the building.

The highest level of complexity in organizing the service and structural systems might be found in a large hospital. Case study 4 of the VA Hospital shows examples of how separate service systems are articulated within the space provided by the structure and enclosure systems. The structure was specifically designed to facilitate and define the service systems so that they could be placed without conflicting with one another. In simpler buildings there may be opportunities for the total integration of the structural and service systems, but the number of cases where this is an efficient arrangement is very limited. On the other hand, in specific buildings, such as those designed by Louis Kahn, there is demonstrated an attitude toward the design of serving and served spaces, in which structural and mechanical spaces are complementary and articulated.

If we can predict the service requirement of each area to be served and then design a fully integrated combination of structure and services, then a very handsome and tightly designed building may result. The potential for future flexibility within such a building is limited, however, when it is compared to a building with separately articulated systems, each designed to their own rhythm.

Totally integrated buildings are dependent on a simple and clear set of functional requirements whose pattern can be expected to endure for a long

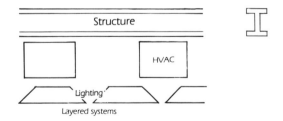

Layered systems

Figure 9.33 The floor-to-ceiling sandwich typically contains the required components in either a layered (*top*) or integrated (*bottom*) mode where they all share the same vertical space within the sandwich. Concrete panel construction typically calls for a layered approach. Steel construction may be designed both ways.

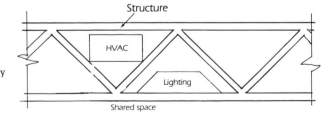

Shared space

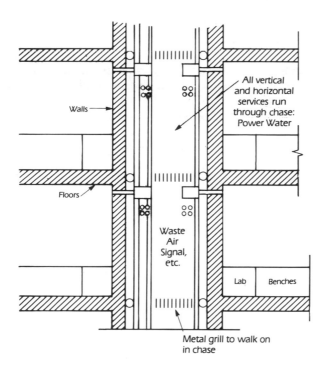

Walls

All vertical
and horizontal
services run
through chase:
Power Water

Floors

Waste
Air
Signal,
etc.

Lab   Benches

Metal grill to walk on
in chase

Figure 9.34 Vertical chase with metal grills to walk on provides access to horizontal and vertical services which support the service requirements of the adjacent rooms. This approach provides great service flexibility with relatively limited room flexibility.

time. The space between finished floor and ceiling typically provides a horizontal slot that includes within it all the requirements for structure, air movement, environmental control, electrical distribution, lighting-ceiling components, sprinklers, and devices for fire separation. This floor-to-ceiling sandwich acts as a kind of service umbrella which permits subdivision of the space for any given configuration and use. The supporting columns or other vertical elements, level changes within the building, and vertical shaft space for services provide constraints on how the space may be subdivided. But for any nonresidential building, the design of the building and location of elements within the overall generic space serviced by the floor-to-ceiling sandwich determines the user's range of freedom and flexibility to change the function of the space. The resultant building constraints may be quite substantial in relation to space layout and services. For example, if you count on natural lighting, this involves considerable limitations for interior spaces, or if all spaces in a single orientation are part of one thermal control zone, the variety of activities that can take place in different rooms on that exposure will be limited to those that have analogous thermal requirements.

The way in which spaces are subdivided with regard to circulation patterns will present constraints relating to egress requirements as well as to the organization of that space into useful rooms. The type of module appropriate to educational requirements is very different from one that is appropriate for office buildings. In one case a significant module might be 30 × 30 feet while the other might be 5 × 5 feet. In the design of spaces whose future is unpredictable, a large enough module must be provided so that useful spaces can be formed using the basic building block. If the partitions of an educational facility can only be placed on a fixed grid of 30 feet, it may become very difficult to organize 25 × 20 foot spaces in such a way that the leftover space has a useful function.

It becomes clear, therefore, that specific building types require different organizational patterns so that space can be efficiently divided and rearranged. The case studies in Part 3 show that there are major differences in the appropriate spatial organization and design modules for office, educational, and health facilities. The technological organization, however, remains very similar, when you consider the wide range of services and facilities provided within the horizontal floor-to-ceiling sandwich. In addition to the type of organization described so far, in which the various service and structural systems share a horizontal block of space, buildings with relatively small floor areas can have service systems that run vertically through the building and feed out to separate areas. Such buildings bear a greater resemblance to residential systems, in which the bathroom-kitchen-service core frequently provides space for vertical movement of services through buildings. In a chemical laboratory building, for example, the nature of the core may call for extremely large and well-organized chases which contain all laboratory services and which provide vertical connections to all laboratories having access to that chase (see Figure 9.34). In areas where a considerable degree of service and change go together, such as a hospital, it is possible to design a walk-on service space, which has been called interstitial space (see Figure 9.35), which provides better access to services. The cost studies done for the Academic Building System (Case Study 3) and the Veterans Administration hospital system (Case Study 4) indicated the life-cycle cost effectiveness of this approach.

The design of institutional or commercial buildings requires accommodation to uncertainty, as well as a projection of how activities are to be serviced to meet the full range of generic requirements appropriate to the specific building type. This means that the building must be designed so that it will function well and be aesthetically pleasing at the time of its opening but still permit a process of evolution. If an office building is built so that any space can become a computer center in the future, the cost may be untenable for the initial owner. We therefore have to develop approaches for the design of service systems that provide for a rational mix of performance requirements. The normal energy requirement for an office building might be 5 watts per square foot, but specific areas might call for as much as 20 watts per square foot. It is therefore incumbent upon the designer and the client to determine what the average capacity of a building will be and make it possible for the maximum requirements to be met in any particular location. Diversity will permit the design of an initially economical building, while the provision of proper access to services will ensure that the maximum requirements can be met. Conceptually the idea is simple but providing for this flexibility demands coordinated decisions about the combined and simultaneous operation of all these separate subsystems. No single building component should be developed with the idea that others will be adapted to it. Rather, a systematic process of progressive decision making must be employed through which all subsystems are designed with compatible functions.

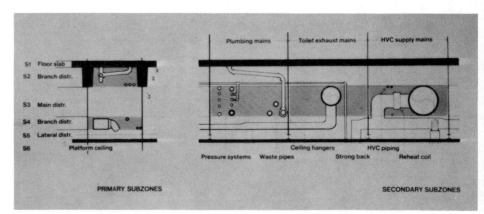

Figure 9.35 Single-story cross section of an interstitial space, which shows the use space being separated from the service space by a floor hung from the ceiling.

In designing a building, you can look at each of the subsystems and begin to call out the basic issues and questions which must be asked about them. In respect to the structure, you must be concerned with the activities that take place in the building, the basic loads which the structure must carry . . . the amount of deflection permitted, the acoustic properties of the structure itself, and the way in which the structure provides a framework, on or through which, to channel all the other service systems which must move within the building. The enclosure system must protect the interior from the weather. It should provide for appropriate ventilation and flow of heat into or out of the building and for natural and artificial lighting; in a sealed building, the internal environmental system must take over and do what cannot be done through the perimeter of the building itself.

Air-conditioning systems must be developed with concern for the different range of activities taking place throughout the building, the size of the control zones required for separate instrumentation and performance, and the degree to which the thermal environment must be ordered. An acceptable variation from the thermostat setting of $\pm 2°$ rather than $\pm 5°$ can make a difference of $10 per square foot to the cost. The amount of fresh air required for ventilation and odor control must be determined. Design of the lighting system must take into account how much light is provided within the individual spaces, the lighting required for each task performed within a given space, and the degree of flexibility for moving the luminaires to meet the task requirements. Finally it must also be borne in mind that heat from the lighting system adds to the air-conditioning load.

Each of the separate systems may work together positively or negatively depending on the season and how they are controlled within the overall building design. The design of the ceiling system must be developed so that it coordinates most closely with the lighting system and provides for acoustic control of room-to-room sound transmission over the ceiling as well as absorbance of sound within a given space. It must also interact with the structure and other components to establish proper acoustic control of impact noise and other unwanted sounds passing from floor to floor. Fire control must be related to the structural design of the building and to the way in which the service systems run through it. Interior partitions, which provide visual and acoustic separation of adjacent spaces, must take into account the kinds of change anticipated. The fixed elements of a building, which provide its exits, vertical shafts, and elevator cores, must be worked out so that the movement of people and goods can be handled efficiently.

In order to establish a flexible, yet coordinated environment, it is helpful to think of a building as a stage which will permit the users to act out their roles whatever the play. In the case of an office building the greatest concern is productivity of the staff. Three tools are required to accomplish the mission of an office building: people, equipment, and environment. All three must be able to work in harmony in any mix and at any point in time.

In developing each of the component systems, we must be concerned not only with the way components work with each other, but how they work within the building. A high degree of acoustic separation in a partition is useless if the sound will go under an adjacent door. If subsystems are to work together to perform a function, the design process must be considered iterative in nature because even assumptions based on experience about structure, air conditioning, lighting, ceilings, partitions, planning grids, and means of access have to be tested. The analysis of possible patterns should show which ones fall short and new variations and groupings can then be tested. It is not always possible to change one subsystem and have the whole package work together. In a building designed so that fire separation is provided by an exposed concrete structure, a fireproof ceiling must be provided if a steel truss is used instead. Many components of a building can be organized and reorganized as groups. For housing it is often easier to choose the structural approach first as a basis for the building enclosure and to then choose an appropriate way to service the building. However, in the design of nonresidential buildings it is better to look at different clusters of subsystems and then make each cluster work by refining the various compatible components. The various clusters can then be analyzed for an acceptable solution in terms of both function and cost. If it is not forthcoming, then another group of compatible components can be tried (see Figure 9.36).

Figure 9.36 Sequence of design must analyze basic human requirements, develop compatible subsystems which have the capacity to respond to those needs, test that capacity, and analyze the costs of those subsystems that can do the job. The information gained from this process allows an appropriate design vocabulary for the project to be developed and information to be gathered for a recycling of the process as the search continues for a match between needs and resources.

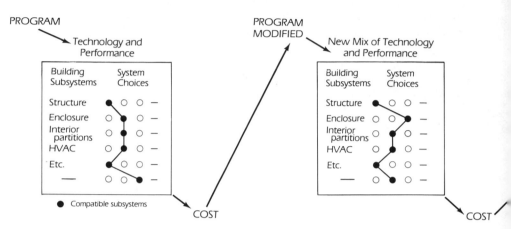

Chapter Ten

Labor

The selection of an appropriate building technology to meet user requirements must obviously take into account the labor resources available for putting that technology in place. The availability of suitable personnel trained for the constituent tasks becomes a matter of major concern in situations where, for example, there are too few carpenters or welders. When there are labor shortages, even modest demands for increased building volume may well set prices skyrocketing. When we were working on the Elmwood Housing Project in Detroit, we had to pay to bring in additional outside labor, but the new workers soon learned that a great deal of overtime was available elsewhere, and they quickly moved on. The need for additional outside labor substantially increased the price of the job without improving the project. The ability to relate the construction approach to the availability of the pool of skilled labor thus assumes great importance, particularly when the construction industry heats up or cools off periodically for economic reasons or to respond to various incentive programs.

In the typical construction process, confrontation with labor rather than partnership with the unions is common. In part this is because the design and construction professions all have an opportunity to decide whether or not to work on a particular project in a given context. For example, a general contractor or an electrical subcontractor may or may not choose to bid on a project, depending on the job conditions. An architect may or may not elect to compete for a commission depending on whether the client's conditions or goals are in accord with his or her principal design interests. But the electricians' or steel workers' unions have no such opportunity. Individual architects and contractors may opt out of certain jobs, but if the project is to be built at all, the essential trades must participate. Once a building has been designed, it is in everyone's common interest to get it built. But, while everyone else on the job is there because they want to be, construction workers are called upon to perform the work without advance notice about the particular scope and demands of the job. As a result, we often encounter resistance because the workers do not have the option of declining the job. Moreover, the professional architect or engineer knows in advance the conditions around which the plans will be drawn, and the contractor in bidding the project knows if special skills are to be exercised or particular risks to be taken. In contrast, the labor unions are asked to have their people report for work on a given day, and they may then be confronted with new installation procedures and products. Since there is insufficient lead time for them to evaluate any new procedures with respect to union work rules, significant changes may trigger jurisdictional disputes, normally resulting in a work stoppage at the building site.

When the unions are characterized as recalcitrant or are blamed for holding up job progress, the inequity of their situation should be borne in mind. Although the professional or contractor may have a similar reaction, it tends to be overlooked, since there is always a replacement or there is time built into the process to resolve such difficulties. He or she is not faced with a fait accompli or the issuance of an ultimatum to start work immediately on a project that has no precedent.

In a systems approach, it is possible to evaluate ahead of time the nature of any innovative products that might be used and the methods for their installation. In many of the programs described in the case studies, shortly after the commencement of the project (during analysis of the user needs), we invited the participation of union advisory committees. They were asked to evaluate the program and study the basic goals of the project, the nature of the performance requirements that would achieve those goals, the products that would have to be developed to meet the performance specifications, and finally, the work rules required to install the products.

Just as we had significant discussions with other professionals and with the subcontractor groups on jurisdictional issues, we had substantial input from the building trades. By helping the unions understand the aims and objectives of the program and by giving them time to respond, we found that, in many cases, problems based on the jurisdictional requirements of the various unions could be submitted to the jurisdictional boards for determination of crew composition and work rules before work began. Five such jurisdictional disputes were resolved for the SCSD project before construction started on the first building; this was unprecedented.

In the development of the SCSD program, the building trades agreed that when the mock-up building, which demonstrated and tested the new products before their use in practice, was constructed, the contractors and subcontractors could use whatever crew composition they needed to get the job done. They also agreed that once the prototype was built, conflicts in the jurisdictional areas would be resolved. The test building for our systems thus became the test building for the building trades as well. In this way, we had the opportunity to optimize technology and labor independently, as well as their interaction. As a result of this kind of two-way communication, the designers gained insight into the impact of new design approaches on the work rules of the various trades and then plugged this knowledge back into the design process.

Our experience with labor also taught us the value of incentive programs in improving morale and controlling time and cost. Programs which set appropriate targets for performance and then reward the individual worker can increase productivity on the site and, therefore, reduce overall construction time.

The new components which have major implications for the way building trades work are the ones that change previously established work roles of the various trades, particularly as they relate to one another. In our systems programs, we have found that if a program creates a disadvantage for a single trade and if that trade is still needed to complete the job, then there will be trouble. If you want to make a change that has a negative impact on plasterers, be sure not to use any plaster at all in your building. It is quite natural and understandable for any trade to be concerned about the setting of precedents that adversely affect not only their role but their status, just as any architect, engineer, or contractor would be concerned if the U.S. government, for example, set up precedents in hiring that ran counter to the normal practices under which these disciplines currently work. If many changes are to be made, they must be orchestrated so that they affect everyone equally. Even though roles may change, status must be preserved.

The work in the SCSD project was organized so that each participant had to make some significant changes, but also so that no single trade or profession was compromised in favor of another. The architects were expected to design buildings using previously developed and purchased components supplied by the school districts. The same was true for the structural, mechanical, and electrical engineers. The general contractor could not select the subcontractors for those component products that were part of the building system. The individual subcontractors had to install those products without being able to take bids from the industry to determine who the suppliers would be. They had to work with specific manufacturers on the installation of their products.

The individual building trades also had to cope with a variety of significant differences. For example, the structural system was made up of light gauge metal. Normally, installation of metal of that gauge fell within the province of sheet-metal workers but, in this case, the structural work had to be done by the iron and steel workers. The sheet-metal workers, on the other hand, had a metal ceiling and lighting system to install which gave them work by way of compensation. The electricians, not too pleased by the nature of the combined work crews required for lighting-ceiling components, were agreeable to the low brightness lighting system that, in effect, called for wall-to-wall lighting fixtures in order to obtain the right luminous environment.

These trade-offs went on up and down the line. There were areas for potential technical innovation in the plumbing field, but if the bathrooms were prefabricated off-site, we still had to rely on the plumbers to connect these systems, but if we had no offsetting advantage to offer the plumbers' union, it was obvious that the work would not get done. This area of development, therefore, was not included in the program. When we evaluated all the activities and all the participants in the building industry, it turned out that in this case, the electrical subcontractors were perhaps the most unresponsive to change, then came the structural engineers, and then the millworkers — not necessarily the sequence one would have anticipated.

The key, however, was that everyone was asked to bend and to do so in a way that maintained their status while their roles changed. To orchestrate this kind of activity, we had to understand the nature of the territories carved out by each trade and then sequence the activities so that one trade could begin and end its work independently of the others; otherwise time is lost and costs escalate. Effective design calls for sequencing activities so as to limit interdependencies. A trade-sequencing schedule is as important as the materials delivery schedule.

When we recognize that the unions' concern to protect their individual territories is as strong as the professionals' need to guard their prerogatives, we can very easily understand why work stops at 8 o'clock in the morning when a union facing quite new procedures on the job is given no prior warning or preparation. If we can project the nature of the desired changes in advance, we may well find, as we have on many of our projects, that the unions are actually more flexible than the professional and contracting groups. This is not to say, of course, that, in given locations around the country, we do not find specific union groups being more recalcitrant than anyone else. But this is a matter of local variation rather than an essential part of the way in which the industry works.

In the SCSD project, the head of the building trades in California was willing to form an advisory committee that met with us throughout the project. The building trades were concerned that our call for the use of newly developed industrialized products might have some negative impact on the amount of labor used on the job. But they understood that we were not asking for new products capriciously and that we were trying to relate our program to urgent curriculum needs and user requirements defined by the educators. They were concerned that the subdivision of work between the trades might discriminate against one or another of the unions or that the unions might be asked to sacrifice more than other participants in the program. But as the program developed and they saw that there were going to be as many concessions demanded of the contracting and design professions as there were of the labor unions, they helped us develop a process that permitted us to get significant approvals in advance of construction and in which not one single day was sacrificed to work stoppages on any of the California schools. In fact, once those precedents were established, to our knowledge not one day was lost anywhere in the country on any project incorporating the SCSD components.

Chapter Eleven

Resource Allocation

The use of the systems approach to design permits the proper formulation of the equation for resources and user requirements. On any project, it is thus possible to determine how the job should be organized in relation to the four-function model, how to allocate resources to meet specific user needs and aspirations, and then to design the building, knowing that there are sufficient resources to accomplish the task. The systems process is one that makes it possible to array the constituent decisions in the planning, programming, and design process in an appropriate sequence and context, beginning with the design itself and ending with the evaluation of the completed construction so that new information may be organized for subsequent projects.

In this process, trade-offs can be made at a number of different points along the way. Decisions about how the building will function and be operated must be made before a program can be set. At the very least, guidelines must be set forth before the design can start and design options must be studied before the program is finalized. The design implications of program options can, in their turn, influence a client's priorities. In any project of reasonable complexity, it makes no sense to set down the results of one phase of the design process and hand off the baton to the next, as though a relay race were being run. Because design is an iterative process among the desirable, the creative response, and the affordable, we must make sure that all the appropriate information goes along with the baton. A systems process may apply to any project whether it uses conventional techniques or not. The materials may be high-tech in nature, or 2×4's on 16-inch centers. Energy conservation may be a major issue, or staff utilization even more important. The nature of the problem determines the direction for the solution. There can be no vested interest in the use of self-help, building trades, or factory processes. The concern must be with problem solving. The scale and kind of project do not affect the basic approach, although they significantly influence the specific techniques and building processes.

In developing the approach now set forth in this book, some of our larger-scale programs allowed time for thought and reflection. The results have been cited in the text as examples and are described in greater detail in the case studies which follow. The same principles, however, have also been applied to single buildings which do not necessarily feature high-tech approaches. We must differentiate between the merits of a systems approach to design and the application of prefabricated, factory-built, or high-technology approaches to the solution of a particular problem. The exploration of the use of indigenous materials and self-help techniques is just as important as the exploration of new techniques for energy conservation, use of solar energy, and prefabrication. These explorations, whether developed as a result of large-scale systems programs or the individual experience of building one's own home, all contribute to a body of knowledge which yields an ever-widening range of alternatives from which to select the appropriate direction for a specific project. Work done in developing new technologies or improving old ones is valuable to any designer in increasing his or her awareness of the possible. When allocating resources for a single project, we must understand the cost and performance implications of various decisions. With a given budget and a program requiring a specific number of square feet, we may elect a middle level of performance for structure (as shown in Figure 11.1), a low level of performance for partitions, and a high level of performance for air-conditioning (as seen in Figures 11.2 and 11.3). A similar selection process must be undertaken for all the components which go into the building, until the total cost developed for the whole project matches the project budget. For example, longer spans might be desirable, but if the program can be met and sufficient flexibility can be obtained with the 30-foot span, this may well be sufficient. Concern for an effective thermal environment and reduced operating costs may lead to a very high price for the air-conditioning system and may involve economizing on both interior and exterior partitions. This type of decision making relates not only to the precise needs of the client but also to his or her aspirations, which must be reflected in the selection process. The palette of materials, the development of different types of spatial relationships, the variety of room types and sizes beyond those specifically needed to fulfill

Structural Spans: Options for Cost Adjustment

Primary spans	Secondary spans	Cost/OGSF
1. 20 feet	20 feet	$ 7.30
2.	30 feet	$ 7.50
3.	40 feet	$ 7.80
4. 30 feet	20 feet	$ 8.20
5.	30 feet	$ 8.50
6.	40 feet	$ 8.80
7. 40 feet	20 feet	$ 8.75
8.	30 feet	$ 9.00
9.	40 feet	$ 9.20

ASSUMPTIONS: Steel frame
Two stories + basement
Total enclosed area
No "interstitial space"
Rectangular plan
66,000 square feet
Includes spray-on beam and column fire protection
Includes 1½-inch metal deck + 3½-inch topping

NOTE: Finishing of columns is additional and ranges from $.20/OGSF for 20 × 20 foot spacing to $.10/OGSF for the 40 × 40 foot spacing.

Figure 11.1 Analysis of cost for structure. The 30 × 30-foot bay was accepted for this project. (OGSF = outside gross square footage.)

Partitions: Options for Cost Adjustment

Generic System	Construction Type/Standard	Finishes 90 percent	Doors + Glass 10 percent	Cost/ Linear Foot	Cost/ OGSF
1. Portable	E. F. Hauserman "Ready Wall" metal sandwich	Colored, washable	Solid core, Single glass metal frame	$24.50	$1.97
2. Demountable, steel	Donn Products Co. "Crusader" steel panelled	Colored, washable	Solid core, single glass metal frame	$26.60	$2.14
3. Demountable, gypsum	Vaughan Walls gyp. composite	Colored, vinyl covered	Solid core, single glass metal frame	$22.50	$1.80
4. Replaceable gypsum	2½-inch boards Sheetrock on each side of metal studs	Field painted	Solid core, single glass metal frame	$18.50	$1.50 ◄

ASSUMPTIONS: 9 feet, 0 inch floor to ceiling.
Approximately 5300 linear feet of partitions
Sound transmission coefficient (STC) = 38

Figure 11.2 Interior partitions were reviewed, and the lowest cost alternative was selected, not because it would best meet the users' requirements but because the money saved was needed to meet both budget and function requirements of other building subsystems.

HVAC: Options for Cost Adjustment

Generic systems	Initial cost/OGSF	Relative operating and maintenance cost/OGSF	Cost zone of control/OGSF	Comments
1. Central double duct	$ 9.50	$ .75	$ .11	20–25-year life ◄
2. Central, single duct reheat	$ 8.50	$ 1.00	$ .09	20–25-year life
3. Central variable volume	$ 6.75	$ .90	$ .075	20–25-year life
4. Roof-top multizone	$ 6.00	$ 1.30	$ .12	25-year life

ASSUMPTIONS:
1. Heating—1.25 CFM/OGSF
2. Cooling—256 OGSF/Ton
3. Basement + 2 floors. 3 (210 × 105) = 65,000 square feet
4. Assume 10 zones of control for all systems except roof-top units which are assumed to have 5 to 6 zones of control.

NOTES:
1. Cost of controls included in initial costs.

2. Cost of life cycle must be based on same time frame and includes replacement of unit parts after 15 years.

3. High costs escalated to 15-year point at 8 percent per annum; any comparison, however, should take note of the impact of time on the value of money. Future costs should be discounted.

4. Present life cost comparison: Options 1 and 3 are approximately equal when total life costs (include initial construction costs) are discounted by Stanford's 9.0 to 9.5 discount rate. Options 2 and 4 are approximately 10 percent higher in cost. Present values do not include escalation factor. This is largely offset by Stanford's unusually low discount rate.

5. Reduced mechanical space required.

Figure 11.3 The highest cost HVAC system was selected because of its life-cycle benefits and because the function of the building is dependent on very accurate control of the thermal environment.
(OGSF = outside gross square footage.)

the function are all part of the response to the client's needs and aspirations. Appropriate options that carry different price tags must be developed for consideration within acceptable thresholds of performance. Nondemountable interior partitions may be inexpensive, but if flexibility is a major concern, then they will have to be torn down from time to time and new ones put in their place. The importance of demountable partitions as opposed to an efficient air-conditioning system with efficient environmental controls may well determine where the client will choose to put his or her money. But even the less desirable partitions must still function well enough to meet the given needs of the program, regardless of the sophistication of other systems in the building.

In developing this type of threshold information and making appropriate trade-offs through the systems approach, it becomes possible to lead the client and the designer to confront and resolve hard questions. Only when this approach is effectively developed, can we embark upon the design process in full command of our vocabulary, instead of at its mercy.

In the process of designing a building, we may well find certain modifications appropriate for emphasizing or enhancing a particular design concept. But in order to assure reasonable project control it must be possible to offset the cost of such changes, which may increase area or span or call for more expensive finishes in other areas of the building. The development of this type of budget information is analogous to the cost-control techniques used in construction management where the costs for completed subcontracts and the estimates for those yet to be done are always kept in balance with the total budget. If one area gets out of hand, compensations must be made in others. Contingencies, as they are used in construction budgets, may also be appropriately expressed in design terms. When a building is designed to a tight budget and where every penny is allocated to the lowest acceptable performance threshold, there is little or no room for adjustment if any changes occur during the design process. Alteration of performance levels is a more realistic method of cost control than a reduction in square footage when the project is already under way.

Used appropriately, these tools should not inhibit the designer, but rather should become second nature. When you first learn to drive a manual-shift car, you first have to think about which gear to shift to, but later the process becomes automatic and you drive without thinking about the gears. In the same way, as a designer you must understand and assimilate within your own nature the processes that enable you to shift gears as you go through the design process, in control at all times of whatever may be necessary to accomplish the job. Without fluency, you cannot compose freely. Undisciplined composition is, all too frequently, a paper exercise.

The development of information on the cost and performance of different components is best developed in your own practice, taking into account local and regional factors and the nature of the industry. Experience in developing cost estimates on projects (if charted according to the procedures shown in Chapter 7) makes it possible to build a database. Its purpose, within the specific context of the individual office, is to allow you to determine the desired and affordable performance levels before design begins, and then, through the design process, to actually deliver the predicted cost and performance. The control of this process is essential to the survival of the historic role of the architect on behalf of the client: to organize the use of the client's resources so as to construct a building which fulfills the four-function model.

Program, designs, and related costs for one of our past projects provide an example of how programs and design options may be costed from the outset of the work. See Figures 11.4 through 11.9.

PROJECT	Project Type: OFFICE BUILDING	Sheet 1 of 4
		Issue: 1
COST PLAN	Location:	
		Date: 3-16-■■■

| Outline Project Description: | Capability |
| | Date Assumed: |

Statistical Criteria

FLOOR AREAS

Occupiable area:

			Design Efficiency Targets:	
Office	519,200 square feet	55.0 percent	Net-gross area ratio: 74 percent	
Court-computer (raised floor)	2,000 square feet	.2 percent	Building envelope—area ratio = .32	
Cafeteria	17,000 square feet	1.8 percent	Number of levels assumed:	
Parking	12,900 square feet	1.4 percent	Below grade:	2
	——	——	Above grade:	15
Support (SSA)	90,800 square feet	9.6 percent	Penthouse:	1
Commercial	15,400 square feet	1.6 percent	Total:	18
Auditorium	10,000 square feet	1.0 percent	Site area assumed:	83,044 square feet
Storage (warehouse)	30,000 square feet	3.2 percent	Footprint area:	67,100 square feet
Reserve	—— square feet	—— percent	Roof area:	67,100 square feet
Net occupiable floor area:	697,300 square feet	74.0 percent	Exterior closure area:	271,500 square feet
			Perimeter—basements:	1,250 linear feet
Building support area:			Perimeter—typical floor:	980 linear feet
Custodial	3,380 square feet	.4 percent	Story heights—basement:	32 linear feet
Toilets	12,700 square feet	1.3 percent	Story heights—typical:	12 linear feet
Mechanical (inc. shafts)	99,500 square feet	10.5 percent	Day size assumed:	30 × 30
Horiz. circulation	73,000 square feet	7.7 percent	Seismic zone:	1
Vert. circulation	36,700 square feet	3.9 percent	Parking spaces	
Construction	18,700 square feet	2.0 percent	Exterior:	0
Gross floor area:	942,800 square feet	100 percent	Interior:	43

Figure 11.4 Area required to meet program program for GSA Jamaica Federal Office Building. Part of a national award-winning design and cost submission.

INTERIOR SPACE UTILIZATION

Typical Floor—Four Work Service Units per Floor

WSU	–Open office	5,800 square feet		
	–File space	2,200		
	–Entrex	200		
	Subtotal	8,200		
	Minus file	(2,200)		
	Subtotal	6,000	(Four WSUs per floor)	24,000
Supv.	–For six WSUs	2,500	(Prorated for four WSUs per floor)	1,666
Support	–Photo	200		
for six	–Conf./training	1,200		
WSUs	–Inquiry	1,500		
	–Supply	500		
	–Vertical	300		
	–CPU	500		
	–Circ/exp.	1,700		
	–Operational review	2,400		
Sub	Subtotal	8,300	(Prorated for four WSUs per floor)	5,560
File	Per floor	12,000		12,000
Vending	Per floor	175		175
Vim	Per floor-1150			
	(minus 150 for shaft) =	1,000		1,000

	Net square feet:	44,101

| | Shafts and mechanical | 3,900 |
| | Nonoccupiable area | 6,900 |

| | Total gross square feet | 55,400 |
| | Occupiable/gross ratio | 80.1 percent |

Figure 11.5 The space program was worked out in detail for this submission in the 6-week period allowed for the competition. Shown here is a more detailed program for the work service units (WSUs) required by GSA.

10. Electrical Systems

Emergency power from a standby generator will be provided for the following systems:

(a) Fire protection
(b) Fire communication and alarm reporting system
(c) Exit lights
(d) Egress lighting
(e) Elevators on a selective basis

Electrical Systems

Electric Service: Two service takeoff will be provided at 277/480 volts from sidewalk vaults and building network compartments to building main service switchboards.

Distribution will be at 277/480 volts, for fluorescent lighting and 3-phase motors, through riser closets to electric closet panelboards. 120/208 volts for incandescent lighting, receptacles, and appliances will be provided through stepdown transformers and associated panelboards.

Emergency Power and Distribution: A diesel generator unit will provide emergency standby power through automatic and, if necessary, manual transfer switches to emergency lighting, critical equipment, and elevators. The manual transfer switches would make emergency power available to less critical equipment if so desired.

Underfloor Distribution: A complete system of underfloor raceways will be provided for all office areas. The system will consist of 3 compartments, fully accessible trench headers (low voltage power, signal, and telephone) emanating from the closets on each floor feeding out to electrified cells. The exact spacing of electrified cells will be determined as part of a study of the furniture layouts for the floors.

The underfloor distribution system will be designed for the follow-in wire or cable capacities:

Electrical: ¼ square inch per 100 square feet
Signal: ¾ square inch per 100 square feet
Telephone: 1 square inch per 100 square feet

Figure 11.6 This example of a summary of the electrical criteria was prepared for all building subsystems in order to price the competition design.

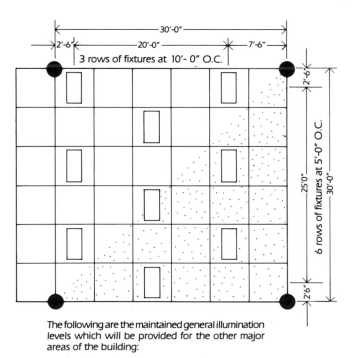

The following are the maintained general illumination levels which will be provided for the other major areas of the building:

Warehouse space	20 footcandles
Computer room	60 footcandles
Cafeteria	30 footcandles
Conference/training	30 footcandles
Lobbies	30 footcandles

Figure 11.7 The implications of the criteria were spelled out for costing and for client awareness of what was included in the budget estimate as illustrated by this typical lighting layout. (O.C. = on center.)

Project:	ESTIMATE NO: Date: March 16, 1981				
Group (Level 2) Cost Center: A. CONSTRUCTION (ECC)	Budget Date:	Concept Estimate Date:	Tentative Design Estimate Date:	Pre-bid Cost Estimate Date:	Bid Analysis Date:
01. Foundations 02. Substructure 03. Superstructure 04. Exterior closure 05. Roofing 06. Interior construction 07. Conveying systems 08. Mechanical 09. Electrical 10. General conditions and profit/escin.		2,684,200 870,800 14,174,400 6,431,500 380,000 5,098,000 3,942,000 11,110,000 5,224,000 21,840,700			
Net Building Cost: 11. Equipment - food service 12. Site work		71,755,600 500,000 250,000			
Progressive cost	$	$72,505,600	$	$	$
Target cost Difference from target cost	$ $	$70,000,000 $ 2,505,600	$ $	$ $	$ $
1983 Cost per square foot Gross floor area	$/SF SF	76.90 $/SF 942,800 SF	$/SF SF	$/SF SF	$/SF SF

Cost Summary (Level 2)
Comparison

Figure 11.8 The estimated cost of the design was $72,505,600 for a specified number of square feet and specific performance levels. This was less than 5 percent over the GSA budget and was acceptable within the framework of the competition.

Figure 11.9 (a) The winning design. (b) Some program changes on the part of the client, namely, a desire to alter some of the performance criteria and the need to further reduce the budget, required that the design be revised to a more compact scheme. In each case the cost-performance analysis determined what could and could not be done in the design.

Part Three

Design

Chapter Twelve

Case Studies

The seven case studies were selected to describe in some detail the developmental projects which were the most instrumental in the formulation of the concepts presented in this book. As each case study could in itself be the subject of a separate volume, *certain points emphasized in one case study may be mentioned briefly or not at all in the other case studies.* Therefore, the studies should be viewed as complementary to one another.

The last case study, that of Canaday Hall, was selected as an example of the application of the systems approach to a conventional design project. The weighting of six development projects to one conventional project is not related to the applicability of the philosophy but rather to its impact on the formulation of concepts.

In addition to the developmental projects there were a number of study and research endeavors which were also influential in the formulation of ideas. One of the first was for the National Bureau of Standards and dealt with an analysis of the organization of the building industry. This was followed by the In-Cities Experimental Housing project that analyzed a mix of social, economic, and technical scenarios which could be combined in various ways to provide housing in 25 separate cities. More recently, another study on research directions and strategies for building research at the National Bureau of Standards which led to a final report entitled "Beyond the Performance Concept," and a variety of energy-related research projects have also provided the experiential base for the book.

CASE STUDY 1

The SCSD Project _____

The origins of this project came out of my experience working at the Building Research Station in England for a period of 2 years on Fulbright Fellowships. It was during this period that I became engaged in work on modular coordination at the Research Station and began to learn something of their principles of coordinating building products in terms of their actual dimensions. The work, which was part of an 11-nation European program, was set up through the Organization for European Economic Cooperation, which sought to coordinate various building products and sizes throughout western Europe. The basic requirements for tolerance control, for compatibility of various building components, and for development of a coordinated vocabulary which would provide design freedom were established during this period. My book, the *Modular Number Pattern*, published by Alex Tiranti in 1958, gives an account of some of the major findings of this work.

While this basic research activity was taking place, I also had an opportunity to observe the first rate work on the prefabrication of school buildings being done in the county of Hertfordshire in England. Work on the design of the schools was initiated through the county's own architectural office, with private architects working on those schools which were beyond the capacity of the county's own office. Given the substantial market, the county architects were able to develop a closed building system, and specify all the coordinated components with which to build the varied and substantial buildings in the program. More than 400 schools using industrialized components were built over an extended period of time in Hertfordshire. The various cycles of research and development of a given set of systems hardware, its utilization in test or prototype schools, and then its implementation in a wider construction program were gone through many times. Through this work considerable knowledge was gained and sound

value was obtained in providing good schools quickly and economically.

The effectiveness of this program made a lasting impression on me, and when I returned to the United States, I began to look for a way to develop an analogous technical program in this country. After several years of searching, I was able to obtain the support of Educational Facilities Laboratories, Inc. (EFL), a subsidiary of the Ford Foundation, in response to programs initiated in various parts of the country that called for stock plans to reduce school costs. The English experience showed quite definitely that there was a great deal more that could be done by working with coordinated ranges of standard components than designing a single stock plan and fitting it to a variety of different sites where slope, orientation, and configuration differed. The costs of adapting any given plan to a variety of special situations were higher than they would be starting from scratch with a completely new design.

In trying to develop a system which would make it possible to use coordinated components for school buildings, we found that there were considerable differences between the United States and Great Britain. First, there was no single educational authority in the United States that was large enough to provide the laborpower and resources needed to develop such a system or to provide the market around which industry could coalesce to manufacture the needed components. Second, the quality of school construction in the United States was generally quite high, and individual architects working for separate school districts provided a higher level of services than any governmental agencies performing a design role. It was, therefore, necessary to look for a way in which a group of school districts could develop such a system. The districts would work together as a multifaceted client, each of whose designers had his or her own ideas as to what good design might be.

It appeared that the only way to coordinate

such a client group was to establish a new framework—combining many clients to search for a better school building. This meant postulating the nature of the basic educational requirements in terms of performance criteria and providing appropriate methods to control the design implications of the performance specifications. In this way, the individual architects who had to work with the resulting system would not have someone else arbitrarily determining their palette.

It was through this mechanism that it was eventually possible to organize a group of school districts and form them into a single consortium, The First California Commission on School Construction Systems, which was an official body set up by the elected boards of 13 separate school districts. Under the Joint Powers Agreement, two or more school districts could do together what any single district could do alone. The concept was that this would be an ad hoc group put together for the purpose of developing new components which would meet basic educational requirements within the state's cost ceiling for state-aided construction. This state support was available to school districts who had already voted school bonds up to 100 percent of their legal bonding limit. They were, therefore, districts with limited monies available in need of state support.

This program was initiated at a time when there was considerable evolution in the pedagogical world. The advent of team teaching and individualized instruction required a wide variety of approaches to education, creating major demands on facilities. In California particularly, more factors were being recognized as essential for producing a satisfactory educational environment within schools, especially in terms of lighting. But with the demands of changing educational techniques, new stress was also being placed on the thermal and acoustic requirements. The fact that the school systems were undergoing a period of transition also demanded considerable flexibility so that educational programs could continue to evolve in response to changing requirements. The interest of the various school districts in joining this program were predicated in large measure on the fact that their assessment of available funds versus their needs for flexibility, environmental quality, etc., left them with an imbalance. Thus they became extremely interested in finding any way to procure responsive and economically efficient schools.

The program that we recommended, via SCSD, provided an opportunity for a number of school districts to work together to obtain potentially better value for the school building dollar. After making an average of five visits to each of the school districts involved, and before obtaining final board approval, we were able to get a sufficiently large group of districts to work together as a single entity in the SCSD program. Armed with this market, we could then go to industry and solicit bids for components which would meet the needs of the school districts. This then became the base around which the SCSD program was organized. It should be noted that the dollar value of components for which innovation was needed represented about one-half the cost of a school.

A team was formed to work on behalf of the various school districts in establishing the basic educational requirements that would be met by the system. This would be done by working with the various curricula and with department heads in each of the member school districts to translate the resulting requirements into a single set of performance specifications by which all of the districts could respond positively to meet their specific educational requirements. Once the specifications were prepared and approved by the various school districts, those components would then be put out for competitive bid to determine the system's suppliers and the very details of the system itself. The bidding was a two-stage process — the first stage was for design and technical approval and the second was a price submission. This ensured that all technical criteria were met regardless of price competition. This process was followed, and the system tested in terms of the compatibility of the various components in a prototype building in which many of the full-scale environmental tests were performed. In addition, many separate laboratory tests were performed at various testing facilities throughout the country. The approved products were then used to build the various schools.

Establishing User Requirements

If we had tried to set a single pattern of user requirements which would meet the needs of all the districts or to obtain a consensus from all of the districts that a single pattern was appropriate for the design of a system, we would have failed at the outset. There are many different concepts of education within an individual school district, in fact, within any given school.

Our program was shaped by the districts' recognition that no matter what their specific concept of education was at the time, potential for change over time must be taken into account. We therefore took the point of view that the diversity of requirements set a range of needs that the basic building system must be able to meet if it were to survive over time. Flexibility became the only concept through which we had a chance of responding to the very diverse requirements of the various school districts. In effect, it became a prime requirement of the system that the full range of educational requirements, as set out by each individual school district, must be met by a single set of components which, in the hands of an able designer, could be used for any school district and provide a unique design tailored to its specific educational requirements.

The individual districts were extremely pleased to find that the group of components developed for SCSD did in fact have sufficient flexibility to respond directly to their own needs. School boards were particularly pleased by this flexible approach. In many cases superintendents did not have a long tenure within a given school district, and it was not unusual for the next superintendent to have a different approach to education, which often meant that the considerable amount of money already spent in fixed bricks and mortar was for an outmoded facility. However, once the full range of requirements was determined and the degree of flexibility needed over time was emphasized, these requirements could be translated into performance terms.

From Requirements to Performance

One of our first tasks for initiating the process was to determine the size of the market and the types of guarantees necessary to attract appropriate manufacturers to participate in the program. We also began to look at the level of innovation and coordination that could be demanded of the industry for meeting the basic user requirements. We had to have a sense of what levels of innovation were feasible.

This was accomplished in two ways: (1) We established performance specifications which were reviewed with people in industry. (2) We also worked on the design of a variety of individual component approaches ourselves, using various conventional building components in new ways to meet our specifications. We did this in order to get an idea of the cost implications of the performance specifications as well as to check the component's ability to meet the actual requirements. This was a key factor, because, as we went into the program, we had a committed market for schools which would be built to much more severe performance specifications than any previously constructed, with or without a state aid format.

We therefore had to be extremely careful to ask for levels of performance which would make the industry stretch to come up with

appropriate components, but which were neither impossible to deliver nor potentially too costly. The nature of the bidding process allowed us to organize, select, and give interested manufacturers the opportunity to comment on the nature of our specifications. Many specifications were changed during this process to ensure that the districts would get the best value for their money. We emphasized calling for levels of performance that were in line with natural break points in terms of cost and performance trade-offs; we did not call for an unnecessarily complex level of technology in order to get insignificant performance improvements. In acoustics, for example, if we asked for a level of acoustic isolation between adjacent rooms just 1 or 2 decibels higher than was actually required, the cost would have increased by about a dollar per square foot at a time when schools were built for less than 20 dollars per square foot. It was important, therefore, to balance the various aspects of the total system with the amount of money available to the various school districts.

This balance was accomplished through a wide variety of cost trade-offs; in the process, we became particularly concerned with the expenditures for providing specified lighting levels within existing school buildings. These specifications were developed in very sophisticated ways in California (where there was considerable concern about providing good lighting), supported by appropriate research on lighting requirements for educational purposes. As a result of this work, a variety of new lighting systems which used up to 6½ watts per square foot had been developed in California to meet those requirements. Since this resulted in very high energy consumption, state-aided school districts, which had very limited budgets, were in fact spending tremendous amounts of money for just a single component, not only in terms of first cost, but in terms of the life cost of operating those facilities. As far back as 1963, when we took our first bids on SCSD, we saw that 1 watt per square foot in the average 1800-student high school (which would contain about 150,000 square feet) was equal in cost to a teacher's yearly salary. Today it would account for the salaries of at least two teachers. It became obvious as we began to develop improved lighting specifications, that just over 3 watts per square foot would be required. At that time this represented potential saving in operating costs equal to 6 percent of the teaching staff salaries.

This was our first major foray into the area of life-cycle bidding, which has now become a hallmark of more recent systems projects. Its impact was very significant, even at a time when energy considerations were not given much thought.

The Prebid Conference

It is interesting to note that at our prebid conference about half of the lighting industry participants stated very vocally that our specifications could not be met because of the laws of physics, but the other half kept quiet. The basic purpose of these prebid conferences, as mentioned earlier, was to provide us with an opportunity to review with industry the expected performance requirements, to emphasize the size of the immediate market provided by the 13 school districts, and also to discuss the generic nature of components designed to meet SCSD criteria, which would in fact have substantial markets elsewhere.

Another significant reason for the prebid conferences was to get the manufacturers of different components to talk with one another. The very nature of a systems program, which required compatibility between different subsystems, call for industry to play an unaccustomed role. They had previously looked upon design professionals as having the total job of coordinating the various components. The industry would put a product on the market, and whether it would be used with other related subsystems was determined primarily by the design initiatives of the architects and engineers. But with SCSD, the performance requirements frequently called for a number of different components to work together in an optimal manner. This could not be achieved by using ad hoc products, but rather called for careful coordination. For many companies, working together in this manner was quite traumatic, and we used the vehicle of the prebid conference to introduce various component manufacturers to one another. In fact, at the time of the design submission, we required that each company list those companies that made other components that would be compatible with their products. Compatibility was only accepted when components manufactured were cross-listed, and we asked manufacturers if they wished to be formally introduced to the companies that made components compatible with their own. In this respect, we played the role of matchmaker. We used coffee breaks, lunch breaks, and so on, during the 2 day prebid conference to get different company representatives to talk to one another with a view to establishing basic cross-compatibility.

Bids were eventually taken only from groups of manufacturers that established the compatibility of their various subsystems, so there was a single bid for structure, air-conditioning, and lighting systems, and they all worked together. We were not interested in the low bid for any single component, but rather in the low bid for a total package that met all our performance requirements. By requiring a single bid for those three major subsystems, we were able to get over 50 different bidding combinations from manufacturers of compatible components. Partitions, casework, and the rest of the components had to tie in and be compatible with the structure, air-conditioning, and lighting-ceiling systems.

Bids were received within the price framework required by state-aided school construction and, in fact, came in substantially under those figures. They provided for an average structural span twice that of the normal structure to provide for flexibility; demountable instead of fixed partitions; an effective air-conditioning system in place of ineffective heat pumps or a system which lacked cooling capacity; and a lighting-ceiling system which worked within the laws of physics. These developments were quite significant in terms of their technical implications for school construction. It is interesting to note that they had a major impact on school construction across the country, and eventually schools using these components were built in all 50 states. There were literally thousands of schools across the country that incorporated one or more of the separate components manufactured by competing companies that modeled their new product lines on the successfully bid systems.

Prototype Testing

Once bids were received, a development process was initiated to produce the individual components, to perform the appropriate tests on them, and then to build a prototype building in which large-scale testing could be carried out on the lighting, acoustic, and the thermal environments. This prototype building was used for testing purposes for more than a year and then given to Stanford University, on whose land it was built, for its own future use. The testing program took about 9 months, during which time many questions about the most economical way for industry to meet the various performance requirements were answered. Major tests were undertaken for structural safety, lighting, fire protection, etc. In these cases, some new ground was broken in the use of items such as flexible ducts, methods for protecting enclosed plenums within the structural ceiling sandwich of the building, and techniques for mounting operable partitions so that they could be opened and closed easily without destroying the acoustic separation between adjacent spaces they were designed to provide.

All of these developments, and many more, required fine tuning and an extensive development program which took more than a year to complete. Once completed, the components were then ready for use by individual architects in the design of specific buildings.

The Finished Product

The architects incorporated into the design of their individual projects that mix of components which related to the specific needs and design approach of each school district. The vocabulary established by the components provided sufficient flexibility so that, of the first seven schools which opened in September of 1966, five won citations at the annual A.I.A.-A.A.S.A. convention in Atlantic City that year.

There were, in a number of cases, problems with specific architects or consultants who, instead of working with the system, tried to use the system to do specific things for which it was not designed. They created a series of problems for themselves and their school districts by trying to work outside the capacity of the system.

The architects had responsibility of designing the buildings with the basic system components and detailing the interface requirements to relate them to the conventional products that would be used to complete the school. Slightly more than 50 percent of the cost of a school was represented by system components; the rest of the work—basic site work, exterior walls, plumbing, power wiring, etc.—was done conventionally. These designs were then put out to bid to general contractors. The general contractors, in effect, were assigned the contracts for system components on which bids had been previously received. The component contractors, in effect, became nominated subcontractors to the general contractors, and the general contractor bids were for completing the remainder of the project. The same unit prices for subsystem components were given to all general contractors by the successful component contractors. This process caused considerable concern on the part of some subcontracting trades, such as the electricians, a portion of whose work was bid conventionally while another portion was included in the lighting-ceiling installation. There was a fear that we were trying to set a precedent for taking away a major portion of the electrical subcontractors' work. This, in fact, was not the case as was shown subsequently.

In organizing this process, there were a number of areas, already mentioned, which caused the industry concern. Reasoning and logic, combined with the overall purpose of providing more effective school facilities, provided the basis for holding the program together when some of the practices necessary to create and organize a market for systems construction were not in line with some individual's perceptions of their own best interest.

All of the schools were designed and constructed to open on time and within budget. For state-aided construction, there was no possibility of exceeding budget, as funds would not be available. The schedule of the entire SCSD program is outlined below:

December 1961	Feasibility study begins
July 1962	Feasibility established
September 1962	SCSD team begins actual project
April 1963	Performance specifications and contract documents published
January 1964	Bids received; successful bidders nominated
June 1964	Product literature begins to become available to architects
July 1965	First design completed and bid
September 1966	First seven schools open
February 1968	Thirteenth and final school opens

Illustrated History

The SCSD system was developed to meet the changing educational needs of school districts within the context of tight budget requirements. Concepts of teaching and improvements in educational technology were continually evolving, and the need for a responsive physical environment was critical. Team teaching, individualized scheduling, and many other pedagogical techniques were developed to meet educational needs. At that time, the teaching of biology changed from a study of death (where everything was pickled) to a study of life; language laboratories became a focus for teaching the student to speak as well as to read; the teaching of high school mathematics had even more recently incorporated the computer. Instead of thinking of students as being taught in groups of 30 that moved in lockstep, SCSD identified a variety of large and small instructional groups, all of which had to be serviced.

As we looked at the evolving space requirements, it was not possible to select either of the situations depicted in the two top sections of Figure CS 1.1, but rather to understand that the use of space would continue to change. In fact, we could see that many of the school districts would find it necessary to change space configurations frequently. These changes would eventually call for the use of internal spaces which would require more sophisticated environmental systems.

The SCSD project team worked on behalf of the First California Commission to prepare educational requirements, translate them into performance specifications, obtain bids from industry to make the components, certify the components acceptability, and manage the total process. Each school district would hire its own architect to design the specific school using the system components. The successful manufacturers obtained a volume purchase contract from the First California Commission, portions of which were assigned to the various general contractors as they were selected by the individual school districts to build the specific projects. The process for the SCSD project was selected after analyzing the many available options.

The availability of time and financial support from The Educational Facilities Laboratories, Inc., were crucial to the project's success. Different conditions would have required other strategies. Figure CS 1.2 indicates how time, resources, and expectations for development results vary and must be taken into account for any project.

After the First California Commission was formed and the educational needs were understood, the task of translating those needs into performance criteria began. Initially, the component requirements were set for the structural, ceiling-lighting, HVAC, and partitions. Later, casework and lockers were added.

Planning Module. The structural subsystem had to allow the various district architects the freedom to plan the structure of the individual schools on a 5- × 5-foot horizontal and a 2-foot vertical module or multiples of these modules. All subsystems had to relate to these modules. The 5-foot horizontal grid was derived largely from the development of the SCSD approach to the lighting-ceiling subsystem. The 2-foot vertical module was felt to be in scale with teaching space requirements and promised to be economical for structure and partitions (i.e., since teaching spaces were large, a more refined vertical module was felt to be unnecessary). All subsystems had to acknowledge requirements that permitted the district architects to plan the design of interior spaces on a horizontal 4- × 4-inch module.

The system had to allow for many building configuration options which would provide an appropriate design vocabulary for the individual school districts and their architects. The basic requirements for the structural system that would provide this variety may be summed up by the design condition shown in Figure CS 1.3. For example, if an inside and outside corner can be accommodated on a single column, the expected design variations are permitted. Specifying the detailing components for this task called for a high level of technical capability.

The lighting-ceiling subsystem included the total aggregate ceiling construction from wall to wall plus all lighting, acoustical, and ceiling members, including flat opaque ceiling panels. It also had to provide for introduction and return of air if not otherwise provided by the HVAC subsystem.

Different lighting requirements were specified for the academic and nonacademic areas. The vocabulary for design purposes specified a number of different approaches, each of which must meet the luminous criteria. In the academic areas, three separate designs had to be provided: luminous ceiling, direct lighting assemblies, and semi-indirect lighting assemblies. In addition, components for gymnasium lighting and subsidiary areas such as corridors were also to be included. Figure CS 1.4 illustrates the three different ways by which the academic criteria had to be met.

The specifications required were:

Average illumination at the work plane had to be maintained at a minimum of 70 foot candles.

Illumination at the work plane at any point more than 4 feet from the walls had to be no more than 25 percent below or above the average illumination level.

Maximum brightness of any area in the direct glare zone could not be more than 350 footlamberts (see Figure CS 1.5).

Maximum brightness of any area in the reflected glare zone could not be more than 500 footlamberts (see Figure CS 1.6).

Prior to SCSD, the intensity and brightness criteria were difficult to meet using available components, except by using architecturally unacceptable fixtures which were suspended well below the ceiling and which reflected light off the ceiling, or else by using very costly and sophisticated systems. The former technique required high ceilings; even then the fixtures were not infrequently used as chinning bars by the students. The latter technique could not be afforded by a state-aided program. New components had to be developed to meet our criteria. The successful bidder provided for light levels from 35 to 210 footcandles, with 19 different ways that the 5- × 5-foot grid could be filled in. The overall impact of the new approach was to provide for a low-brightness and low-contrast lighting system (see Figure CS 1.7). The lighting-ceiling systems also had to provide an appropriate acoustic environment within the classroom, and, in combination with the partitions, sound separation between rooms.

The HVAC system included the full range of equipment plus all the plumbing, controls, and wiring needed to service the equipment. The performance criteria are outlined below:

Temperature	±2 degrees at breathing level and at 6 inches above the floor
Outside air	Minimum 8 cubic feet per minute per person
Air velocity	Between 20 and 50 feet per minute
Solar heat gain	6000 Btu per hour per 200 square foot of exterior wall

The outside temperature range for design purposes was assumed to be 30 to 100 degrees. The successful bidder used an expanded temperature range in designing subsystem components so that they would apply to school districts any place in the country. Figure CS 1.8 illustrates some of these criteria which would obviously be modified today given our higher fuel costs and emphasis on energy conservation.

The thermal performance requirements had to be met within a mechanical service module of 3600 square feet, which we figured to be the largest useful single educational space appropriate for educational purposes without a specially designed stepped floor. Within this area, up to eight separate control zones could require individual performance irrespective of neighboring requirements. One zone might be cooled while another was heated. Figure CS 1.9 illustrates eight similarly sized control zones. (The successful bidder provided means to control up to 12 control zones with one mechanical service module.)

Anticipating rearrangement of the space divisions within the mechanical service module during the lifetime of the building, we required that the HVAC subsystem permit a great variety of rearrangements without modification of equipment, distribution of other subsystems, or sacrifice of prescribed performance criteria.

The poor performance of the then existing mechanical equipment in the participating districts' schools prompted us to evaluate bids on the HVAC system on a life-cycle

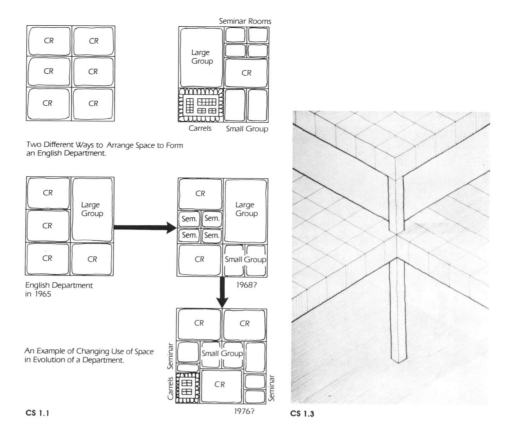

Two Different Ways to Arrange Space to Form an English Department.

English Department in 1965

An Example of Changing Use of Space in Evolution of a Department.

CS 1.1

1968?

1976?

CS 1.3

CS 1.1 Initially a conventional double-loaded corridor plan might be changed to provide for various sized teaching spaces where all the rooms still have a similar relationship to an exterior wall. If it becomes desirable to have internal rooms, the complexities of servicing the various spaces with respect to light, heat, and air increase considerably.

CS 1.2 Chart depicts various levels of development which can be called for depending on the time available and the market size.

CS 1.3 Key design condition to assure system flexibility.

CS 1.4 The semi-indirect light is reflected from the ceiling coffer, the luminous ceiling has a plastic diffuser at the bottom of the coffer, and the direct light has twice the number of lamps in every other coffer.

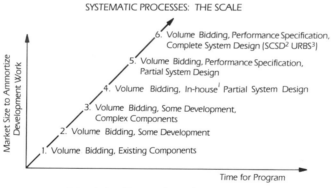

SYSTEMATIC PROCESSES: THE SCALE

6. Volume Bidding, Performance Specification, Complete System Design (SCSD[2] URBS[3])

5. Volume Bidding, Performance Specification, Partial System Design

4. Volume Bidding, In-house[1] Partial System Design

3. Volume Bidding, Some Development, Complex Components

2. Volume Bidding, Some Development

1. Volume Bidding, Existing Components

Market Size to Ammortize Development Work

Time for Program

1. i.e., designed by owner's consultants.
2. School Construction Systems Development project.
3. University Residential Building Systems project.

CS 1.2

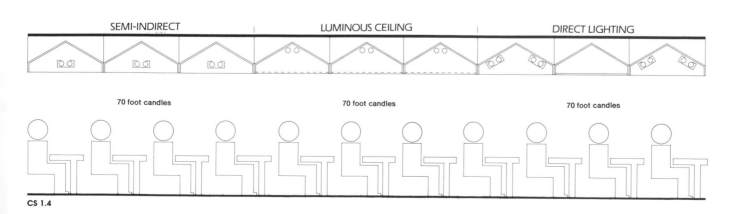

SEMI-INDIRECT   LUMINOUS CEILING   DIRECT LIGHTING

70 foot-candles   70 foot-candles   70 foot-candles

CS 1.4

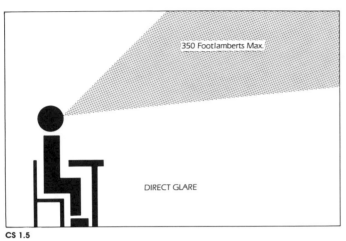

350 Footlamberts Max.

DIRECT GLARE

CS 1.5

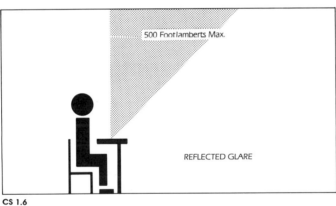

500 Footlamberts Max.

REFLECTED GLARE

CS 1.6

CS 1.5 The direct glare zone is from 0 to 45 degrees; above this angle the eyebrow shields the eye from glare.

CS 1.6 The reflected glare zone is from 45 to 90 degrees; to be source of discomfort, the light from this angle must be reflected from a desktop, papers, books, etc. The typical reflectance factor used for these items is 70 percent, which accounts for the variations in brightness levels.

CS 1.7 The low brightness scheme shown on the right reduces glare as compared with more usual lighting system and was designed to provide an improved luminous environment for academic purposes.

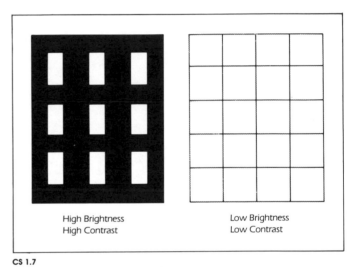

High Brightness
High Contrast

Low Brightness
Low Contrast

CS 1.7

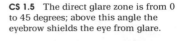

Outside air: minimum 8 cfm per person
Total air supply: minimum 30 cfm per person

Solar heat gain: 6000 Btu per hour per 200 sq. ft. of exterior wall

Air velocity: between 20 and 50 fpm

CS 1.8

CS 1.8 HVAC criteria used for SCSD bids taken on a life-cycle basis. (fpm = feet per minute; cfm = cubic feet per minute.)

CS 1.9 The 3,600-square-foot mechanical service module may have one to eight control zones averaging 450 square feet each.

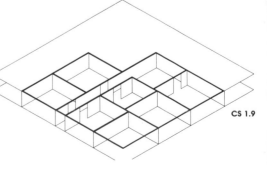

CS 1.9

basis. A maintenance contract was required and was used to establish parity between the bidders. This contract had to include periodic inspection and replacement of parts on failure and as necessary for preventive maintenance.

These structural, lighting-ceiling, and HVAC component systems were bid by subcontractors working together as explained above. We selected the bids that resulted in the lowest total price for the three component systems and that also met the total system criteria.

The interior partition subsystem included those elements which provided vertical separation of spaces from floor to ceiling inside the building. The following types of partitions were provided:

Fixed partitions: Partitions which would be permanent.

Demountable partitions: Partitions which could be moved to a new location with minimal reworking of the partitions themselves or the components to which they were attached.

Demountable or operable partitions: Partitions which could be moved at will along their line of placement and, in addition, were independent of the building structure and could be relocated elsewhere. (Previously available operable partitions were fixed to and supported by the building structure, rendering them the least relocatable partitions in the school.) Two types were required: panel and accordion. The panel-type operable partition made it possible to include a door in the panel.

The various types of partitions are illustrated in Figure CS 1.10. Dimensional criteria called for a partition planning module of 4 inches for fixed and demountable partitions. The horizontal dimension of panels for fixed and demountable partitions had to accommodate a 3-foot door and relate to the 5-foot structural module. The vertical module for floor-to-ceiling heights was available in 2-foot increments from 10 to 16 feet. Fixed partitions were provided in all modular heights only. Doors had to be 7 feet high.

Performance criteria for the fixed and demountable partitions were:

Partitions had to be designed so that the facing on one side of a partition could be changed independently of the facing on the other side.

Demountable partitions had to be designed so that school district personnel could relocate, install, and/or replace individual panels.

Fixed and demountable partitions had to permit both horizontal and vertical passage of services, a critical point for effective demountability.

The following panel faces and finishes had to be provided: basic panel (durable but finished for chalk or tackboard use in a range of 25 colors), chalk panel, tack panel, glass panel, back-up panel (unfinished).

Performance criteria for the operable partitions were:

An operable partition had to be movable by a trained crew in not more than 1 week.

Operable partitions had to be self-supporting; however, they could be stayed laterally by attachment to a structural member.

Operable partitions had to be designed so that they could open or close with the exertion of not more than 25 pounds pressure, the typical force that could be developed by a 95-pound teacher on a waxed floor.

The compatibility between the lighting-ceiling-and-partition systems was critical, as the key to planning flexibility lies in this relationship. The two subsystems had to allow the partition components to be rearranged on a 4-inch module within the 5-foot structural module (see Figure CS 1.11). The lighting-ceiling subsystem also had to be designed so that the presence of an interior column would not require more than one 5-foot lighting module to be omitted.

Once the bids were received, we began to test whether the performance criteria were met. Structural tests were begun with a full-scale handmade structural bay (see Figure CS 1.12). Structure and ceiling components were tested for their ability to meet the fire requirements (Figure CS 1.13). The HVAC system was tested for a period of 1 year at the mock-up building. Figure CS 1.14 shows 100-watt light bulbs in a test room used to simulate the body heat of the average teenager for various test sequences. The SCSD system is shown in Figure CS 1.15.

The mock-up building, constructed with handmade or prototype components, was designed to test the compatibility of the components and their environmental performance. The building was constructed at Stanford University (see Figure CS 1.16).

The orthotropic structural system designed for Inland Steel Products Company by architect Robertson Ward and The Engineers Collaborative emphasized ease of shipping, speed of erection, and careful coordination with other components. Trusses and deck sections were hinged, with connections to be welded when erection was completed. All columns were of constant outside dimension and all trusses of 30- to 75-foot span had identical geometry and a 3-foot vertical dimension; only the gauge of the steel changed to provide for the differing load requirements.

To save weight, the designers replaced the top chords of the trusses with the steel deck so that the deck was stressed. The Inland system used less steel per square foot of building than any other steel system for which we received a bid. Figure CS 1.17 shows the basic structural components.

To conserve shipping space, the components arrived at the site folded up, as shown in Figure CS 1.18. They unfold as the truss deck sections are erected (Figure CS 1.19), and the hinged deck is finally flipped (Figure CS 1.20) as the structure is completed and ready for site welding.

The lighting-ceiling system, which was also designed by architect Robertson Ward for Inland Steel Products Company, used a small number of standard components to provide a wide variety of lighting intensities and visual effects.

A uniform two-tube fluorescent lighting fixture was used with three optional plastic diffusers. The metal coffer could receive one-, two-, or three-bulb fixtures, and the top section of the coffer (which was removable for access to the ceiling space) could be inverted. The lighting-ceiling system was fastened to the structure every 5 feet by a "spider" to which the ceiling runners were attached. The spider (see Figure CS 1.21), which compensated for the camber or deflections in the trusses, provided a thermal break between ceiling and structure for fire protection purposes and provided lateral support for the partitions. It was a key element in the design of the whole system, tying the components of many companies together in a responsive manner. The spider was developed by Fastex Division, Illinois Tool Works, Inc., for Inland Steel Products.

The flat metal pan system was provided plain or with perforation to increase acoustic absorption, and the ceiling was suitable for both interior and exterior use. The top panel of the coffer could also be perforated for acoustic absorption. The mineral wool layer above the ceiling thus served both for fire protection and for acoustic separation.

The three basic academic lighting systems were produced by simple rearrangement of the basic components. The direct system with two 2-tube units per coffer used half the number of lighted coffers and provided the same lighting intensity as the other two systems, as shown in Figure CS 1.22. Photographs of the spider supporting the ceiling system and the semi-indirect lighting system are shown in Figures CS 1.23 and CS 1.24.

The Lennox HVAC system was developed with a self-contained heating and cooling unit sized to match the mechanical service module. Depending on load, the unit could serve from 2500 to 5000 square feet of space. The roof unit fed directly into mixing boxes below it, which in turn provided air to the fixed ducts. Air was returned to the system through the open plenum.

Patterns of standardized fixed and flexible ducts, combined with relocatable supply and return diffusers, allowed for great freedom in arranging control zones (see Figures CS 1.25 and CS 1.26). The cooling unit was completely separate from the heating and ventilating unit, so that cooling could be added as an option and installed at a later date. The designers were careful to isolate the vibrations of the HVAC equipment and the glass-fiber duct system from the light steel structure, which made for a very quiet system.

The basic HVAC unit came to the site in

CS 1.10   The partition system.

CS 1.11   Reflected-light ceiling plan. Relationship of partitions to ceiling system.

CS 1.12   Single-bay structure built to test erection procedure and tolerances. The next structure was constructed for full-scale load testing.

CS 1.13   Ceiling test performed in furnace at Ohio State University.

CS 1.14   Tests were performed in rooms of various sizes on the interior and exterior of the building with seven different plan configurations developed in the course of the year.

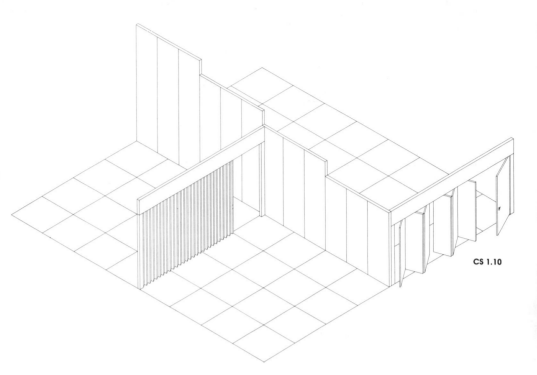

CS 1.10

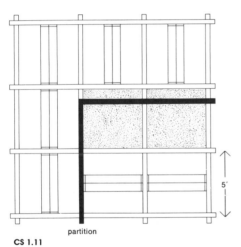

partition

CS 1.11

CS 1.12

CS 1.13

CS 1.14

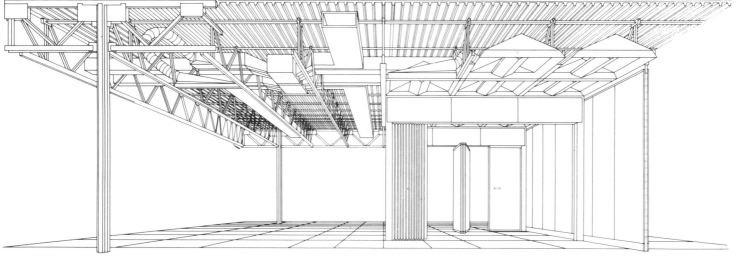

CS 1.15

CS 1.16(a)

CS 1.15 Drawing showing the integrated components of the SCSD System.

CS 1.16 (a) SCSD mock-up building; (b) this building is now the Stanford University Credit Union.

CS 1.16(b)

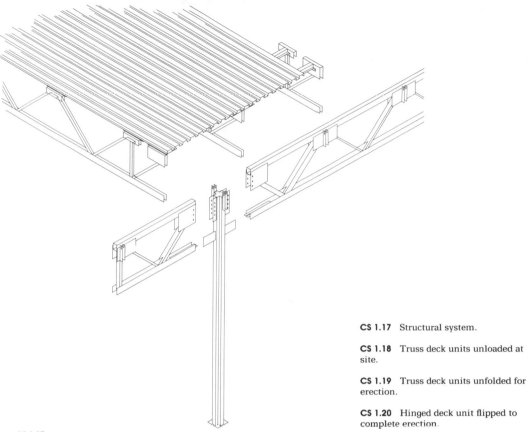

CS 1.17

CS 1.17 Structural system.

CS 1.18 Truss deck units unloaded at site.

CS 1.19 Truss deck units unfolded for erection.

CS 1.20 Hinged deck unit flipped to complete erection.

CS 1.18

CS 1.19

CS 1.20

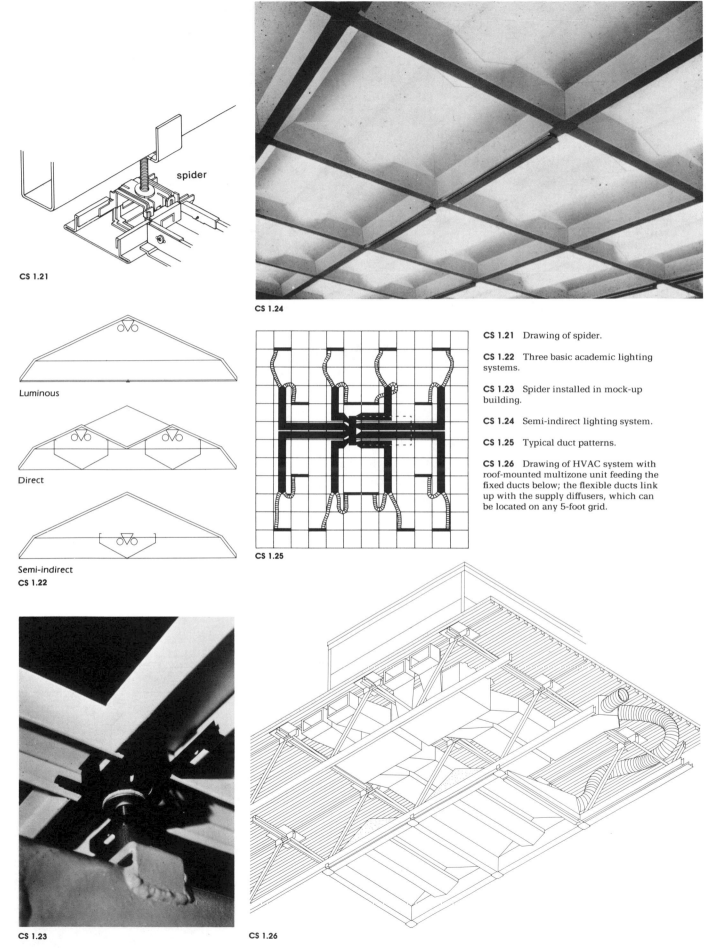

CS 1.21

Luminous

Direct

Semi-indirect
CS 1.22

CS 1.23

CS 1.24

CS 1.25

CS 1.26

CS 1.21 Drawing of spider.

CS 1.22 Three basic academic lighting systems.

CS 1.23 Spider installed in mock-up building.

CS 1.24 Semi-indirect lighting system.

CS 1.25 Typical duct patterns.

CS 1.26 Drawing of HVAC system with roof-mounted multizone unit feeding the fixed ducts below; the flexible ducts link up with the supply diffusers, which can be located on any 5-foot grid.

two sections, with the compressor unit separate. This unit could be lifted onto the building by crane or even by helicopter (Figure CS 1.27). Figure CS 1.28 shows the unit in place on the mock-up building.

All components were located within the structure-ceiling sandwich in such a manner that no two components had to share the same space (see Figure CS 1.29). The fixed and demountable partitions developed for SCSD by the E.F. Hauserman Co. consisted of 40-inch-wide panels of steel-covered gypsum board which snapped onto a specially designed metal stud (see Figure CS 1.30). The studs were clipped to floor and ceiling channels, and the top of the stud incorporated a telescoping section which allowed for 2 inches of structural deflection.

A variety of colors and finishes were provided, including a floor-to-ceiling chalkboard surface. Small magnets or magnetic tape were used instead of thumbtacks for holding display material.

The operable partitions had their own supporting structure, so that the weight of the partitions was not carried by the building structure. In the accordion operable partition, designed by Hough Manufacturing Company, the support structure was raised by a crank-operated cam in order to release the acoustic seal and allow free partition movement. The panel operable partition, which was designed by Western Sky Industries and subsequently sold to Hough Manufacturing Company, had a retractable top and bottom seal which accomplished the same purpose. Figure CS 1.31 shows the various demountable and operable partitions as used in the mock-up building. The drawing in Figure CS 1.32 shows the SCSD components described in this case study.

The DeLaveaga Elementary School, designed by our office, was one of seven projects to open in September 1966. Other architects retained by the various school districts designed the other 12 schools in the program. Figures CS 1.33 to CS 1.35 show site plan, floor plan, and classroom cluster, respectively, for the DeLaveaga school. Figures CS 1.36 and CS 1.37 show some exterior and interior views.

Since the SCSD project, the system has been used in many large-scale programs, such as the one we managed for the Regents of the University of Alaska. After organizing a program to install dormitories quickly for the University of Alaska at Fairbanks (see Figure CS 1.38), we began a program for building eight projects on seven campuses in Alaska within a 2-year period (see Figures CS 1.39 and CS 1.40). All projects were completed on time and under budget.

Other system components were used in Alaska along with those of some of the original SCSD manufacturing companies who bid on the SCSD program. A wide variety of other component systems were made available which met the SCSD criteria; the systems that had the second and third lowest bids in the SCSD program are shown in their initial applications in Figures CS 1.41 and CS 1.42. Other components were developed and bid in follow-on programs in Florida and in other localities.

As a result many components which met the SCSD criteria became available for general use. Typically, they were specified by individual architects designing single schools for a single client. The Colonel Smith Middle School, located at Ft. Huachuca, Arizona, which we designed in joint venture with Flatow, Moore, Bryan and Fairburn Inc., is one such example. Actually thousands of schools and noneducational buildings have been built using SCSD and SCSD-inspired components, which are now considered part of the traditional building industry, even though they can be used most effectively in a systems mode (see Figures CS 1.43 and CS 1.44).

CS 1.27 HVAC unit put in place by helicopter.

CS 1.28 Installed HVAC unit on mock-up building.

CS 1.29 View of structure-ceiling sandwich of mock-up building. Each service is programmed to its own space.

CS 1.30 Section through partition system showing the snap-in properties designed for flexibility.

CS 1.31 Partitions.

CS 1.27

CS 1.28

CS 1.29

Accordian operable and panel operable

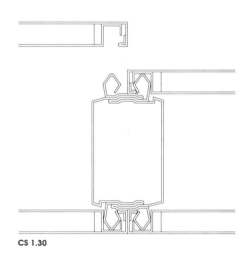

CS 1.30

Panel operable

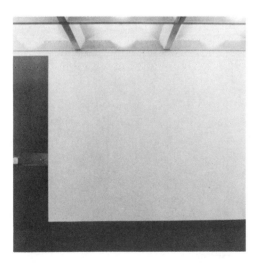

CS 1.31

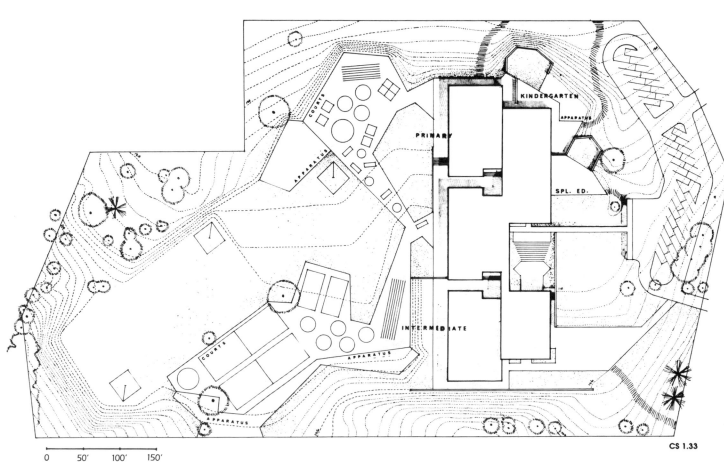

CS 1.32 Composite drawing of SCSD system.

CS 1.33 Site plan.

CS 1.34 Floor plan.

CS 1.35 Six-classroom cluster.

CS 1.32

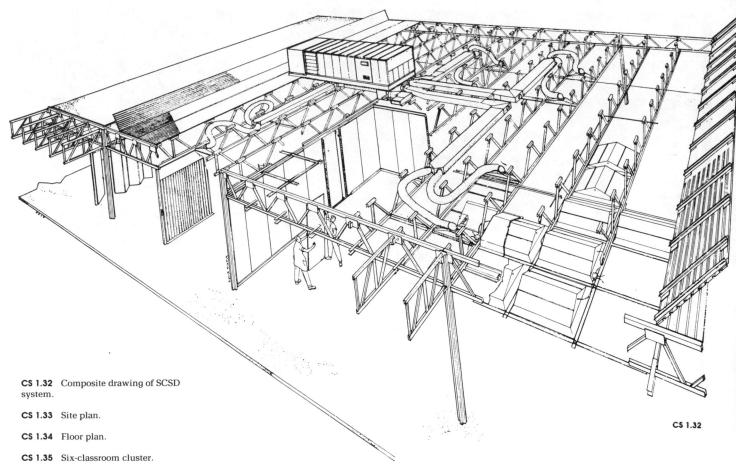

KINDERGARTEN

APPARATUS

PRIMARY

COURTS

APPARATUS

SPL. ED.

COURTS

APPARATUS

INTERMEDIATE

APPARATUS

0   50'   100'   150'

CS 1.33

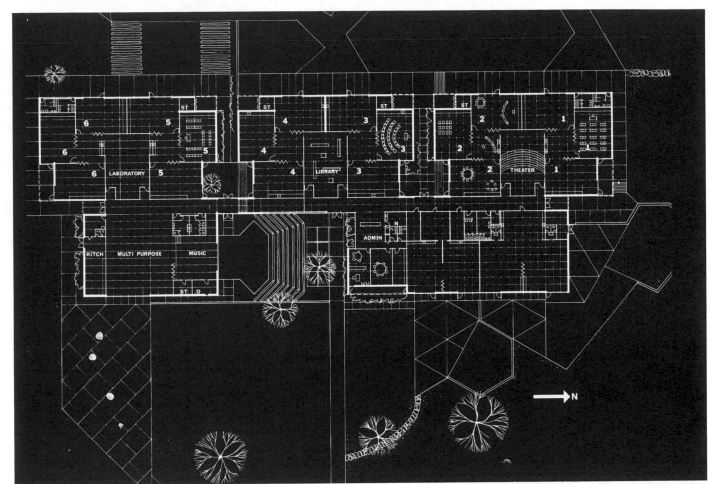

CS 1.34

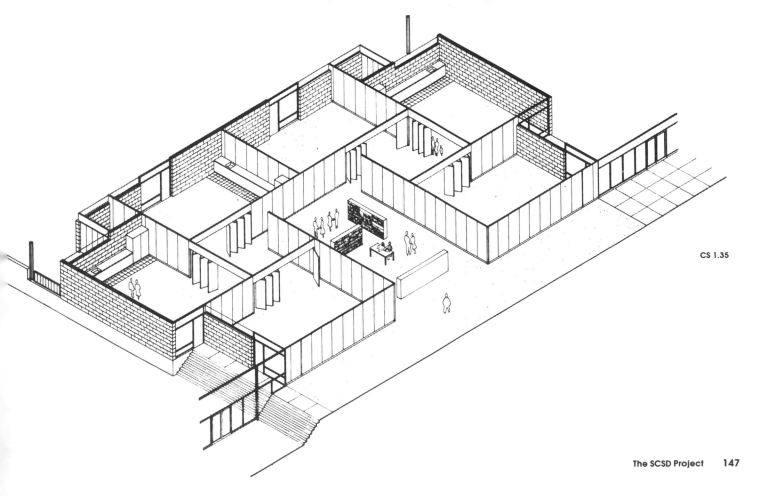

CS 1.35

CS 1.36 Classroom clusters from playground.

CS 1.37 Typical classroom and common space for each group of three classes at the same grade.

CS 1.36

CS 1.37

CS 1.38 Dormitory housing units prefabricated in Oregon.

CS 1.39 Components shipped to Anchorage.

CS 1.40 Library building under construction at Anchorage.

CS 1.41 Space grid system.

CS 1.38

CS 1.40

CS 1.39

CS 1.41

CS 1.42

CS 1.43

CS 1.44

CS 1.42 Concrete system.

CS 1.43 Exterior view of school.

CS 1.44 Library.

CASE STUDY 2

The University Residential Building System (URBS)

In the mid-1960s, the University of California predicted a substantial increase in the size of its many campuses. Higher education was free to California residents, and the university Regents wanted to make higher education available to everyone. As individual campuses increased in size, new residence halls had to be built. A standard room rate for residence halls was applied throughout the entire state and, as new facilities became available, room rates throughout the entire state had to be raised in order to pay off the bonds invariably used to build the new residence halls.

In previous years, student requirements had been carefully analyzed, but the results did not necessarily live up to expectations. In one such case, it was found that a major student complaint was the lack of reasonable levels of acoustic privacy between the dormitory rooms. In order to reduce sound transmission, new criteria for increased wall thickness were developed. Unfortunately, these criteria were not properly implemented or understood.

Sound transmission through party walls was indeed prevented by the partitions, but the heating and/or cooling of the double-loaded rooms was invariably facilitated by returning air underneath the door and into the corridors which acted as return air ducts. The undercutting of doors thus became the primary route for acoustic disturbance. The students' complaint of lack of acoustic privacy, however, was assumed to relate to the party wall. And so, funds were spent to provide thicker walls without resolving the acoustic problem.

If we were to sum up the university's requirements for the University Residential Building System (URBS), they were:

1. Control the increase of student rents
2. Provide flexibility for changing lifestyles to ensure occupancy, and thus ensure that the bonds could be paid off
3. Meet appropriate functional requirements of the students

4. Improve the students' environment with respect to heat, light, and sound.

In URBS, the emphasis on the development of a program for life-cycle costing became more clearly articulated than was the case in the SCSD program. The university had good records on the first cost of its facilities, the cost of operating and maintaining them, and on the costs of necessary major repairs and alterations. Similar programs were also organized in food service and other areas to control costs.

At the start of the program, the university was willing to guarantee the building of some 4500 student places, using a building system which would meet its financial and performance requirements. At the time that commitment was made, the projected volume of construction was sufficiently in excess of 4500 places to make the commitment appear safe. The project began for the University of California with support, on a matching basis, from Educational Facilities Laboratories, Inc. (EFL), and from the University of California.

Our first step after being retained by the university was to visit the various university campuses and other representative campuses throughout the country in order to ascertain the basic user requirements and evolving trends. Meetings were also held with various social scientists and university housing officials to understand the variety of individual group living patterns. People such as Martin Trow, at Berkeley, and Theodore Newcomb, at Ann Arbor, added much to the project.

Except for the valuable insights of a few perceptive people, most information came from various surveys that had been undertaken for a variety of universities, during the course of which some 25,000 students had received and filled out questionnaires about student preferences.

The way in which those studies were conducted provided limited choices for the students responding to the questionnaires. Approximately 70 percent of all students wanted a double room, and 30 percent desired a single room. The weighting toward double rooms was very heavy for freshman students and tailed off in direct proportion to their time at the university. Our discussions with students, student representatives, and administrative personnel at each of the campuses indicated substantial concern about continuing the then current living patterns.

This concern was reinforced by the apparent success of a number of singular experiments at other institutions throughout the country, where a variety of student living patterns other than single or double rooms were being tried. The introduction of suites shared by small groups of students or the equivalent of student houses was very popular wherever they were tried. Through a series of progressive steps, the numbers of students sharing these community living facilities decreased from student houses of 25 to the low 20s, then to 18, 15, 13, 12, 10, 8. Actually the smaller living units were always laid out as suites in larger buildings rather than as discrete houses.

In our sessions with students to ascertain their preferences and requirements, it soon became apparent that their perception of possible patterns was based on those that they were aware of, and the very small number of experimental living facilities throughout the country was generally unknown to students of the University of California.

Therefore, we began, with drawings and models, to describe the possible variations in living accommodations in order to determine the students' relative interest in each of them. In an initial case, working with a group of students aware of only the traditional double or single rooms, we advanced just one additional concept, that of the split double, where two single student rooms are joined by a common door (the common motel design). The students have the option of treating them as single rooms or of using one room for sleeping and another for living

151

activities. Directly, 70 percent of the students favored the split double with the remaining 30 percent divided between single and double rooms.

Our concepts of developing flexible environments for student housing began as a result of these studies. In this regard, we began to look at a number of different scenarios, including the use of graduate student apartments and faculty housing as options for future residents within residence halls, in order to guarantee full occupancy during the life of the mortgage.

Given the varied range of possibilities for single and group living, we found the basic criteria for determination of blocks of flexible space were the requirements for health and safety. The fire marshal, in effect, determined that a maximum of 10 students could share a maximum of 2000 square feet with a single door to the corridor.

The design of flexible living units, in which interior partitions could be located according to student preferences, became a main thrust of the program. The closest analogy to the concept is the office building where one tenant rents a block of space and has it partitioned to meet his or her specific requirements. A maximum group of 10 students could, in fact, move internal partitions and casework in any pattern they wished in order to determine and express their particular lifestyle.

Although this concept might entail many administrative constraints, the translation of basic user requirements into performance criteria and eventually into building products was done in such a manner that the level of flexibility was respected. The ease of movement varied with the nature of the components, and sufficient stability was provided so that room patterns could, in fact, be established which would have the capacity to endure from year to year, as well as to undergo any type of change (see Figure CS 2.2).

New criteria were established for the thermal, luminous, and acoustic environments (Figure CS 2.4). Room dimensions were developed to accommodate many different ways of locating the basic complement of student furniture (Figure CS 2.3), and the walls were equipped to allow cabinetry to be hung from the partitions as an alternative to standing it on the floor.

The students' desire to make their rooms their home led us to develop many techniques for the personalization of space. For example, our design made it possible for students to snap fabrics or wallpapers on to the walls without damage. In fact, a student could paint a mural, and it would be removable at the end of the academic year. A student wishing to line a room with red velvet could do it very easily. The partitions could receive a variety of different surfaces and textures. Tackboard or chalk panels could be used by students as they desired, and the panels could even be traded between students in response to their specific interests.

One of the design team's underlying interests was to avoid forcing students to accept a "canned" living environment. The acoustic criteria established appropriate levels of privacy. The criteria for lighting levels at a student's work surface, meant that new lighting fixtures had to be designed since at that time no lamp could meet the criteria. Developing appropriate thermal controls for temperature and ventilation was very important. While we wanted the students to be comfortable in terms of providing proper temperatures, we did not want to provide so much heat that they were forced to use windows for cooling or vice versa. At all stages of this program, there was considerable concern for life-cycle costing and reducing student rents.

The student rent of approximately $900 per year was used to amortize bonds ($300), operate and maintain the residence hall ($187), and pay for food service ($413). The university, in essence, ran the residence halls to break even.

Our analyses of different patterns of student living revealed that one of the strongest elements in determining the design of residence halls on a double-loaded corridor was the access to the communal bathroom facilities at each level. The logic for using communal bathrooms shared by 20 to 48 students was that it cost less per student to build these large bathroom facilities. Students, on the other hand, did not care for them nor for the specific living patterns that they engendered. We analyzed the cost of providing smaller, shared baths and found that when both first cost and operating costs were taken into account, the shared bathrooms turned out to be significantly cheaper in terms of cost to students and were infinitely more desirable in relation to their lifestyle. The economics of this and a group of other items was described in Chapter 3.

The project was organized to obtain bids for compatible components for the building's structure, ceiling, air conditioning, and partitions to produce the related spatial, environmental, and finish characteristics necessary to meet evolving student requirements. The university provided the basic market and specifications, and teams were formed within the industry to bid for the work based on the major compatible subsystems just mentioned, as well as bathrooms and casework.

The successful bidder designed a compatible system that used a concrete ceiling and floor that allowed for two-dimensional movement of air within the structure-ceiling sandwich. This bidder was very concerned that the thermal properties of this structural system provide an effective radiant environment while being able to meet specific air temperature requirements via a ducted supply system designed to provide air from that ceiling above the windows on the exterior perimeter of the building. (Figure CS 2.15 describes the successful system.)

Bids for the other two subsystems, bathrooms and casework, were not obtained at prices that justified the university's commitment to those components. The requirements that were developed for a unique group of bathroom fixtures (see Figure CS 2.11) did not have sufficient market to make their procurement economical. It appeared that the university's total volume amounted to much less than a week's work on the part of a fixture manufacturer, and the development of new tools and dies for the manufacture of unique fixtures could not be amortized on the basis of such a small market.

At our highest potential, we could commit ourselves to 1000 to 1200 bathrooms, but it appeared that some 25,000 would be needed before the unique type of fixtures that we wished to obtain could be purchased economically. The system, however, was designed to be built using conventional plumbing and other appropriate trades to do the work in the event we could not procure the specially designed bathroom units. And this was in fact how the job proceeded. The total system was erected as described in Figures CS 2.16 through CS 2.18, and residence halls were completed at the University of California, San Diego, using the URBS system.

At about this time, the University of California entered into a period of considerable conflict with state authorities. New construction was reduced to almost a negligible amount, and the projected market for the URBS components dried up. This change in market conditions was *not* unique to higher education in California, as the rate of new construction for universities across the country was drastically reduced. As a result of this reduction, the URBS system never had the same opportunity for growth and further use as did the SCSD school building system. The developed system has some unique capabilities which can be used for a wide variety of different building situations. The advantages of the URBS system, vis-à-vis the traditional techniques for building student housing, are related to flexibility, environmental performance, and the response to a sophisticated set of physical requirements.

The URBS buildings were constructed using a construction manager and a phased process for putting up the residence halls. This process was used to build the University of California residence halls at San Diego at the same time that a similar procedure was used by the State University, New York, Stonybrook campus, to build a surge building. The Stonybrook facility was designed to start and launch new university departments until they reached a size sufficient to build separate buildings for their activities. It is interesting to note that the SCSD components provided the basis for constructing the Stonybrook project. In addition, the fixed prices we had for the URBS project, based on unit quantities that would meet the performance specifications, made it possible to control costs sufficiently for an institutional client to be willing to embark on the uncertainties of a phased-construction project. These two projects apparently were the first two institutional buildings in the country to be built by a phased-construction process using construction management. The large percentage of the total building cost represented by the prebid components, when combined with site and foundation work, comprised well over 50 percent of the total project cost and made it possible to predict a successful completion within the budget.

Illustrated History

The typical plan types included: double-loaded corridor, linear core, point tower, house plans, and row-house apartments (see Figure CS 2.1). Flexibility was essential to meet changing student requirements. The flexible maximum area permitted by code was 2000 square feet, which could house up to 10 students. The system's dimensional properties were related to the minimum room sizes which would permit a variety of arrangements for students' furniture (Figure CS 2.2). Built-ins or rooms that allowed only one layout were anathema to most students (see Figure CS 2.3). But irrespective of layout, each room's performance characteristics had to allow an appropriate work and living environment (see Figure CS 2.4).

The system was seen as a grouping of compatible component systems that would meet the performance criteria. The key components were the structure, ceiling, heating, ventilating and cooling, and partition component systems (see Figure CS 2.5). The bathroom was also designed to house the vertical service lines (see Figure CS 2.6).

Bids were taken on a life-cycle basis to assure that students would get the lowest possible rent and the client would get the best value (see Figure CS 2.7). Requirements were set forth for each of the component categories (a few examples are shown in Figures CS 2.8 to CS 2.11).

In order to develop the air-conditioning system when the exterior design of a specific building had not been started, it was necessary to develop a set of performance criteria under which the skin of the building would eventually be designed. Otherwise, the performance of the air-conditioning system could not be determined. By using a life-cycle basis, we also focused interest on energy consumption — an unusual emphasis in the 1960s (see Figure CS 2.12).

The system was conceived as having many ways in which the components could be put together and still meet the criteria. Some alternatives are shown in Figure CS 2.13. Existing buildings were analyzed for construction costs, and a database of cost and performance information was assembled so that criteria could be set for the functioning of the total system at an acceptable price. Costs were developed by component category and not by building trade. This database is crucial to any problem-solving approach to design (see Figure CS 2.14).

The successful system properly integrated all of the components and had a number of unique features, including a radiant floor system with ducted supply and plenum air return. Air movement takes place within a structure-ceiling system that provides concrete surfaces for both ceiling and floor (see Figure CS 2.15).

The URBS system was used in the design of Muir Hall at the University of California, San Diego. The building was constructed using precast concrete planks which were put in place with reinforcing bars sticking up out of the planks (see Figure CS 2.16). Planks were frequently loaded with other needed materials to reduce the number of required crane lifts (Figure CS 2.17). The plumbing, electrical conduit, and ducts were then set in place. Cylinders were placed over the protruding reinforcing bars and the services placed in between (Figure CS 2.18).

Formed metal pans were then placed into the cylinders that covered the various service systems and created the air return plenum. When all the metal pans were in place, additional reinforcing bars were located to tie the structure together. Concrete was then placed on top of the pans and into the cylinders. This provided a poured-in-place top portion of the structure which tied together the various precast planks. The structure provided for an air return plenum as a by-product of its design. The hard floor and ceiling which resulted were a direct response to the specifications. The completed building is shown in Figure CS 2.19.

CS 2.1 Typical plan configurations for student housing.

CS 2.2 The pattern of student living accommodations can undergo many changes within the same space.

CS 2.3 Possible furniture arrangements in 110-square-foot single room.

CS 2.4 Basic environmental criteria for a student room.

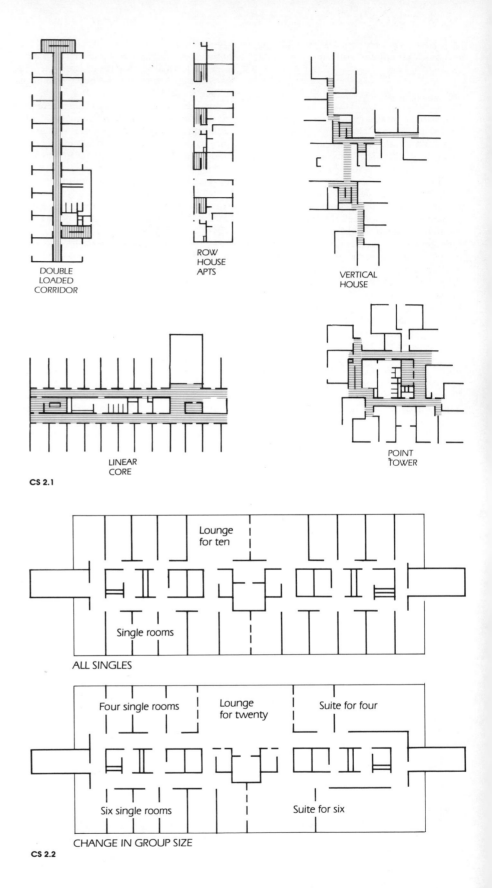

DOUBLE
LOADED
CORRIDOR

ROW
HOUSE
APTS

VERTICAL
HOUSE

LINEAR
CORE

POINT
TOWER

CS 2.1

Lounge
for ten

Single rooms

ALL SINGLES

Four single rooms

Lounge
for twenty

Suite for four

Six single rooms

Suite for six

CHANGE IN GROUP SIZE

CS 2.2

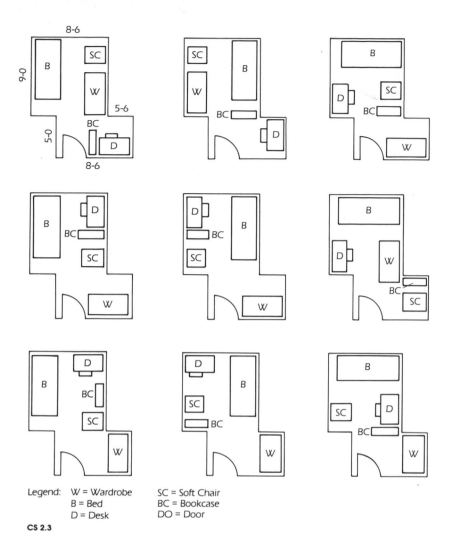

Legend: W = Wardrobe   SC = Soft Chair
B = Bed   BC = Bookcase
D = Desk   DO = Door

CS 2.3

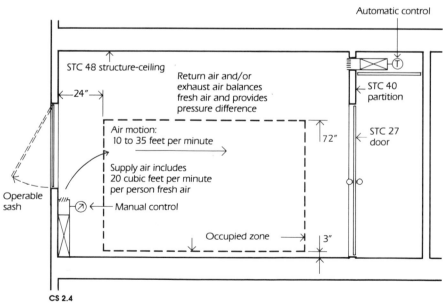

Automatic control

STC 48 structure-ceiling

Return air and/or exhaust air balances fresh air and provides pressure difference

STC 40 partition

24"

Air motion: 10 to 35 feet per minute

72"

STC 27 door

Supply air includes 20 cubic feet per minute per person fresh air

Operable sash

Manual control

Occupied zone

3"

CS 2.4

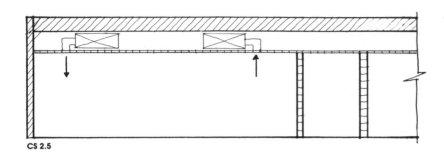

CS 2.5

CS 2.5 The compatible components: structure, HVAC, ceiling and partitions.

CS 2.6 The bathroom as a center for vertical services.

CS 2.7 Life-cycle bid formula for selection of HVAC component contractor.

CS 2.8 Scope of structural system established.

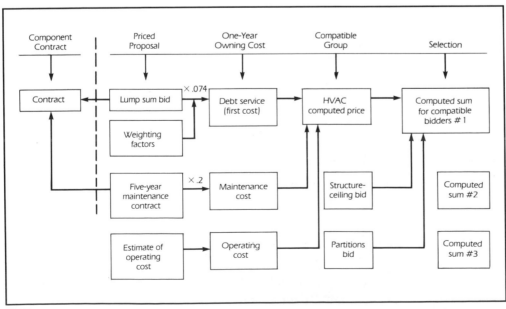

HVAC   Plumbing   Electrical Communications

CS 2.6

Roof structure

Floor structure

Shear-resisting elements

Columns

Stairs

CS 2.8

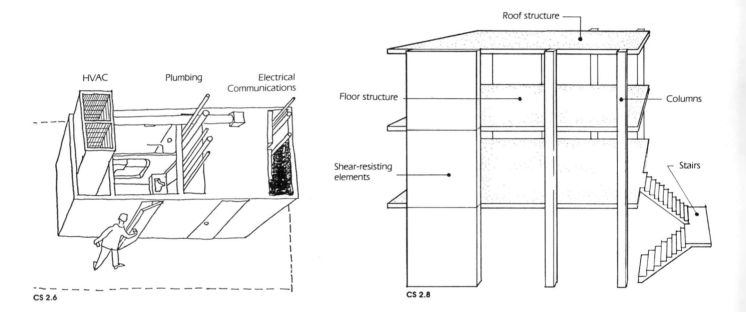

Component Contract	Priced Proposal	One-Year Owning Cost	Compatible Group	Selection
Contract	Lump sum bid × .074	Debt service (first cost)	HVAC computed price	Computed sum for compatible bidders # 1
	Weighting factors			
	Five-year maintenance contract × .2	Maintenance cost	Structure-ceiling bid	Computed sum #2
	Estimate of operating cost	Operating cost	Partitions bid	Computed sum #3

CS 2.7

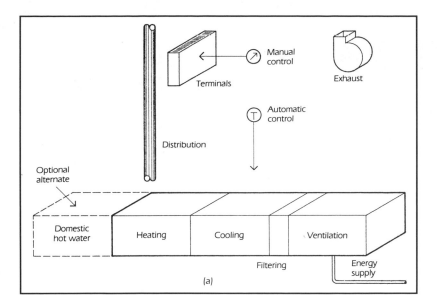

CS 2.9 (a) Scope of required components for HVAC system. Criteria stated in Figure CS 2.7 had to be met within a framework of providing for (b) up to 12 temperature control zones for each 2000 square foot area and (c) up to five zones for recirculation of air.

Manual control

Terminals

Exhaust

Automatic control

Distribution

Optional alternate

Domestic hot water

Heating

Cooling

Ventilation

Filtering

Energy supply

(a)

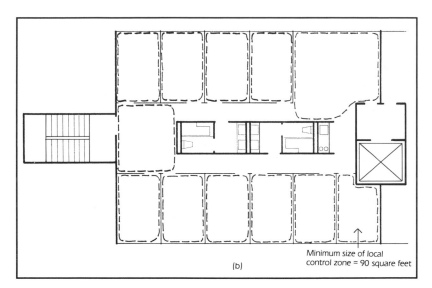

Minimum size of local control zone = 90 square feet

(b)

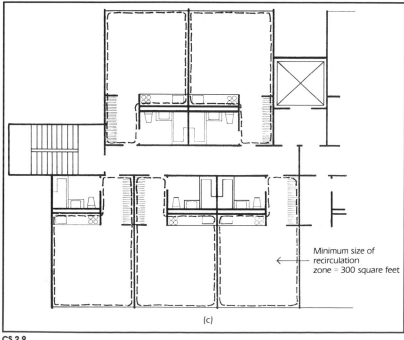

Minimum size of recirculation zone = 300 square feet

(c)

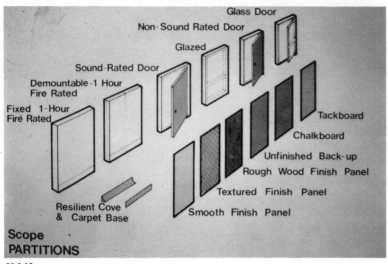

CS 2.10

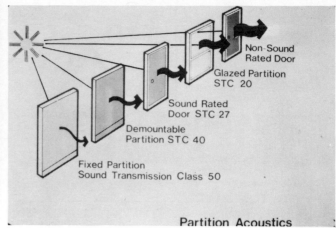

Partition Acoustics

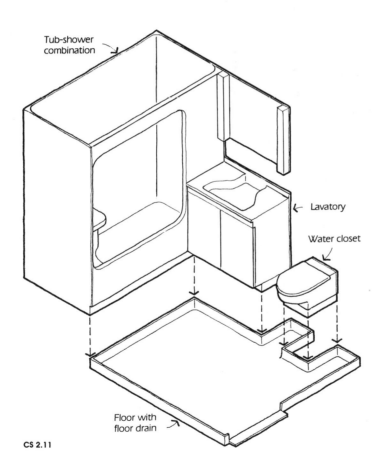

CS 2.11

CS 2.12

CS 2.10 The types of partitions required and the related acoustic criteria.

CS 2.11 Basic bathroom components—mock up.

CS 2.12 Portion of criteria for energy conditions at exterior wall.

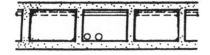

COMPOSITE

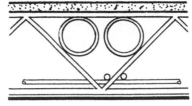

INTEGRATED

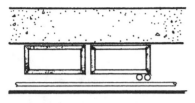

MONOLITHIC/CONCEALED

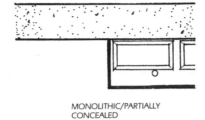

MONOLITHIC/PARTIALLY
CONCEALED

CS 2.13

CS 2.13 Structure, ceiling, and HVAC alternatives.

CS 2.14 In breaking down costs by component rather than by trade content, we were able over time to assemble a file which provides information for costing a project at a predesign stage of work. Decisions on how to allocate resources for the design effort may be predicted in advance, thus reducing later surprises.

CS 2.15 URBS components.

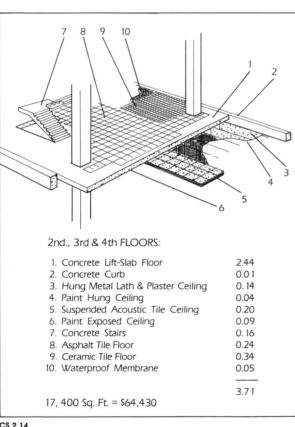

2nd., 3rd & 4th FLOORS:

1. Concrete Lift-Slab Floor	2.44
2. Concrete Curb	0.01
3. Hung Metal Lath & Plaster Ceiling	0.14
4. Paint Hung Ceiling	0.04
5. Suspended Acoustic Tile Ceiling	0.20
6. Paint Exposed Ceiling	0.09
7. Concrete Stairs	0.16
8. Asphalt Tile Floor	0.24
9. Ceramic Tile Floor	0.34
10. Waterproof Membrane	0.05
	3.71

17, 400 Sq. Ft. = $64,430

CS 2.14

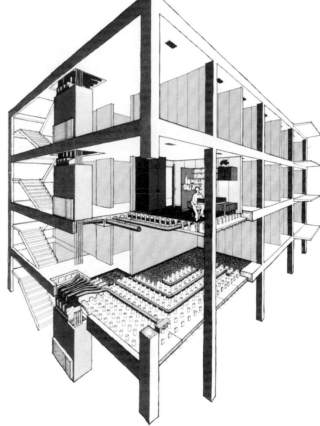

CS 2.15

The University Residential Building System (URBS) 159

CS 2.16 The precast plank is both a part of the structure and a form for the remaining work.

CS 2.17 A single crane supported work on a cluster of buildings. The work was staged to promote efficiency in terms of both people and equipment.

CS 2.16

CS 2.17

CS 2.18 Photographs of the construction process showing work done on top of the precast planks. *Left:* Ducts are set in place. *Below, left:* The formwork is completed. *Below, right:* The concrete is poured.

CS 2.19 Completed project.

CS 2.18

CS 2.19

CASE STUDY 3

The Academic Building System (ABS)

By the time we began working on the Academic Building System (ABS) project, it had become evident that major educational clients could no longer guarantee future precise markets. The University of California began to realize that their effort to control the market for student housing via the URBS project was running into difficulty because of reduced projections for student demand and that they should not once again make a similar long-range commitment. At the same time, the cost of continually altering existing laboratory buildings on the various campuses of the University of California provided a clear indication that new components and new design approaches were needed, if the university was to provide an appropriate environment for its various research- and science-based activities.

During the early stages of the ABS project, we learned another lesson in regard to the difficulty of providing long-range guarantees for future markets which would allow the development of programs of sufficient size and scope to generate innovation. The development of a new building system for Pittsburgh City School District was initiated as a result of that city's desire to racially integrate its public school system. As already described, by the time the construction documents had been prepared, the community no longer wanted to integrate their schools. The end result was the decision not to build the new schools. The time it took to carry out the total planning, systems, and building design programs without tangible results was long enough that the nature of the community itself changed and hence the basic user requirements. These lessons were not lost on us as we began working to put together a team for the ABS project. EFL once again was willing to be a sponsor, but in this case, it was concerned that its resources be spent beyond the State of California. A team was therefore put together, with the states of Indiana and California each contributing $200,000 to match a similar grant from EFL.

These monies were then matched by another grant from HEW, which provided sufficient funds for a major thrust toward the design of a new system for university science and engineering facilities.

Once again we began by visiting dozens of different university campuses throughout the country, as well as making intensive visits to both California and Indiana. User requirements and patterns of use over a considerable period of time were studied, norms developed from the past, and projections made for the future. As a result of these efforts, a user requirements report was prepared relating science and engineering facilities to trends and developments in the field of teaching and research. A history of individual laboratory buildings over a 40-year period was developed in order to understand their costs of maintenance, operation, and alteration; costs were then projected based on trends that we identified. These data then made it possible to develop the basic requirements for design of the system.

In the case of ABS, however, it was apparent at the outset that neither of the two university systems could precisely guarantee a specific market within a given time period, making it necessary for us to develop this system without an aggregated market at our command. A series of strategies were developed and reviewed. It was eventually agreed that it would be possible to design a building system which used available products in a new and more controlled manner in order to achieve the required flexibility and meet the myriad of specific user requirements. We then became the system designers working with demonstrated industry capabilities rather than looking for industrial innovations.

In visiting the various campuses, both in and out of the two state systems, we saw that with the development of new areas of knowledge, the various departments were breaking down along specialized lines. In 1919, for example, there was a single department of engineering in the California state educational system. However, when we studied the Berkeley campus, we found 19 separate engineering departments, each with its own administrative staff, curriculum, and space. Over the intervening years, there had actually been 23 different departments, some of which split, while others disappeared. In each case, the requirements for teaching space, laboratories, and research opportunities were radically different.

The school's ability to attract new, high-level faculty was frequently related to availability of laboratory spaces for specific research programs, which would attract key graduate students who, in turn, would be involved in a variety of teaching activities. The evolutionary requirements of these facilities had not proceeded at a normal steady pace over the last 40 years. Rather, the need for flexibility had evolved slowly, and as our society became more dynamic, the rate of facility change increased radically. The analysis of building costs of the Life Sciences building at Berkeley, shown in the Figure 7.2, is typical of the patterns that we found.

It was out of these studies that requirements for considerable flexibility began to emerge. The scope and extent of flexibility was determined on the basis of a detailed analysis of the typical requirements for physical change when buildings were altered. In Chapter 7 the sensitivity to cost was given for typical alteration conditions for each of the various building trades. Accessibility to services was found to be critical. It was not just a matter of providing space, but required a whole variety of support facilities to enable special tasks to be handled individually. For example, some tasks, such as chemistry experiments, might call for special venting, and others might demand cold rooms which had very exact temperature control. This mixture of performance requirements made it necessary for each building to have the capacity to tie in many different service systems in a flexible manner. The establishment of environmental criteria for these special service requirements was, of course, over and above the basic range of requirements for typical educational activities.

We developed performance specifications as though we were going out to bid on the program, calling upon industry to come up with new components. In this case, however, it was evident that we would not be able to develop industrial support for such innovations since we could not project a significant market. For this reason, we had to analyze the costs of providing for the myriad of requirements using available products only. Our design, therefore, relied on the careful coordination of existing components working together in an effective and efficient manner. This coordination depended upon a method of designing a flexible building to meet basic educational needs that was more precise than would normally be possible within the resources available for the design of a single project.

After the performance criteria were developed, we began work on the design of the components. In the process of developing the criteria, however, we had analyzed a wide variety of separate buildings constructed by the two state university systems to evaluate their level of performance and cost. We met with the users of the buildings to determine the effectiveness with which those resources had been applied; and from these studies, we developed the basic concept of meeting user requirements by using products available at a cost appropriate to the university.

The performance attributes of each component system were studied, keeping in mind that there were a wide variety of alternatives. These alternative systems were compared to the proven performance of systems already used within the university facilities. Appropriate combinations of different component systems were evaluated to determine the specific ways by which various components might be combined, and the cost for each combination was calculated. These studies resulted in analyses of the structural, air conditioning, lighting, ceiling, partitions, and laboratory case work systems, as shown in Figures CS 3.9 and CS 3.10.

There were many ways that component systems could be combined: ceiling access for services, floor access along with the ceiling space, vertical service chases, or an interstitial space approach. After reviewing these alternatives (shown in the figures), a decision was made in favor of a combined approach using both a ceiling access and an interstitial space system to meet the wide range of requirements. The ceiling access or shallow system would be used for more conventional classroom activities, and the interstitial or deep system would be used for those areas requiring complex services.

As a result of these studies, we had to undertake a cost analysis of the interstitial system approach, not only in terms of first cost, but also in terms of its operating implications. We set up generic scenarios for change, based on norms previously identified during our user requirements studies on

various campuses. From these patterns, we analyzed the cost of making repairs within an interstitial facility as compared with a conventional ceiling space. It was obvious that the use of the deep ceiling for highly serviced areas within the building had potential for very considerable savings over the life span of the building.

The fundamental principle of the ABS system was its potential for alternative uses of different materials and component systems which could be bid or selected locally for individual jobs, depending on cost at that particular time. This was a critical factor in the selection of the specific systems. As conventional materials were being used, it was important that the system be designed to permit typical approaches, such as the use of fireproof steel, poured-in-place concrete, or precast and prestressed concrete systems, to be bid one against the other in given locations around the country. The development of the basic system called for the provision of a flexible block of space of approximately 10,000 square feet to meet the basic science or engineering requirements.

Within that space, there had to be considerable flexibility so the major vertical service systems for people, air conditioning, plumbing, electricity, laboratory gases, etc., were placed at the perimeter of the space. Typically, two of these space modules could work together within a single fire zone without requiring fire-rated partitions to separate the spaces from one another. In this manner, the structure, vertical services, and various trunk lines suspended from the structure provided the fixed elements of the building system. They could be arrayed in many ways, and their proportions, relationships to corridors, etc., were analyzed so as to obtain the greatest possible assigned square foot area in proportion to gross square footage. The 10,000 square foot basic block was small enough to permit a great variety of building configurations (see Figure CS 3.8).

The selection of materials and the individual design itself would be based on the architect's concept of what would relate to the specific campus. In the development of the basic system, it was considered important that horizontal, earthquake, or wind loads be taken, as much as possible, by the perimeter structure of the building, thus freeing the interior to the greatest possible extent. No shear walls would be used as permanent elements within the building proper to inhibit change.

The air-conditioning branch lines and terminals, the lighting-ceiling system, partitions, laboratory casework and furnishings were all considered as flexible elements to be installed and rearranged as required.

As no two services shared the same space and all crossovers were designed, the service systems could have dedicated pathways that penetrated the structure-ceiling portion of the building. These throughways were organized so that each of the subcontractors installing the service systems would have full access to them and be able to install them in such a way that the university's mainte-

nance or custodial staff could later gain easy access for both service and alteration requirements.

In developing the design approach for these systems, we first used small drawings supplemented by models; then we used full-size drawings to show how the service systems would fit through the building. Both before and after the completion of system design, independent consultants were retained to analyze the prospective costs of building the ABS system. Since the reports in both cases were favorable, we then began to look, with the universities, for buildings where we could apply the system for prototype testing purposes.

The system was ready by the beginning of 1970, a time when university construction had tapered off very considerably. In these circumstances, it was fortunate that we had not assembled a guaranteed market in order to develop new and more refined components. It was, in fact, difficult to even find a test building at the University of California. At the Indianapolis campus of both Indiana and Purdue Universities, a new building was needed to act as a surge facility. It was anticipated that many departments would be housed in the building initially and that, as they grew and matured, they would move to other facilities built for their specific purposes. Additional new departments would then be lodged within the building, and the process would be repeated many times before the building itself might be devoted to a single department.

The building, which has become known as the Science, Engineering and Technology Building, was designed as a three-story structure consisting of two space modules per floor with all vertical services running outside the flexible portion of the building. It was also designed so that pedestrian passageways could connect this facility with others to be built later, utilizing the same or an analogous system, so that the campus could expand over time around a pedestrian street linking the various buildings together. It was built for flexibility, and within the first year, two new departments moved into the building: a school of hotel management which required extensive kitchen facilities and a department of metallurgy whose crucibles demanded special exhaust facilities. These changes and others were handled simply and directly.

Illustrated History

The system was designed to provide flexible teaching and laboratory space within an easily serviced and effective working environment. Reducing the cost of altering specialized laboratory facilities was our prime focus because high operating costs were becoming an increasing problem while good teachers were requiring first-class facilities. Various buildings and specific projects were analyzed to determine the cost of changing the building subsystem in order to get a profile of the pattern of required alterations and their attendant financial impact (see Figure 7.1, p. 70).

The majority of changes involved the plumbing system; the cost of access to the plumbing lines and the subsequent repair and patching of walls and ceilings was a major item (see Figure CS 3.1). This information, coupled with the result of our user requirement investigation, allowed us to establish criteria for each of the component systems (see Figure CS 3.2). The structural system had to provide for a limited number of bay sizes (see Figure CS 3.3). The HVAC system and the other service systems were designed so that no two services would share the same space within the structural-ceiling sandwich (see Figure CS 3.4). The partition and ceiling systems were designed to work together and to facilitate the passage of services (see Figure CS 3.5). All of these subsystems were designed to work within a framework of building blocks called space modules which averaged 10,000 square feet (see Figure CS 3.6). The space modules themselves could take a variety of shapes with their maximum length-to-width ratios limited to 4:1 for service distribution efficiency (see Figure CS 3.7). The modules could be assembled in a variety of different ways to form any desired building shape (see Figure CS 3.8).

Three examples of our many approaches are shown in Figure CS 3.9. These are: (a) floor access plus ceiling access to services, (b) ceiling access alone, and (c) a deep service or interstitial space using a walk-on ceiling.

Many other configurations were also studied before a decision was made to use a combination of ceiling access and interstitial space. The ceiling access was deemed appropriate for nonlaboratory spaces, and the walk-on ceiling was required for flexibility in the laboratory spaces (see Figure CS 3.10). The total system was designed accordingly (see Figure CS 3.11).

The system was then ready for use in the design of a prototype facility at the Indianapolis Joint Campus of Purdue and Indiana Universities. The three-story building was designed to be built in two phases with a strong circulation element which would not only connect the two phases but would allow the building to be tied to future campus facilities (see Figure CS 3.12).

The services were laid out generically within the building to meet both the requirements of the opening configuration and to provide for future changes (see Figure CS 3.13). The structural frame was designed to take shear loads and, along with the external vertical circulation and service elements, to free the interior space of all fixed elements except for columns.

The building is seen from two different views in Figure CS 3.14, which shows how the pedestrian circulation and flexible space were treated.

CS 3.1 Typical distribution of alteration costs with the cost of the plumbing services requiring 42 percent of all alteration costs.

CS 3.2 An example showing an integrated service distribution system.

CS 3.3 ABS structural bay sizes.

CS 3.4 Drawing of service systems indicating the attention to detail needed to provide a flexible and accessible building system.

CS 3.5 The hung ceiling which receives the partitions *(top)* and is designed to meet fire requirements allows changes to occur more economically than the design approach *(bottom)* which uses partitions from floor to structural slab as a way to meet code requirements for fire separation.

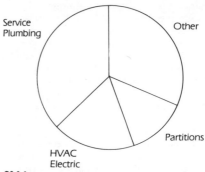

CS 3.1

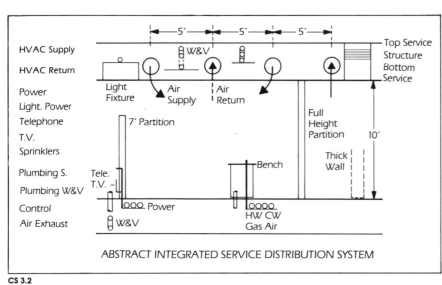

ABSTRACT INTEGRATED SERVICE DISTRIBUTION SYSTEM

CS 3.2

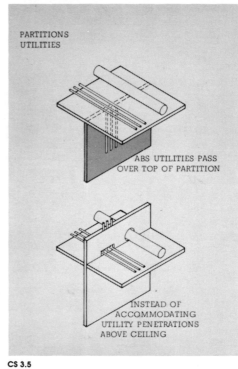

PARTITIONS
UTILITIES

ABS UTILITIES PASS
OVER TOP OF PARTITION

INSTEAD OF
ACCOMMODATING
UTILITY PENETRATIONS
ABOVE CEILING

CS 3.5

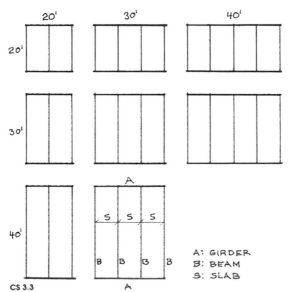

A: GIRDER
B: BEAM
S: SLAB

CS 3.3

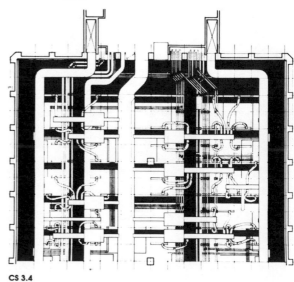

CS 3.4

CS 3.7

SPACE MODULE

- Single Story Area of 10,000 S.F.
  ±2,000 S.F.
- Variable Length to Width Ratio Up to
  2:1 For Use alone. 4:1 For Use in
  Connection With Another Space Module.
- Maximum Side Length 200 Ft.
- 10 Ft. Length Increment in Both Directions.

CS 3.6

CS 3.8(a)

CS 3.8(b)

CS 3.6 Space module.

CS 3.7 Space module shapes.

CS 3.8 Various combinations of space modules.

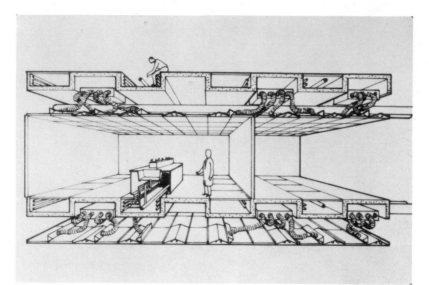

CS 3.9(a)

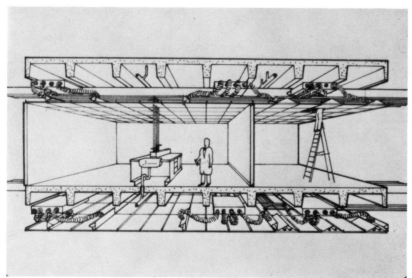

CS 3.9(b)

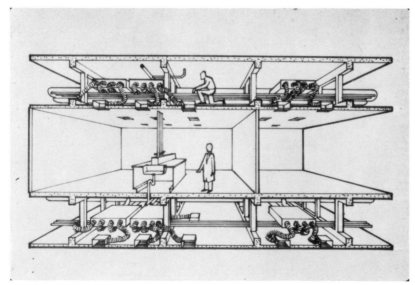

CS 3.9(c)

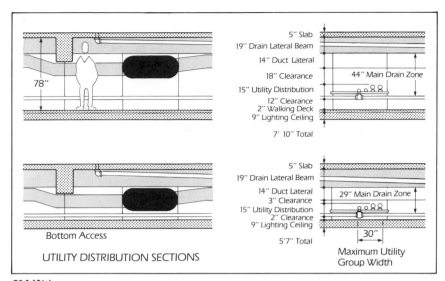

5" Slab
19" Drain Lateral Beam
14" Duct Lateral
18" Clearance — 44" Main Drain Zone
15" Utility Distribution
12" Clearance
2" Walking Deck
9" Lighting Ceiling

7' 10" Total

78"

Bottom Access

5" Slab
19" Drain Lateral Beam
14" Duct Lateral — 29" Main Drain Zone
3" Clearance
15" Utility Distribution
2" Clearance
9" Lighting Ceiling

5'7" Total

30"

Maximum Utility
Group Width

UTILITY DISTRIBUTION SECTIONS

CS 3.10(a)

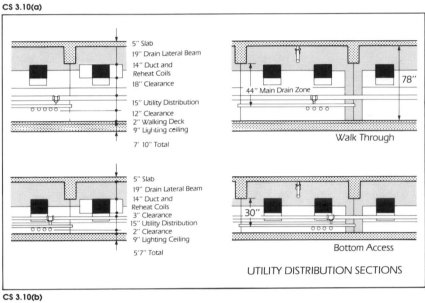

5" Slab
19" Drain Lateral Beam
14" Duct and Reheat Coils
18" Clearance
15" Utility Distribution
12" Clearance
2" Walking Deck
9" Lighting ceiling

7' 10" Total

44" Main Drain Zone

78"

Walk Through

5" Slab
19" Drain Lateral Beam
14" Duct and Reheat Coils
3" Clearance
15" Utility Distribution
2" Clearance
9" Lighting Ceiling

5'7" Total

30"

Bottom Access

UTILITY DISTRIBUTION SECTIONS

CS 3.10(b)

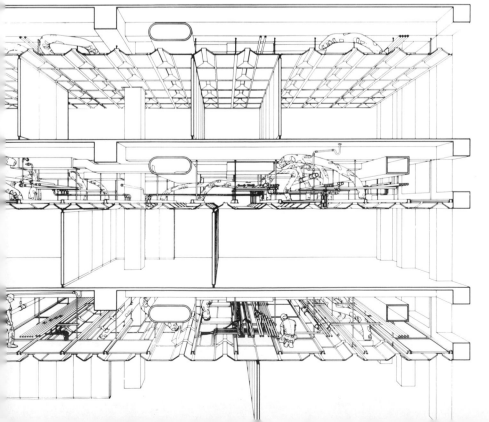

CS 3.11 Drawing of ABS system showing a combination of the shallow ceiling for the top floor and the deep or walk-through space for the lower floors. Both ceiling conditions were required for ABS: the deep space was used for laboratory areas and for those floors where the highest degree of flexibility was needed.

MATHEMATICS   GEOLOGY

ENGINEERING

ELECTRICAL ENGINEERING

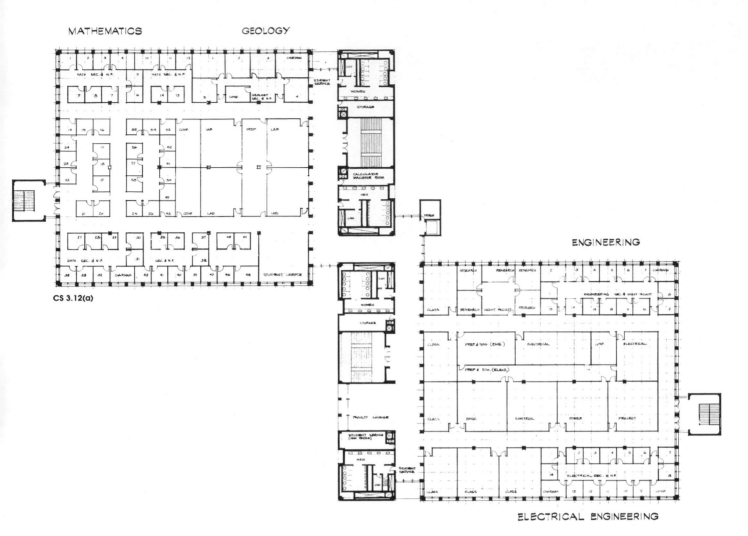

CS 3.12(a)

CS 3.12(b)

CS 3.12   The plan provides for a major service corridor to connect various campus buildings. The basic design is shown in the model of phases one and two.

CS 3.13

CS 3.13 Photograph of interstitial space showing the organization of all service lines in a rational manner. This space can be reached, changed, and serviced easily. The design for the operation and maintenance of a building is as important as any other function if the building is to work well over time.

CS 3.14 Science, Engineering and Technology building at the joint campus of Purdue and Indiana Universities.

CS 3.14(a)

CS 3.14(b)

CASE STUDY 4

Veterans Administration Hospital Building System _____

About a year after the Academic Building System project began, the Veterans Administration became interested in developing a building system for VA hospitals. Their interest was motivated by the rapid rate of hospital obsolescence and the increasingly high cost of remodeling facilities to meet changing needs.

Unfortunately, the Veterans Administration, with the largest health care system in the United States, is not able to predict its hospital construction schedule within a time framework that would permit it to aggregate a market over the many regions in which facilities will be built. Congress appropriates funds for design, or perhaps for design and working drawings, and then at another time, for construction. While the Veterans Administration may request specific facilities to be built on a given schedule, by the time congressional appropriations are provided, there is not enough time to develop the building system. For this reason, the VA became intrigued with the approach we were using in the ABS project, since it called for a design approach that would work in widely divergent sections of the country without a commitment to an aggregated market. After going through the usual procurement process, we, in a joint venture with Stone, Maracini & Patterson, were selected to develop a hospital building system.

We began by trying to understand the basic needs of the VA by visiting a wide range of different facilities. We used a departmental basis to analyze their requirements for different levels of performance, energy needs, air conditioning, space, and rate of change, as well as the use of efficient anthropometric sizes that would permit those activities to be housed within an effective but efficient area. From these requirements, we were able to establish the nature of basic modules that might be used for the design of hospital facilities. The basic module in our design was a space module of approximately 10,000 square feet. The hierarchy by which the mod-

ules were created is shown in Figure CS 4.8. The actual configuration of the space module had many different permutations, but they were all based on using a limited number of different structural span sizes.

When reviewing the basic planning requirements for the VA building system, we took into account a major requirement: providing simple access to service systems for alteration and maintenance. This was accomplished by permitting considerable flexibility within the space modules themselves and by allowing different levels of services to be installed later. Each service had basic areaways reserved throughout the total building to allow future installation of those services as required in the future. The development of this flexible approach was derived from studies analogous to those made on the ABS project.

Our analysis of hospital service networks convinced us that the complexity of the hospital requirements called for installation of the networks in interstitial space for both layout and access. We were convinced that the pattern of two structural floors for one usable floor, used in the Salk Institute in San Diego and in a number of other facilities was too expensive. Another approach, tried elsewhere just prior to this project, was an interstitial floor that serves two levels, one up and one down, but it caused tremendous complexity in the design of the service systems. The third prevailing approach to providing interstitial space was catwalks lined with service walls. However, these walls acted as barriers to future change. Our analyses of these systems led us to the conclusion that the most economical way to provide for interstitial space was a walk-on ceiling.

A hospital is essentially a building made up of a variety of small spaces. We therefore developed a group of secondary structural spans that range in length from 40 feet 6 inches to 58 feet 6 inches, with primary structural beams of 22 feet 6 inches. These spans were large enough to permit appropri-

ate combinations of different rooms, and by using this type of repetitive module, we could size maximum ducts, conduits, and plumbing and locate them in specific places within the interstitial space in such a manner that no two services could or would occupy the same space.

The main trunks and branches of each of the services had their own particular levels, and the connections from the trunks to the branches would always be of a predetermined configuration (see Figure CS 4.13). Thus each separate service was given its own location. During the development of the system, we also worked with full-size drawings. Someone standing in front of the drawing would try to locate conduits, ducts, etc., and we could judge whether there was sufficient working room to do so. At a later state in the work, when the design direction was set, a mock-up of the most densely serviced areas was prepared so that we could then see, full-size, how the system would work and make minor adjustments (see Figure CS 4.17).

Since we were dealing with a design system rather than with a group of industrialized components on which preset unit prices could be obtained, our ability to cost design alternatives quickly and easily was essential. We found, as in the case of ABS, that it was essential to design a basic system which could be built with any material. The coordination of all the components, therefore, was done on the basis of product sizes using the maximum space requirements for the particular task at hand (i.e., poured-in-place concrete beams as opposed to fireproof steel, which would have thinner members). The limiting factor in the height of the interstitial area was the 5-foot top-of-ceiling to underside-of-structure dimension, which would allow workers to work standing up between the beams in the interstitial space. The system, once designed, was tested; it was shown that basic user requirements could be met and the functions altered to meet realistic levels of change within an appropriate cost context and so the system was "frozen with respect to the design approach."

The VA was satisfied with the system because it provided a range of services which could be tailored for a specific use at any point in the building and permitted easy access to the services for maintenance, operations, and potential alteration. Their concern was that hospitals should no longer be designed to meet a specific set of user requirements related to a specific time, place, and pattern of care, because staff and basic programs often changed by the time the facility is completed.

The user needs were studied on a departmental basis; once the proper service networks were established, the basic space module dimensions were determined by a careful study of the nursing portions of the building. It was here that minor dimensional variations were critical. A group of different arrangements were analyzed within each of the different types of space modules to assure the VA that a limited number of structural bay sizes would provide for all its possible needs. Figure CS 4.5 shows the type of studies on which the determinations were based. The various relationships of beds, bathrooms, corridors, etc. were analyzed, and the relevant permutations were incorporated into the 11 basic space modules. The user requirement studies of the service portion of the hospital then showed that the space modules sized for the various bed patient needs could easily accommodate the other departments.

The concepts that we developed were costed initially by our own specialists and then by an independent cost-estimating firm. Positive results in terms of cost targets were revealed. Because the design could meet the varied medical requirements, provide for change, and provide a single comprehensive building system which could be constructed economically in different localities and which incorporated flexibility to meet changing medical requirements, we decided that the design stage was over. With the completion of the system design, the VA decided to utilize and test it in the design of a prototype hospital at Loma Linda, California.

The Loma Linda VA Hospital is a 500-bed teaching and research facility designed to replace the previous VA hospital which collapsed in the 1971 Los Angeles earthquake; it was to be rebuilt on the same site. Earthquake requirements were therefore a major concern in design of the hospital. It was planned as a symmetrical low-rise four-story structure which could meet both the requirements of the basic program and the requirements of earthquake design in a high-risk area. The core services of the hospital were placed in the center of the building with courtyards from the second through fourth stories providing access to natural light for the nursing wings, which are at the perimeter of the building. A separate nursing home wing and central plant protrude from the basic block of the hospital, which is made up of repetitive space modules stacked one on top of the other. Once the building was de-

signed, a model of a typical service area was constructed so that potential bidders at a pre-bid conference could see that the building and related services were precisely designed.

We had hoped that by laying out well-coordinated service systems, we would realize significant cost savings. Since the building finally cost $57 million, well below the target price of $60 million, it seems that we succeeded. Subsequent discussions with subcontractors indicated that there were considerable efficiencies in the installation of service subsystems in the building. The building was completed ahead of schedule, in December 1977.

Illustrated History

The Veterans Administration building system for hospital design had to provide many different building configurations appropriate to the program, site, and climate across the country. Figure CS 4.1 illustrates the variety of obtainable configurations.

User requirements were analyzed to determine specific needs in terms of the primary relationship of function, environment, and service, as well as appropriate room sizes and building modules. Figures CS 4.2 to CS 4.4 show examples of each of these factors.

Because a hospital is made up of many small rooms, it was important to determine appropriate building block sizes within which departmental activities could be properly organized. Various departments were studied to determine the dimensions they would require. Figure CS 4.5 shows an example of a nursing wing. Eleven different space modules which had the capacity to meet the basic user requirements with a limited number of structural member sizes were developed (see Figure CS 4.6). Each space module was analyzed for its specific relationship to a variety of hospital requirements and conversely all requirements were reviewed to be sure that they could be accommodated effectively. A wide range of Veterans Administration and other hospitals built in the United States and abroad were then studied to see whether the space modules would permit duplication of those facilities. Invariably this could be done (see Figure CS 4.7), and the organizing concept of using space modules became an accepted focus for the building system. There were many permutations by which space modules could be arranged, and their design application to known requirements appeared to provide for appropriate solutions.

The system is composed of typical structural bays which are combined to provide the required area for a space module. Two or more space modules plus a service bay for vertical risers form a service module, which is a fully integrated unit of space with both horizontal and vertical service capabilities. The average size of each module is 10,000 square feet. Two such service modules, or about 20,000 square feet, comprise what was called a fire section. Special fire walls and other fire protective requirements limit pos-

sibilities for reorganization of space between two fire sections. The flexibility within a fire section, however, is substantial, and the area is large enough to accommodate any set of user requirements. Figure CS 4.8 illustrates the system's space module concept. The service module is defined by three basic building subsystems of the building shell which are: structure, ceiling, and partitions. The basic service systems are heating-ventilation-cooling, plumbing distribution, and electric power distribution. These six subsystems, shown in Figure CS 4.9, provide the skeleton and arteries for the design of the total hospital. The six subsystems were designed to be totally compatible with each other. Figure CS 4.10 shows the basic structural system. Five structural bay sizes, all of which are 22 feet 6 inches wide, are included. Their lengths range from 40 feet 6 inches to 58 feet 6 inches in 4 foot 6 inch increments. In addition, the length of the bays may be extended by 18-foot cantilevers.

The ceiling system provides a 1-hour fire resistive walk-on platform for service access. It is suspended from the structure and provides anchorage for the partitions as shown in Figure CS 4.11. The introduction of a walk-on but nonstructural ceiling which could hang from the structural floor or roof slab was one of the key concepts in developing an economical interstitial space system. Figure CS 4.12 shows the partition system. The 2-hour fire partitions are permanent. All other components of the partition systems are considered adaptable.

Figure CS 4.13 shows how the space between the platform ceiling and the building structure was vertically subdivided to separate all the service elements and eliminate conflicts. The module studies below indicate the horizontal allocation of service routes with people access provided on the periphery of the service module. The service bays on the end of the service module handle the vertical service line requirements, provide space for mechanical equipment, and take in fresh air for the air-conditioning system. Figures CS 4.14 to CS 4.16 show through model studies the location and coordination of the HVAC, electrical, plumbing, combined service, and structural subsystems, as well as an end view of the interstitial space. Notice that the center structural beam is dropped so that the plumbing lines can pass over it. Also the large HVAC ducts are next to this dropped beam so that access to the services is along perimeter access routes and one then moves in from either side of the space module to the center. Figure CS 4.17 shows a full-size mock up of the service zone built to test the concepts of fit and accessibility.

Following completion of the design of the Veterans Administration system, the joint venture of Stone, Marracini & Patterson and Building Systems Development, Inc., was selected to design a prototype hospital at Loma Linda, California. This project was to replace a hospital destroyed in the 1971 Los Angeles earthquake with a new facility on the same site. The project was therefore designed to meet the most critical earthquake standards with a low and very symmetrical design as shown by the model in Figure CS 4.18.

In order to obtain the lowest possible bids, we had to convince potential bidders that all of the services were in fact designed so that no two service lines would occupy the same space. For this reason one of the 32 similar space modules used in the design of the building was built with all the trunk lines shown in place (see Figure CS 4.19). It was shown to the contractors at a prebid conference to demonstrate the system and most specifically the coordination of all the subsystems. The results were good in terms of cost, construction time, and completion time, all of which were ahead of target, and the client has been interested in furthering the system's approach and concept in its new and more recent work.

The hospital's typical plan is shown in Figure CS 4.20. The building is a rectangle with wings for central plant and nursing home facilities. The upper three levels are punctured by courtyards to let light into the interior of the building so that the patients' rooms can be placed on an increased building perimeter. Figure CS 4.21 shows the building's entrance. A typical two-person bedroom is shown in Figure CS 4.22. Notice that the console units next to the beds are designed to cover wall-mounted service lines to make them easy to reach and to alter. The interstitial space is shown in Figures CS 4.23 and CS 4.24.

The same level of study and model analysis should be done on appropriate individual projects. Figures CS 4.25 to CS 4.27 show the building, study model, and service organization in the penthouse of the completed Tufts Veterinary Medical School's Large Animal Hospital at Grafton, Massachusetts, as an example.

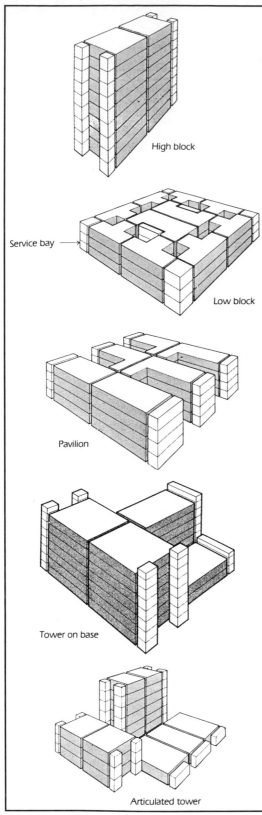

High block

Service bay

Low block

Pavilion

Tower on base

Articulated tower

CS 4.1

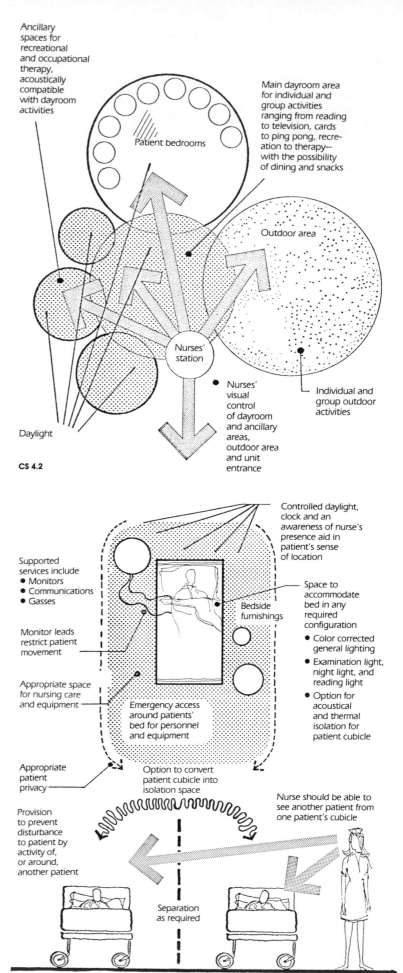

Ancillary spaces for recreational and occupational therapy, acoustically compatible with dayroom activities

Main dayroom area for individual and group activities ranging from reading to television, cards to ping pong, recreation to therapy-- with the possibility of dining and snacks

Patient bedrooms

Outdoor area

Nurses' station

Nurses' visual control of dayroom and ancillary areas, outdoor area and unit entrance

Individual and group outdoor activities

Daylight

CS 4.2

Controlled daylight, clock and an awareness of nurse's presence aid in patient's sense of location

Supported services include
• Monitors
• Communications
• Gasses

Monitor leads restrict patient movement

Appropriate space for nursing care and equipment

Emergency access around patients' bed for personnel and equipment

Bedside furnishings

Space to accommodate bed in any required configuration
• Color corrected general lighting
• Examination light, night light, and reading light
• Option for acoustical and thermal isolation for patient cubicle

Appropriate patient privacy

Option to convert patient cubicle into isolation space

Nurse should be able to see another patient from one patient's cubicle

Provision to prevent disturbance to patient by activity of, or around, another patient

Separation as required

CS 4.3

CS 4.1 The service module as a building block for alternative building configurations.

CS 4.2 Diagram of primary relationships for a psychiatric unit.

CS 4.3 Diagram of patient environment for intensive care unit.

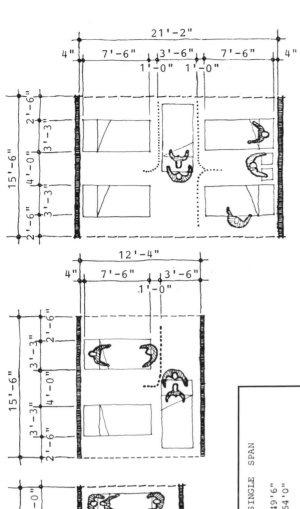

CS 4.4

CS 4.4 Critical dimensions for patient's room.

CS 4.5 Planning zones are established for different functions, and these activities are then related to a group of structural spans. The system has a limited number of bay sizes, all related to a single planning module. All the required functions can be effectively housed by this limited dimensional vocabulary.

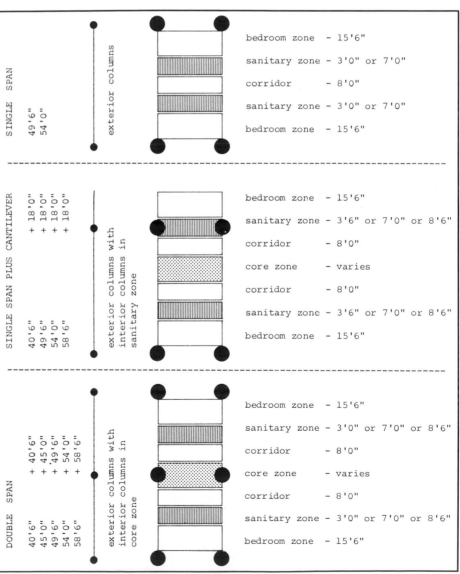

SINGLE SPAN	49'6" 54'0"	exterior columns		bedroom zone – 15'6"
				sanitary zone – 3'0" or 7'0"
				corridor – 8'0"
				sanitary zone – 3'0" or 7'0"
				bedroom zone – 15'6"

SINGLE SPAN PLUS CANTILEVER	40'6" + 18'0" 49'6" + 18'0" 54'0" + 18'0" 58'6" + 18'0"	exterior columns with interior columns in sanitary zone		bedroom zone – 15'6"
				sanitary zone – 3'6" or 7'0" or 8'6"
				corridor – 8'0"
				core zone – varies
				corridor – 8'0"
				sanitary zone – 3'6" or 7'0" or 8'6"
				bedroom zone – 15'6"

DOUBLE SPAN	40'6" + 40'6" 45'0" + 45'0" 49'6" + 49'6" 54'0" + 54'0" 58'6" + 58'6"	exterior columns with interior columns in core zone		bedroom zone – 15'6"
				sanitary zone – 3'0" or 7'0" or 8'6"
				corridor – 8'0"
				core zone – varies
				corridor – 8'0"
				sanitary zone – 3'0" or 7'0" or 8'6"
				bedroom zone – 15'6"

CS 4.5

CS 4.6 Group of space modules developed within the system.

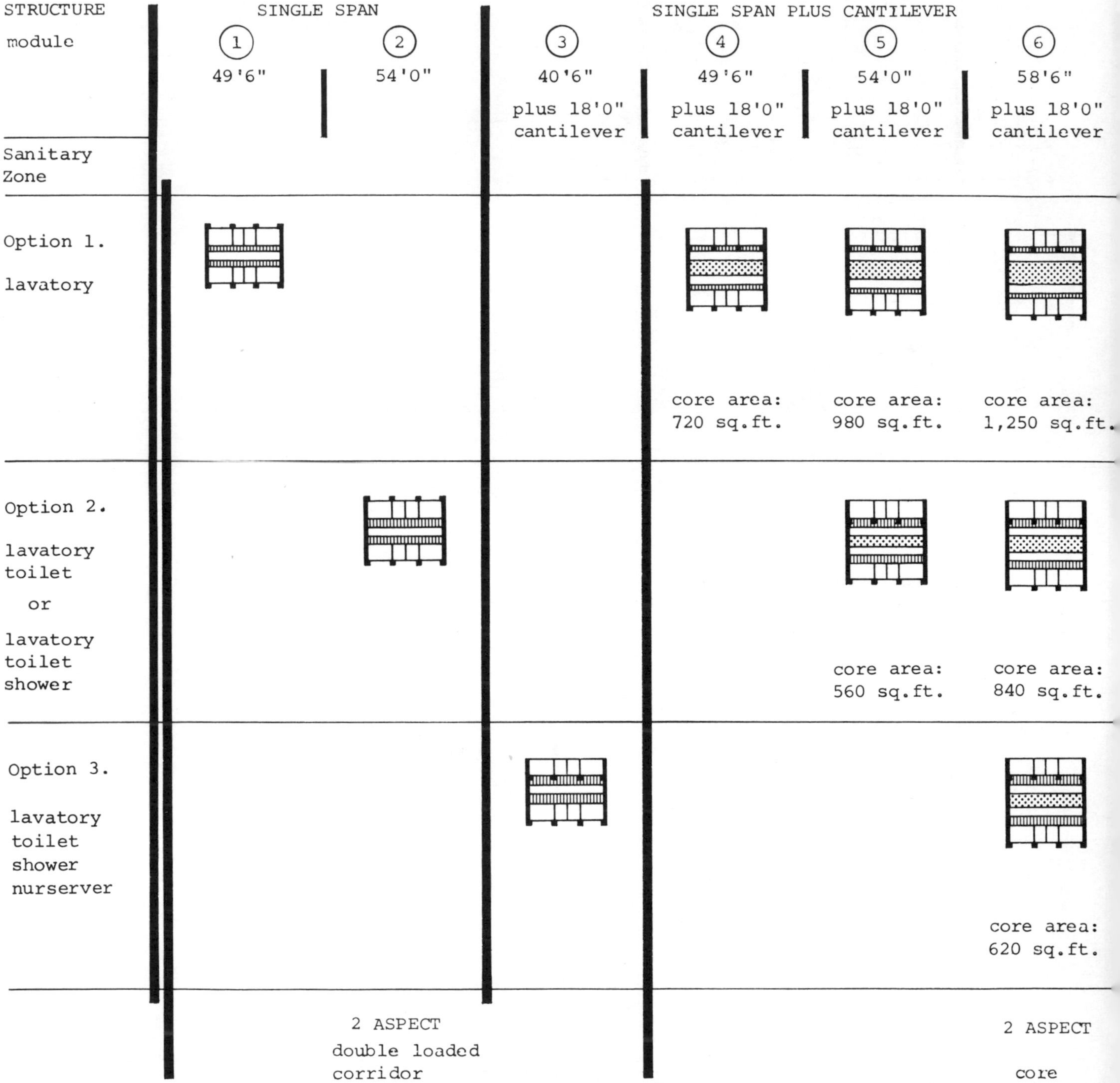

STRUCTURE module	SINGLE SPAN		SINGLE SPAN PLUS CANTILEVER			
	① 49'6"	② 54'0"	③ 40'6" plus 18'0" cantilever	④ 49'6" plus 18'0" cantilever	⑤ 54'0" plus 18'0" cantilever	⑥ 58'6" plus 18'0" cantilever

Sanitary Zone

Option 1.

lavatory

core area: 720 sq.ft. | core area: 980 sq.ft. | core area: 1,250 sq.ft.

Option 2.

lavatory
toilet
   or
lavatory
toilet
shower

core area: 560 sq.ft. | core area: 840 sq.ft.

Option 3.

lavatory
toilet
shower
nurserver

core area: 620 sq.ft.

2 ASPECT
double loaded
corridor

2 ASPECT

core

CS 4.6

Shaded areas indicate Sanitary Zones and Support Zones (core area). Heavy line indicates the potential interface with either a Space Module and/or a service bay and/or additional space (Catalog of Space Module Capabilities).

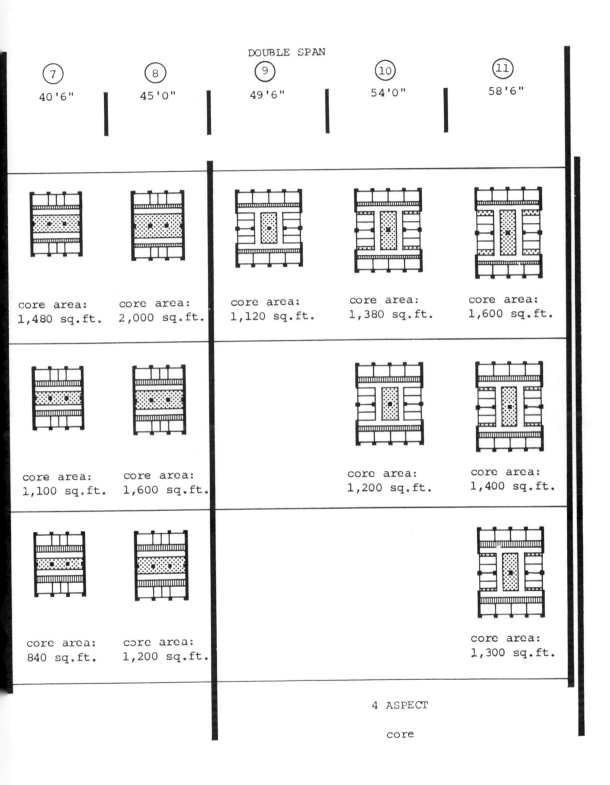

DOUBLE SPAN

⑦ 40'6" ⑧ 45'0" ⑨ 49'6" ⑩ 54'0" ⑪ 58'6"

core area:
1,480 sq.ft.

core area:
2,000 sq.ft.

core area:
1,120 sq.ft.

core area:
1,380 sq.ft.

core area:
1,600 sq.ft.

core area:
1,100 sq.ft.

core area:
1,600 sq.ft.

core area:
1,200 sq.ft.

core area:
1,400 sq.ft.

core area:
840 sq.ft.

core area:
1,200 sq.ft.

core area:
1,300 sq.ft.

4 ASPECT

core

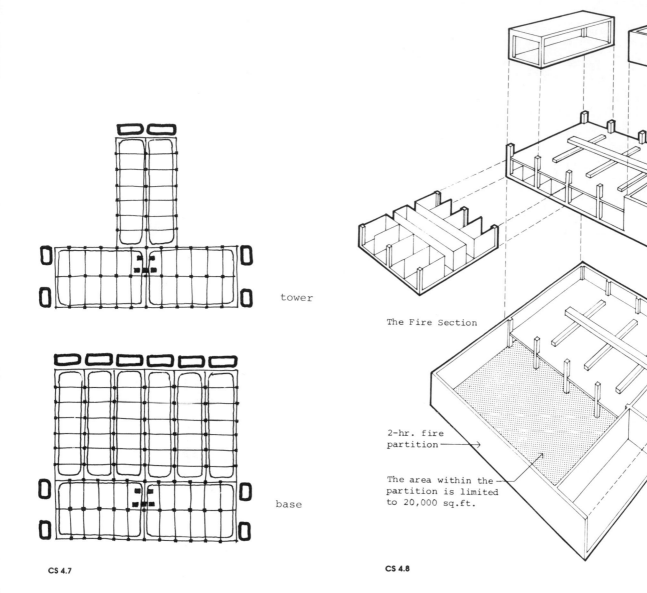

tower

base

The Fire Section

2-hr. fire
partition ————➤

The area within the —
partition is limited
to 20,000 sq.ft.

CS 4.7

CS 4.8

CS 4.7 Diagram showing the
application of the space-module concept
to the VA Hospital in Lexington,
Kentucky, one of many hospitals which
were analyzed and could be duplicated
with the system.

CS 4.8 The modular system.

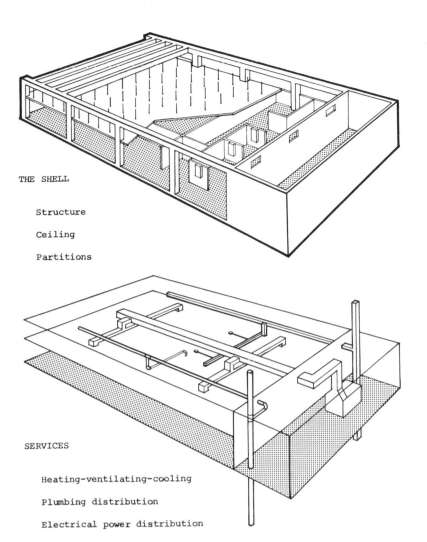

THE SHELL

   Structure

   Ceiling

   Partitions

SERVICES

   Heating-ventilating-cooling

   Plumbing distribution

   Electrical power distribution

CS 4.9

CS 4.9 The six subsystems.

CS 4.10 The basic design of the structural system. Note the dropped beam at the center of the structure; it will facilitate the placement of plumbing lines as shown in Figure CS 4.21.

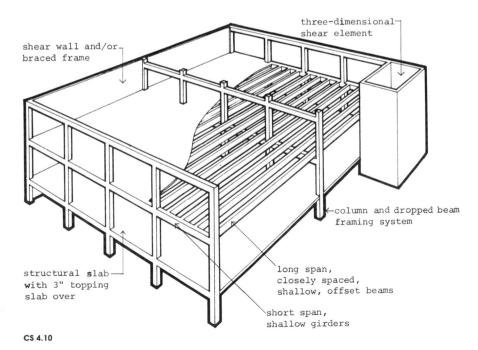

shear wall and/or braced frame

three-dimensional shear element

column and dropped beam framing system

structural slab with 3" topping slab over

long span, closely spaced, shallow, offset beams

short span, shallow girders

CS 4.10

CS 4.11 Basic design of the ceiling subsystem.

CS 4.12 Components of the partition subsystem.

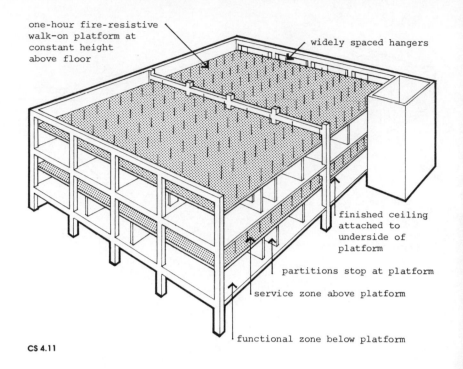

one-hour fire-resistive walk-on platform at constant height above floor

widely spaced hangers

finished ceiling attached to underside of platform

partitions stop at platform

service zone above platform

functional zone below platform

CS 4.11

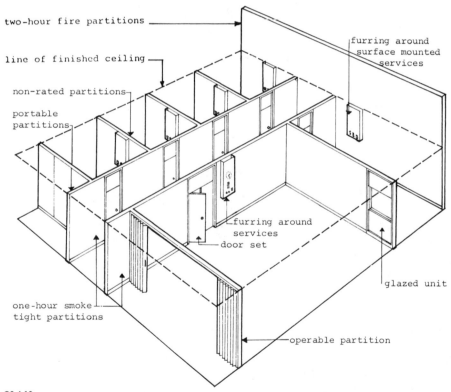

two-hour fire partitions

line of finished ceiling

non-rated partitions

portable partitions

furring around surface mounted services

furring around services

door set

glazed unit

one-hour smoke tight partitions

operable partition

CS 4.12

All dimensions are nominal.

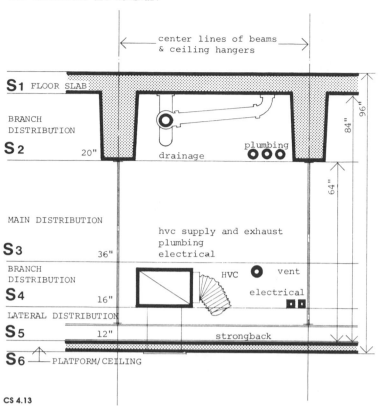

CS 4.13

CS 4.13 The vertical height of the interstitial space is divided into six zones. All services have specific routings related to these zones.

CS 4.14 Study model HVAC system.

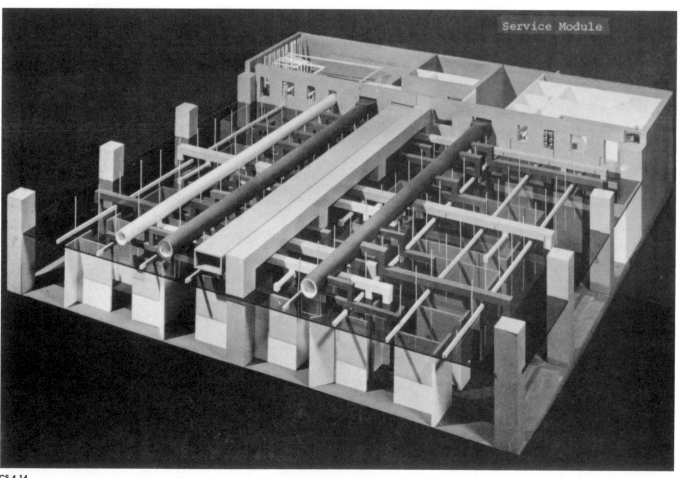

CS 4.14

CS 4.15 Study model shows the integration of all the mechanical, plumbing, and electrical services with the structural system. Notice the plumbing lines running over the dropped structural beam.

CS 4.16 Study model with structure in place.

CS 4.17 A full-size mock up of the densest service area was constructed to test if access could be obtained for the operation and maintenance of all the services. A worker can stand up when working between the beams but would have to duck underneath the beam when walking through the space. This keeps the floor-to-floor height to a minimum.

CS 4.18 Bird's-eye view of model.

CS 4.19 View of service lines in typical space module. The model was taken to building site as well as to the prebid conference to show contractors and workers how we intended it to be built and to indicate that there shouldn't be many surprises at the building site.

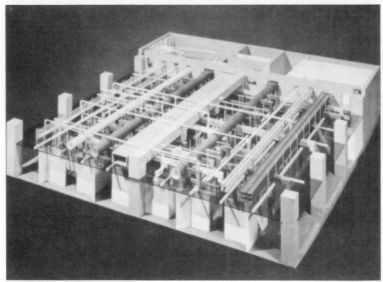

CS 4.15

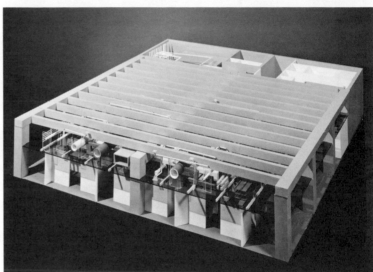

CS 4.16

CS 4.17

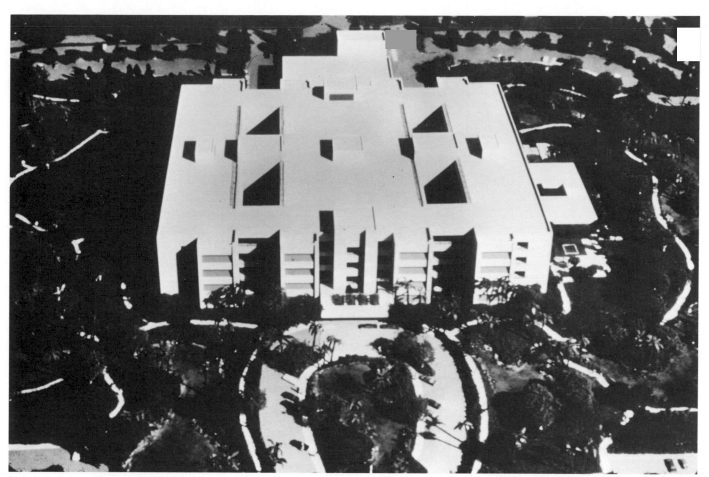

CS 4.18

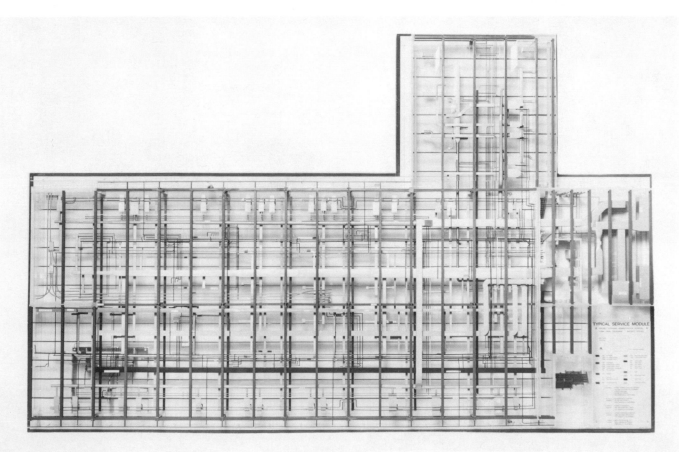

CS 4.19

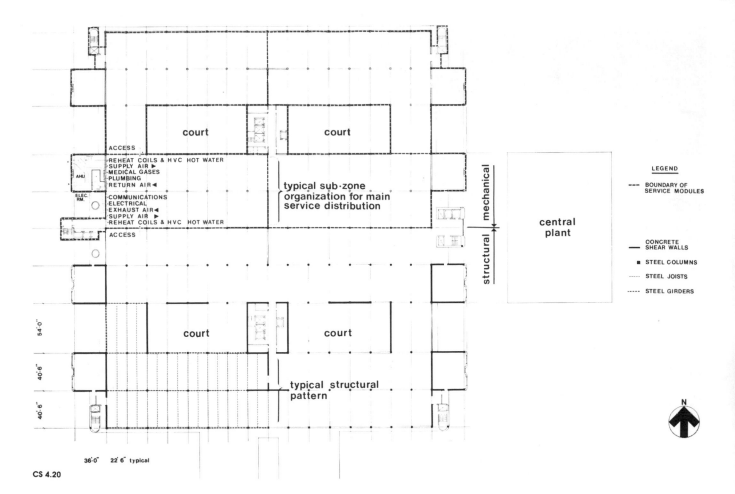

LEGEND

‐‐‐ BOUNDARY OF
SERVICE MODULES

—— CONCRETE
SHEAR WALLS

■ STEEL COLUMNS

···· STEEL JOISTS

---- STEEL GIRDERS

central
plant

structural | mechanical

court   court

ACCESS
REHEAT COILS & HVC HOT WATER
SUPPLY AIR ▶
MEDICAL GASES
PLUMBING
RETURN AIR ◀

AHU

ELEC.
RM.

COMMUNICATIONS
ELECTRICAL
EXHAUST AIR ◀
SUPPLY AIR ▶
REHEAT COILS & HVC HOT WATER
ACCESS

typical sub-zone
organization for main
service distribution

court   court

typical structural
pattern

54'-0"
40'-6"
40'-6"

36'-0"   22'-6" typical

CS 4.20

CS 4.21

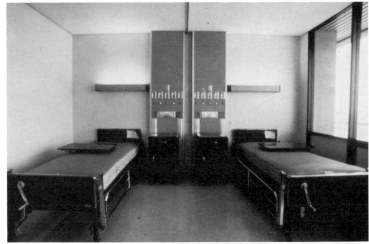

CS 4.22

CS 4.20   Block plans of hospital.

CS 4.21   Side view of entrance. Note the
mechanical service bays — four at each
end of the hospital.

CS 4.22   The console units next to the
beds cover surface-mounted services
which can be removed for maintenance
or alterations. The articulation of the
individual building systems was carried
through in every phase of planning this
project.

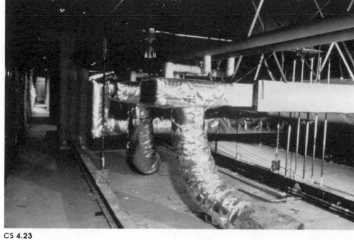

CS 4.23

CS 4.24

CS 4.23 View of interstitial space adjacent to access corridor.

CS 4.24 General view of interstitial space. Note the electrical service drop from main distribution to lateral service location. The discipline is maintained.

CS 4.25 Large animal hospital.

CS 4.25

CS 4.26

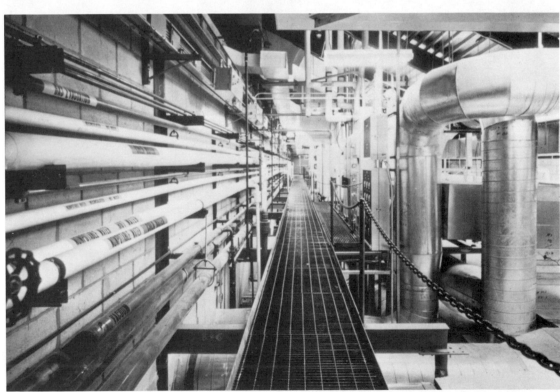

CS 4.27

CS 4.26 Service model used in design
and for prebidding and site instruction
purposes.

CS 4.27 Service penthouse in
completed building.

CASE STUDY 5

Fiber-Shell _____

We first became involved with the development of a fiberglass housing system in the late 1960s while working on a Department of Housing and Urban Development research project called "The In-City Experimental Housing Project." We were seeking new approaches to providing housing in cities throughout the country. We were looking to develop and test specific social, technical, and economic innovations that would improve housing and make it more affordable.

As part of our technical research, we investigated a technique developed by Aerojet General Corporation of Sacramento which was an attempt to manufacture houses by wrapping fiberglass tubes on a mandrel in a way that was analogous to the construction of rocket casings. It quickly became apparent that the concept of winding a house with fiberglass filaments and resin resulted in extremely high costs even when a large market was projected. This was based solely on the material content of the fiberglass and resin. But since the strength characteristics exceeded the structural requirements many times over, we advised Aerojet General to develop a technique which would use the fiberglass more efficiently.

About a year after the conclusion of the In-City Experimental Housing Program, we were retained by Aerojet General to help with their development work. By this time they had developed a concept of making a sandwich consisting of (1) an inner sheet of fiberglass made up of a woven roving of glass cloth wrapped around a mandrel and then sprayed with resin; (2) a core that consisted of phenolic impregnated honeycomb paper which would not support combustion, and (3) repeat layer of fiberglass and resin placed on the outside of the honeycomb paper to form an efficient structural sandwich panel. In order to meet code requirements for fire protection, gypsum wallboard was attached to both the inner and outer surfaces. The outside weathering surface could then be chosen by the individual designer to provide a

waterproof and visually attractive skin. The system therefore allowed the use of conventional products for both exterior and interior surfaces. When compared with typical wood stud construction, the difference was inside the sandwich, leaving the user of the house to work with conventional and familiar materials. This technique was used to construct a prototype room-size module at the Aerojet General factory in order to analyze how this approach might best be carried forward for future development. In keeping with the concept discussed above, a fiberglass tube was wrapped with the woven roving of fiberglass cloth impregnated with resin. Then the honeycomb paper was laid up as shown in Figure CS 5.2 (see page 192) before the final layer of fiberglass was added. The end result of this process was the fabrication of a tube whose ends could then be closed with any desired material. Tooling for actual production, however, was potentially expensive so the process presupposed and depended upon a considerable market.

This developmental work was done in the late 1960s at a time when housing construction exceeded two million homes per year and shortages of lumber resulted in steep price increases. At the same time, the costs of resins and fiberglass were slowly coming down. Aerojet General's system appeared to provide an acceptable substitute for wood-frame construction, which required a viable alternative because of increased lumber prices and general construction trends.

At the time of the first announcement of Operation Breakthrough, in 1968, it became apparent that government support could provide a basis for bringing the Fiber-Shell system to the marketplace. But Aerojet General did not appear to have the resources or interest in doing the required work. We identified an interest on the part of TRW to diversify their activities into the housing market. We introduced TRW to Aerojet and assisted TRW in acquiring the rights to the Fiber-Shell system, as well as key personnel who had been

associated with its development. We then prepared TRW's response to the government's request for a proposal in Operation Breakthrough. The Fiber-Shell system was selected as one of the 22 Operation Breakthrough systems, and we began working with TRW to develop the system in detail.

The development of the Fiber-Shell System in Operation Breakthrough began with Aerojet's latest efforts. The structural properties of the fiberglass sandwich indicated that its high strength could best be used to create a large rectangular tube in which a total house or at least very large segments of a house could be planned. The use of this material for 12-foot-wide room-sized modules or trailer-type units, similar to mobile homes, invested as much or more material in the walls as in the floor and roof, which would constitute an uneconomic use of the system. In looking for dimensions that would satisfy a wide variety of housing conditions, each foot multiple was analyzed for the rooms and clusters of rooms that could be designed, e.g., a dimension that would be satisfactory for a living room might be overgenerous for a bedroom. As we began to look at the possibilities of developing different housing arrangements and configurations with a relatively small number of sizes, it became apparent that we should look for a housing module within which a number of different room-type configurations could fit.

It became clear from the technical requirements of the total system that we needed to design houses using a module that would contain two rooms within a single structural span. Essentially, the exterior walls would be the only bearing walls in the house. A previous project for the design of a wood-box system for the Alodex Corporation had provided us with an opportunity to study the problems of designing houses with room-sized modules. A variety of different box widths and lengths would have been untenable even when working with a rationalized wood technology. This was avoided by the design approach shown in Figures 9.11 and 9.12. The single width of 12 feet was used with varied lengths on a 4-foot module in order to build up an efficient group of three-dimensional building blocks. Houses were built with six to nine separate boxes. The use of such short spans with any material as strong as the Fiber-Shell sandwich would be totally uneconomical, and joining so many units at the building site would be costly and increase the technical problems. Being able to build a house with few or no interior bearing walls allowed us to respond well to our user needs studies, and perceptions of a growing need for flexibility. The fact that the Fiber-Shell system made it more economical to span the whole dwelling unit thus became a significant advantage. The decision to make a prefabricated unit of this size, however, called for house-moving techniques to deliver dwelling units from the plant to the site. This meant limiting delivery to a relatively short distance and, in consequence, locating the factory close to building sites where large-scale projects could absorb the production capacity. This required the development of a manufacturing approach which permitted the factory to be easily moved.

The system was designed around the use of a 21 foot 8 inch width with lengths on a 4-foot module that varied from 12 to 32 feet. The job of designing a mandrel which could make the tubes was quite complex. The testing process was initiated with hand-made samples to be certain that the system would meet all the requirements. This task included dozens of separate tests of structural properties, fire ratings, thermal properties, and adhesion of the sandwich materials to one another, among others. At the same time, there were specific problems that had to be addressed with respect to the manufacturing and handling of a product of that size. A small prototype manufacturing unit was built to check the process. The cross section of the material was made full size so corners could be checked and the total process evaluated (see Figure CS 5.8). When this analysis was completed the full-scale tooling was designed. As had been expected, the anticipated cost for tooling was high and required a significant market for amortization.

The engineering problems were (1) to design a mandrel that would permit easy placement of the sheetrock, woven roving, resins, and honeycomb paper in their proper locations and (2) then to provide sufficient pressure during the curing process to allow a tight bond to form between the woven roving and the honeycomb paper. The latter was the key to the whole process; since the resins were heat cured, the bond could not be established if the surfaces were not in contact when the heat was applied. The cost for the process was so great that we felt that we needed a guaranteed market or a research grant in excess of what HUD was able or willing to commit within the framework of the Operation Breakthrough program. There-fore, other techniques of building the Fiber-Shell tube were investigated to determine if there was an alternative more in keeping with the market that was committed to the program.

An adaptation of a technique used to manufacture the plywood Bristol Bombers during World War II was found to offer the best opportunities for developing a system whose capital investment would be commensurate with the market guarantees provided within the Breakthrough program. It involved constructing the floor, walls and ceiling of the tube from panels which would be fabricated separately. The individual panels had a maximum size of 21 feet 8 inches by 32 feet and were made using a simple lay-up process. A layer of sheetrock was put in place on a jig, and then a woven roving of fiberglass was stretched over the sheetrock and impregnated with resin. The honeycomb paper was then put in place on top of the fiberglass, followed by the woven roving again with the accompanying resins and finally the top layer of sheetrock. In order to close off the panel at the edges and to provide a structural element for joining the panels together, a wood member was set into the honeycomb paper around the perimeter of the panel. The completely laid-up panel was then wrapped in a polyethylene bag, and hot air blown into the bag to set the resins. In order to assure adhesion between the various layers of the sandwich, the honeycomb paper was pricked with needles prior to its placement in the panel and the small vacuum pump was used to exhaust the air from the center of the sandwich, which pulled the materials together. A ½-pound vacuum provided the equivalent of a press that might need hundreds of tons of pressure to do the same job at very substantial cost.

The panels were joined with dowels and adhesives to make a tube. This tube had the same configuration as one that would have been manufactured on a mandrel with much simpler and cheaper tooling. One such tube could then be placed on top of another to provide a typical 1400-square-foot dwelling unit of the type shown in Figure CS 5.14 (see page 195). These units were developed in such a manner that when placed in a row housing configuration, there would be a double wall between adjacent apartments or when a two-story house was built, there would be a double wall between the floor of the top floor and the ceiling of the bottom floor. This provided effective acoustic separation and space for the placement of electrical and mechanical services.

Economic studies undertaken in the development of the system showed that while the use of double walls required extra materials for structure, wall, or ceiling purposes, the ease with which services could be put in place and acoustic requirements met made them more economical than alternative single-wall-type construction methods. The process for making and outfitting the tubes into complete boxes was sufficiently simple that it was possible to do the work in what was essentially a portable factory that could be moved close to the building site. An agreement for the construction of the Fiber-Shell system was made with the building trades which permitted totally outfitted units to be shipped to the site if it was 5 miles or more from the factory. This made it possible to use union labor at factory rates within the plant. All of the interior partitions, finishes, and services were put into the tube, along with a prefabricated bathroom and kitchen unit; the ends of the tube were then closed off, thus completing the dwelling unit at the factory. This made it possible to achieve considerable economies, and the units were moved and put in place by house-moving techniques. At the same time we explored shipping panels to the site for field assembly and completed a successful panel house as part of the Operation Breakthrough program.

The design of the Fiber-Shell houses for the Operation Breakthrough site in Sacramento is shown in the Illustrated History section. As part of the demonstration program, resins and sand were used as an exterior coating and tested to see how well this surface would stand up to normal weathering and especially to ultraviolet deterioration. The favorable results obtained by the chemists in accelerated weathering and other tests working with the then existing resin technology were not confirmed in practice. A few years later, plywood was used to resurface the exterior. Until better weathering of resinous materials is obtained, conventional materials should be used for exterior surfaces in all but test programs. Approximately 1800 units using this system were built after Operation Breakthrough and before the downturn in the housing market in the 1970s and unavailability of mortgage money brought the use of the system to a stop. TRW sold the system at that time to another company interested in its overseas use.

During the period when housing was being built in the early 1970s, the cost of Fiber-Shell in the U.S. Southwest averaged $12.50 per square foot in an open market situation, which was very competitive at that time. However, with the considerable reduction in housing and construction which followed shortly thereafter, the cost of lumber generally decreased by approximately 40 percent. During the same period in 1973, the increase in the price of oil, from which the resins are made, caused resin prices to rise. These two new developments indicated that the bright economic future initially projected for Fiber-Shell might no longer be valid. As a result of this, what was once considered an important technology for use as a back-up to the construction of wood-frame buildings became less attractive. The potential for using the same type of technique with other materials remains unexplored. The technologies of the Fiber-Shell system are of considerable interest and might well be employed with alternate material combinations. With lumber prices high and quality hard to obtain with second growth lumber, the Fiber-Shell process itself may be worth revisiting.

Illustrated History

The concept of developing a house-size tube to be wound on a mandrel was a direct development of the manufacture of rocket casings (see Figure CS 5.1). In this case a woven roving of fiberglass (a fiberglass sheet) was wrapped around the mandrel with honeycomb paper layered on top of this fiberglass layer, and then another sheet was wrapped around the outside. Figure CS 5.2 shows the honeycomb paper reinforced at the corners so that the tube could take moment loads and not collapse like a deck of cards. A shear panel was used for this purpose at a later time in the development of the system.

For the housing system, the inside of the tube was covered with a layer of sheetrock, which was set in place first. A woven roving of fiberglass was then placed on the sheetrock, and resin was then sprayed on. The honeycomb paper was then placed on top of the woven roving, and another layer of resin-sprayed fiberglass and sheetrock was added which resulted in the cross section shown in Figure CS 5.3. Figure CS 5.4 shows a cut of the material undergoing structural tests.

The basic concept was to create house-sized tubes which could be put together in a wide variety of ways with different infill components to complete the house (see Figures CS 5.5 and CS 5.6). Initially the work began with the winding of a room-sized unit, which is shown in Figure CS 5.2. The completed room-sized unit was tested and found to meet all structural requirements (see Figure CS 5.7). The room-sized unit tests plus the work done on panels, as shown in Figure CS 5.4, eventually demonstrated that the structural properties of the Fiber-Shell system were susceptible to conventional design analysis.

At this point, studies were undertaken to determine the best width of the tube and the most appropriate mandrel size. Since the tooling costs were very high relative to the projected market size, only a single width could be used. Once work began on perfecting the manufacturing process, production tools were designed and tested (see Figure CS 5.8). From this work designs were completed for full-scale tooling, and the costs were related to the market guarantees. The Operation Breakthrough market guarantees were insufficient to amortize the tooling costs and so the panel approach was developed to build the units.

The lay-up panel-making process is described in the main text. Figure CS 5.9 shows one of the stages, i.e., the spraying of the resin on the fiberglass from a traveling walkway. This figure gives some idea of the size of the largest panel, which was 21 feet 8 inches by 32 feet.

Figure CS 5.10 shows the fully layed-up panel wrapped in its polyethylene sheets ready for heat to be blown in. Notice the clamps which are spaced around the perimeter to seal the panel and make it possible to draw off the air from the interior, creating the vacuum to provide good adhesion of all the layers of the cured panel. After the panels were made and tested, a tube was constructed by putting the walls and horizontal panels together as shown in Figure CS 5.11 using dowels and adhesives.

The simple connection of the panels required cross bracing until the end walls were inserted or until a shear panel was put in place as part of the infill system. The end walls which close in the tube may be made of any required combination of materials. An example used later in our Breakthrough housing is shown in Figure CS 5.12.

Within the tube, prefabricated kitchen and bathroom cores made on a separate assembly line were installed along with the interior partitions, doors, and casework (see Figure CS 5.13). Internal services within an apartment or house were placed in the infill walls as much as possible, and ducts were placed between the boxes of the two-story units. When units were ready to leave the factory, they were complete except for site service connections (see Figure CS 5.14).

Figures CS 5.15 and CS 5.16 show typical one- and two-story dwelling units built on the Sacramento Breakthrough site. Figures CS 5.17 to CS 5.19 show typical exteriors and interiors. In addition to the use of the tubes, one Sacramento house was built with panels to determine the feasibility of site construction (see Figure CS 5.20).

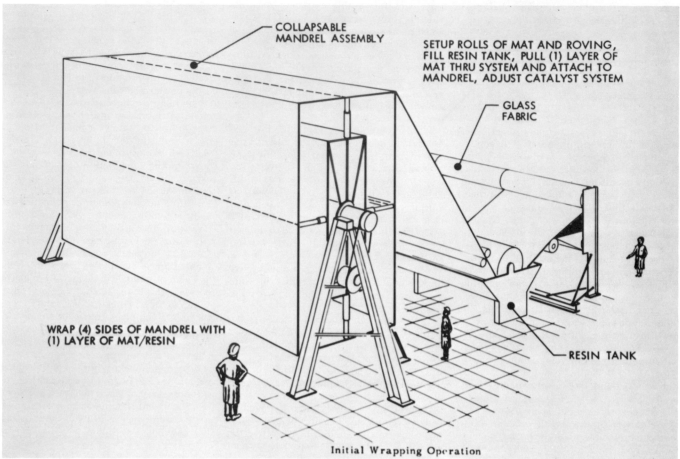

COLLAPSABLE MANDREL ASSEMBLY

SETUP ROLLS OF MAT AND ROVING, FILL RESIN TANK, PULL (1) LAYER OF MAT THRU SYSTEM AND ATTACH TO MANDREL, ADJUST CATALYST SYSTEM

GLASS FABRIC

WRAP (4) SIDES OF MANDREL WITH (1) LAYER OF MAT/RESIN

RESIN TANK

Initial Wrapping Operation

CS 5.1

CS 5.1 Typical tubes made by this process were to be over 700 square feet in size.

CS 5.2 Honeycomb paper applied to the inner layer of fiberglass before the outer layer is wrapped.

CS 5.3 The bond between sheetrock and woven roving and honeycomb paper is made when the resins set up.

CS 5.2

Sheetrock

Resin impregnated woven roving

Honeycomb paper

Sheetrock

CS 5.3

CS 5.4

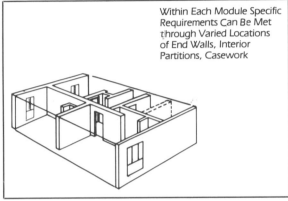

CS 5.5

Within Each Module Specific Requirements Can Be Met through Varied Locations of End Walls, Interior Partitions, Casework

CS 5.6

CS 5.7

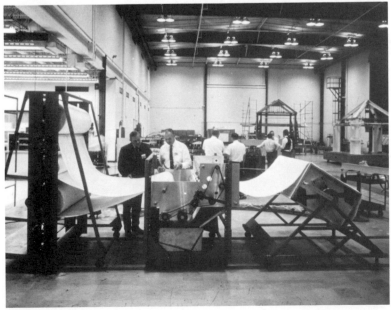

CS 5.8

CS 5.4 Tests were made to determine the structural properties of the material. It is interesting to note that the sheetrock which was not included for structural strength, made a significant contribution to the strength of the panel. This contribution was discounted because the building code doesn't recognize sheetrock as a structural material.

CS 5.5 The design of the tubes permits a variety of different sizes and shapes. Each different shape requires a mandrel which is both complex and expensive.

CS 5.6 Each tube is outfitted with a series of infill components to create the individual rooms. Services are provided as part of the infill package.

CS 5.7 The roof of the unit is loaded, and the deflection is measured with respect to the beam supported by the ladder.

CS 5.8 A sample production line was set up to test the process where the woven roving was impregnated with resin before being wrapped on the mandrel.

CS 5.9

CS 5.11

CS 5.10

CS 5.12

CS 5.9 This photo was taken during early developmental stages when the process used a hand-held spray gun.

CS 5.10 The wrapped and clamped panel is 21 feet 8 inches by 32 feet in size and is now ready for heat to be introduced to set the resins.

CS 5.11 The tube is made from panels and is braced until at least one infill panel is added.

CS 5.12 Infill with bay window.

CS 5.13 Prefabricated plumbing walls.

CS 5.13

CS 5.14

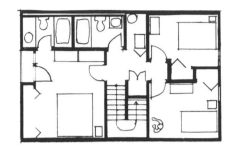

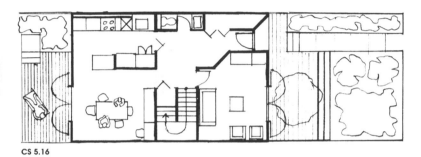

CS 5.16

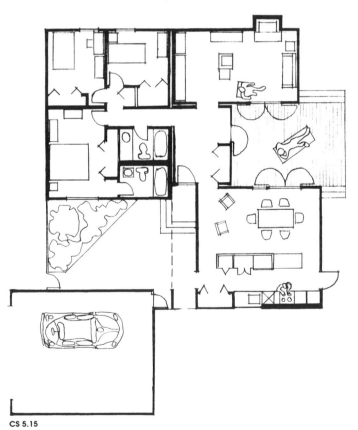

CS 5.15

CS 5.14 A two-box town house completed at the factory and ready for shipping to the site.

CS 5.15 Single-story house.

CS 5.16 Town house.

CS 5.17

CS5.20

CS 5.18

CS 5.19

CS 5.17 Close-up of town houses.

CS 5.18 Town house kitchen–dining room seen from stairs.

CS 5.19 View toward outdoor deck from single-story interior.

CS 5.20 House built of panels on site instead of in the factory.

CASE STUDY 6

GSA Building System

In 1968 the General Services Administration (GSA) began the development of a building system with work done at the National Bureau of Standards on performance specifications. In its earliest stages, we played a minor advisory role to the Bureau of Standards, but as soon as work proceeded, the development of the first-round building systems program was guided by a joint venture of Leo Daly Associates and Nolan Swinburne as system consultants. The program resulted in the construction of three Social Security Administration payment centers. As a result of this effort, the GSA decided to run a second program to continue and expand their efforts. The program called for the reorganization of the specifications as required to take advantage of experiences gained in the first round, to meet the new national perceptions about energy conservation, and to extend the scope of the work, which had dealt only with simple office buildings, to meet the full range of sophisticated needs as were embodied in computer facilities. Our firm associated with Leo Daly in a joint venture, and we were selected to serve as system consultants for the second round of the GSA program.

A primary purpose of this program was to establish a group of prequalified building systems on which the GSA could obtain competitive bids quickly and easily. This would make it possible to reduce the time required for design and construction to a minimum and to obtain fixed prices for construction very quickly because a combination of single-line drawings and performance specifications would be all that was required for competitive bids. This would enable the GSA to find out if the project could be built within the congressional budget or to change the project scope, if necessary, without spending much time and money. A major problem of

the GSA had been meeting congressional budget authorizations. The time from presentation of a project budget for congressional approval to its authorization and completion of contract documents for bidding was unpredictable and frequently involved significant delays. The escalation of costs therefore put many projects over budget; the budget would then have to go back to the Congress again and repeat the cycle, much to everyone's embarrassment. It was hoped that use of a systems approach could shorten the total process once congressional approval was obtained and increase the likelihood of performing within the established budget.

The first-round building program of three Social Security Payment Centers showed the feasibility of the systems approach. The second round, dealing with the Social Security Administration Computer Center and main office building, had as a primary objective establishing the basis for future bidding on projects in such a manner that first cost, life-cycle costs, design and construction time, and quality of the end product could be effectively controlled. In addition, there was a desire to improve and "fine tune" many aspects of the system, especially because a wider range of activities would be housed in the second round of buildings and the October 1973 oil embargo triggered a strong interest in energy conservation.

We began by reviewing the GSA's criteria that had evolved since the first program. In establishing a new set of criteria, we also took into account the results of that program. Whereas the first program dealt primarily with a straightforward office environment, the subsequent program not only had to meet the basic user requirements of the Social Security office building but also those of their

central computer center. In establishing criteria for the GSA, which manages the construction programs for various governmental agencies, we worked directly with members of the Social Security Administration to understand their basic needs and to define them in terms of environmental conditions, space requirements, and need for flexibility. This last item was particularly significant since government reorganizations were constantly taking place, due not only to interests in work efficiency, but because each time Congress passed a new bill that was to be administered by the Social Security Administration, there was some change in the workload.

The magnitude of the Social Security Administration's (SSA) tasks is constantly increasing. In many instances, the SSA finds new ways to get the same job done more efficiently. As an example, it was found that certain jobs that had previously required two secretaries could be done in the same time by one person with a microfilm reader. Other tasks suitable for a computer terminal previously required two microfilm readers or four secretaries. The space and power requirements varied significantly: a secretary usually required 70 square feet of space and a power equivalent of 5 watts per square foot; a microfilm reader required 50 square feet of space and 12 watts per square foot; and a computer station required 120 square feet of space and 7 watts per square foot.

The combination of changing work procedures, the responsibility of administering new legislative mandates, and related administrative reorganizations caused the GSA to pursue optimum flexibility. Our studies indicated that this could be done best through the use of an office landscape approach to office facilities. A landscape approach to the office assumes limited use of full-height partitions, if any, and calls for the establishment of good working conditions through the use of furniture, space dividers, and the proper design of environmental control systems. This makes it easier to rearrange both the workstations themselves and the neighboring space. The establishment of this kind of environment had undergone careful consideration and use by industry for a fairly substantial period of time.

There were many advocates of the approach but also many detractors. The main reason for disappointment with an open office-landscape environment was the difficulty in obtaining a good acoustic environment, especially in regard to speech privacy, without full-height partitions. Flexibility to adapt to changing work conditions loses value if staff productivity suffers.

Research, sponsored by the GSA, helped develop techniques for providing speech privacy between adjacent individuals not more than 10 feet apart. Prior to this program, the acoustic performance of available products required at least 19 feet between adjacent workers, or almost 4 times the area previously required to provide speech privacy. This phenomenal improvement could only be achieved by controlling the performance characteristics of the ceiling, space dividers, flooring materials, and the noises and sounds that came through the air-conditioning system. The generation of background noise was kept at acceptable levels via a separate sound system to mask unwanted sounds. This combination of performance standards for the many different subsystems of the total building system did the job. The implications are quite significant since optimum conditions for flexibility and productivity are no longer mutually exclusive.

These requirements were, however, very difficult to meet. The only way they could, in fact, be met was to make sure that each of the required components met specific and compatible performance standards. It is fair to say that the results could not have been obtained without the GSA serving as the catalyst. In addition to proving an appropriate environment, the service needs, especially for electronic equipment, were spelled out to accommodate the revolution in office technology that is now taking place.

While we examined use patterns and developed the user requirement statements for office buildings with the SSA staff, it became apparent that the first cost of the building accounted for a very small proportion of the total owning cost. The first cost, as mentioned in Chapter 7, typically equals 2 percent of the 40-year owning cost; operating and maintenance costs equal 6 percent, and staff salaries equal 92 percent. In developing user requirements, therefore, it was of paramount importance that individual needs for a beneficial environment be respected. This, then, provided a strong basis for a program which paid careful attention to the lighting and thermal requirements of the working environment and to the provision of appropriate networks for electrical, telephone, and communication services as well as to the

basic space requirements for the people themselves and their ability to individualize their workspace.

Once the basic user requirements had been determined, we began a series of cost-performance exercises to determine how to meet the requirements within the economic context established by the congressionally approved budget. This was done by analyzing cost-performance trade-offs for the various component systems of the building. With regard to structure, for example, cost studies showed that 60-foot spans for the computer center could be justified, even though the Social Security Administration officials actually wanted 120-foot spans. The cost of doubling the span reduced the available resources for other requirements to a point that it would have been impossible to stay within the budget.

Compromises were made all along the line before the performance specifications were finally determined. The final mix of cost and performance had to represent the best application of the available resources to meet the clients' needs. Shorter spans had to be balanced against better lighting, efficient life-cycle costs, good acoustic properties, etc.

At the same time as the program was being set, the procurement and construction process was being defined. The GSA was anxious to have a single source of responsibility for the total performance of the system and was therefore looking for a team leader, which might be a single company or joint venture of a number of companies, that would, in fact, take on this responsibility. This was required by the GSA in order to establish a basis of leadership for future systems projects which would permit a quick and efficient bidding process.

The resulting situation was one in which closed systems were bid that could be put together only in the patterns established by the team leader. GSA, therefore, obtained a group of fast and accurate bids for new projects. Such teams could then bid against one another on systems projects. A more limited basis of competition was also possible in which all of the systems components might not be bid. In a number of cases the GSA has bid interior furnishing systems in this manner.

As in the case of the SCSD program, it was considered appropriate to take bids as part of a two-stage process, first to ensure that the design criteria could generally be met and second to get the price. Bids received were well within the budget estimates established to meet congressional funding requirements, and the low bid system was followed. In this case, the GSA used a construction manager who had the responsibility of managing the entire project, which included obtaining bids for all the nonsystem work, seeing to the installation of the systems components, and making sure that the total job was on time and within budget. Nonsystems components were bid conventionally by the construction manager and accounted for approximately 65 percent of the total construction cost.

The GSA's concerns in the development of

the system were to bid those components which demanded innovation in order to meet the basic user requirements in general and those of the Social Security Administration in particular. The developed components had to be relevant to the needs of other government agencies as well in order to justify the program.

The design of the individual SSA buildings was in the hands of separately selected architectural joint ventures consisting of three firms in each case. For the Metro West Social Security Administration office building in downtown Baltimore, the joint venture team consisted of Welton Beckett and Associates, the Eggers Group, and the Grad Partnership. For the Social Security Administration computer center in Woodlawn, Maryland, the joint venture consisted of Geddes, Brecher, Qualls, and Cunningham; Richter, Cornbrooks, Matthai Hopkins Inc.; and Meyer, Ayers, Saint & Stewart. The individual buildings designed by these two ventures are shown in Figures CS 6.20 and CS 6.21. Together the buildings have over 2 million square feet, which provided the basic market for inducing industry to develop new products. Once the products had been determined by the competitive bidding process, the architects were able to begin designing their buildings with a reasonable concept of the products' final configuration.

The final design of those products, however, had to await the testing and approval program, confirming that they did in fact meet the basic user requirements. As in the case of SCSD, the testing program was an arduous one, with a prototype facility constructed for testing purposes. While this test period was still in progress, the government became interested in using the systems approved on a follow-up project for a Federal Office Building (FOB) in Norfolk, Virginia. In this case the components systems developed in the second round of the GSA program could be bid against one another without having to go through a full development process, since the basic systems had already been designed to meet the performance specifications. Actually, some criteria were changed from the previous SSA program, and old and new systems were given an opportunity to prequalify for bidding on the Norfolk FOB. The total process went quite quickly, and it is interesting to note that the successful team for the initial Social Security Administration program did not win again in Norfolk. The design was done by Vosbeck, Kendrick and Redinger. Our firm, in joint venture with Leo Daly, was selected once again as systems consultant.

As a result of this third round of bidding, there were two separate systems programs with two separate sets of manufacturers working simultaneously on three construction projects. Even though it had started much later, the smaller Norfolk project opened earlier than the larger SSA projects.

The program has resulted in new sets of hardware, now available on the market, which can meet basic needs for office facilities, whether they be public or private, and which fulfill the complete range of performance criteria and economic factors that were determined as being pertinent to an efficient office environment.

Illustrated History

Our participation in the GSA program began with the second of three rounds conducted by the GSA. The three projects of round one were under construction when round two began after the October 1973 energy crisis.

The program, therefore, focused on deepening our understanding of user requirements for a wide range of office and computer activities, energy conservation within a life-cycle cost context, and obviously the GSA's and SSA's concern with productivity. The interest in new office equipment was related to the low increases in productivity found in the office work place (Figure CS 6.1), which may be the result of higher investment per worker in the factory as compared with those in an office. If some redress of this disparity in investment is attempted, many more sophisticated tools will be developed for office use with significant implications for the future in terms of building and service flexibility.

The requirements for the whole system needed to be defined component by component to respond to present, anticipated, and unanticipated needs. Figure CS 6.2 shows the seven components which were part of the system.

In addition, the definition of the system had to be related to the GSA's procurement process for both the system's initial development and its potential for quick and efficient implementation in the future. The initial programs were bid with sufficient time for development. Once systems were qualified, bids would be taken for system components on the basis of schematic drawings only, thus saving much time and obtaining a quick response on costs, so changes in scope could be made if required. Figure CS 6.3 shows the following steps:

1. Systems are qualified on written submission.

2. Development work undertaken to prove specification conformance by test.

3. System components bid by those who have qualified.

4. The nonsystem portions of the building are designed.

5. Construction takes place.

The system bids, taken on a life-cycle basis, related to the formula shown in Figure CS 6.4. Beyond the cost of operating and maintaining the building, the comments made earlier in the book about mission cost are represented by Figure CS 6.5.

Figure CS 6.2 shows the overall system with its subsystems identified. Figure CS 6.6 shows the floor-to-ceiling height. Figure CS 6.7 shows the floor-ceiling sandwich which the system's designers could vary in height to provide the most economical solution. The addition of more space (Figure CS 6.8) would require an additional equalization cost for pipe runs, exterior walls, etc. A heavier structure would require a similar factor to equalize bids (Figure CS 6.9). The structural module size was established as 5 × 5 feet with the eight bay sizes shown in Figure CS 6.10. Performance criteria were established for all attributes of the structural system; an example is shown in Figure CS 6.11. Similar criteria were set for the heating, ventilating, and cooling systems with an example shown in Figure CS 6.12. A bid equalization factor was needed to respond to different energy requirements, which would depend on the design of the total system (see Figure CS 6.13). The lighting system had to respond to specific criteria for background, uniform, and task lighting, as shown in Figure CS 6.14. The space dividers included full-height and partial-height partitions (Figure CS 6.15).

All performance criteria were described and shown in matrix form so that the relationships could be seen. Figure CS 6.16 shows a simplified matrix and indicates how one attribute could affect the design of all the component subsystems. The design criteria were spelled out in "The Peach Book," which laid out the performance requirements to potential system bidders. In addition to spelling out all of the systems design and performance criteria, "The Peach Book" also defined the interface criteria with out-of-system components (see Figures CS 6.17 and CS 6.18).

Bids were successfully received below budget, and the development and testing work began (see Figure CS 6.19). The project is shown in Figures CS 6.20 and CS 6.21.

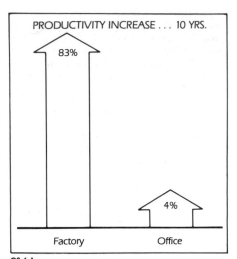

PRODUCTIVITY INCREASE . . . 10 YRS.

83%

4%

Factory   Office

CS 6.1

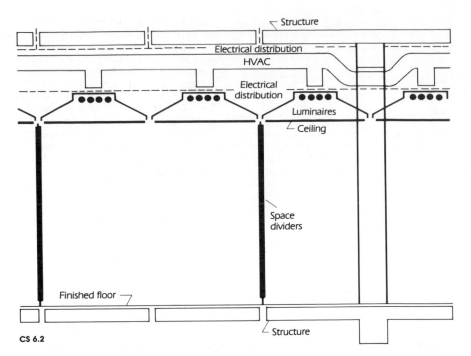

Structure
Electrical distribution
HVAC
Electrical distribution
Luminaires
Ceiling
Space dividers
Finished floor
Structure

CS 6.2

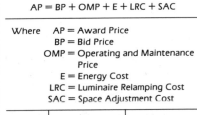

$$AP = BP + OMP + E + LRC + SAC$$

Where AP = Award Price
BP = Bid Price
OMP = Operating and Maintenance Price
E = Energy Cost
LRC = Luminaire Relamping Cost
SAC = Space Adjustment Cost

	OFFERER A BID (Millions of $)	OFFERER B BID (Millions of $)
BP	48.0	45.0
OMP	3.9	3.9
E	29.7	34.0
LRC	.07	.07
SAC	1.3	2.0
AP	83.0	85.0

Offerer A has the "low bid" despite a higher first or bid price

CS 6.4

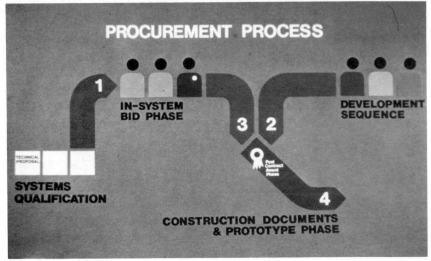

PROCUREMENT PROCESS

1 IN-SYSTEM BID PHASE

DEVELOPMENT SEQUENCE

3 2

TECHNICAL PROPOSAL

SYSTEMS QUALIFICATION

4

CONSTRUCTION DOCUMENTS & PROTOTYPE PHASE

CS 6.3

CS 6.1 Productivity rate improvement of blue collar versus white collar workers in 10-year period, 1965 to 1975.

CS 6.2 Visual depiction of the seven building subsystems that make up the GSA building system. They address structure, services, space division, and interior environment.

CS 6.3 Procedure developed to obtain new products for that portion of the office building where innovation was needed to meet basic user needs within an appropriate cost framework. Products where innovation was not needed were bid conventionally, and both sets of components were combined to design and build an office building. With the products now available in the marketplace, conventional design and bidding procedures can be used to obtain the GSA performance levels for any single building.

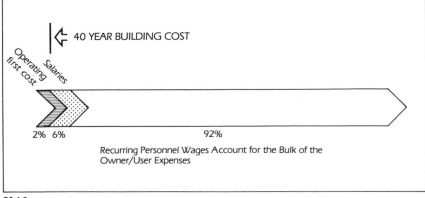

40 YEAR BUILDING COST

Operating first cost
Salaries

2% 6%   92%

Recurring Personnel Wages Account for the Bulk of the Owner/User Expenses

CS 6.5

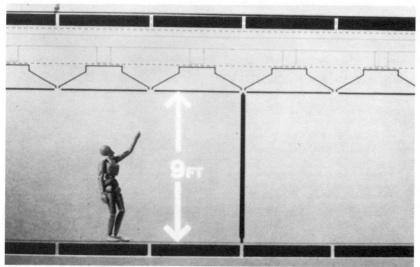

CS 6.6

CS 6.4 Abbreviated description of award formula for life-cycle bid evaluation along with the analysis of the two lowest bids received.

CS 6.5 The importance of staff productivity versus building cost must motivate anyone designing an office building to plan for an optimal environment for the people who will work in the building.

CS 6.6 A 9-foot ceiling height was established for the system.

CS 6.7 The floor-ceiling sandwich height was not fixed in the system criteria.

CS 6.8 Bid equalization factor for depth of floor-ceiling sandwich.

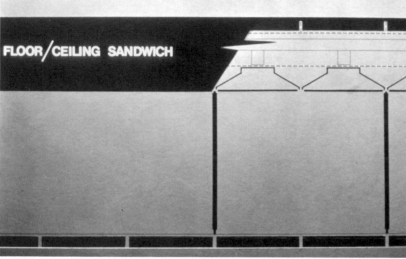

CS 6.7

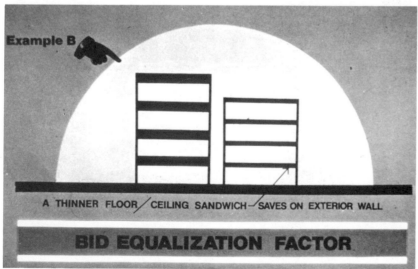

CS 6.8

CS 6.9 Bid equalization factor for building weight, which affects foundation costs. Similar factors were developed for all the critical variables so that when bids were received, different solutions could be compared on a valid basis.

CS 6.10 The system's eight structural bay sizes.

CS 6.11 Structural system performance was called out for loading vibration and deflection among many other factors.

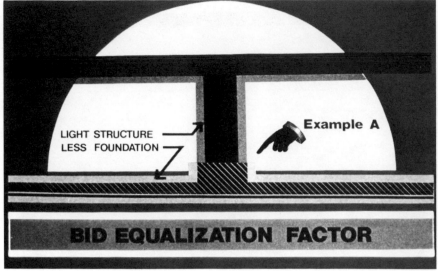

CS 6.9

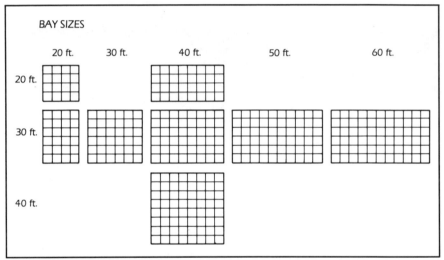

CS 6.10

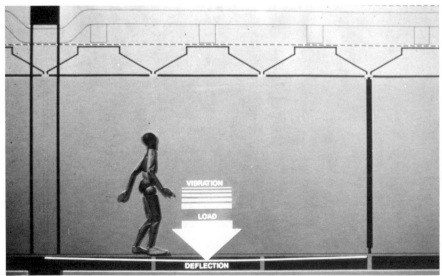

CS 6.11

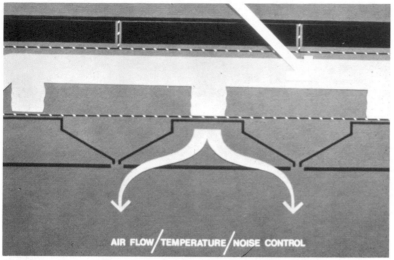

CS 6.12

CS **6.12** HVAC system performance was called out for air flow, temperature, and noise control among many other factors.

CS **6.13** Bid equalization factor for energy requirements of the HVAC system based on total system design.

CS **6.14** Lighting criteria were established for both uniform lighting conditions and for the use of task lighting with its attendant background lighting levels specified.

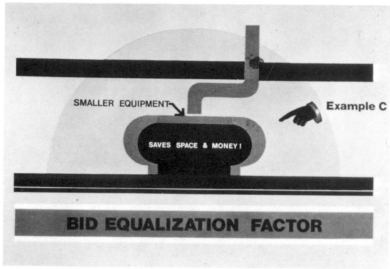

CS 6.13

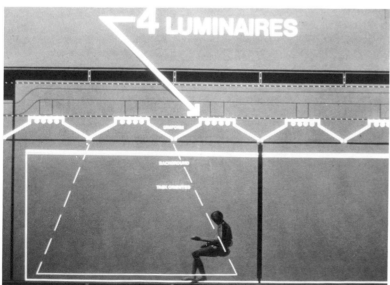

CS 6.14

CS 6.15 The development of a flexible partition and space divider system capable of providing speech privacy was the key to worker productivity.

CS 6.16 The acoustic environment is a result of the structural system's resistance to sound transmission, the noise generated by the HVAC system, how easily sound goes from room to room through the HVAC ducts and the conduits, or holes, created for electrical distribution. Sound can be reflected or absorbed by lighting fixtures and other ceiling components, by partitions (which can impede sound transmission into adjacent spaces), and by the floor covering (which can also reduce noise generated at the floor level). Providing an effective acoustic environment is not in the province of any single manufacturer. It depends on a designer understanding and relating all the components of a building to achieve the desired acoustic objective.

CS 6.17 Coordination drawing for exterior interface boundary plan.

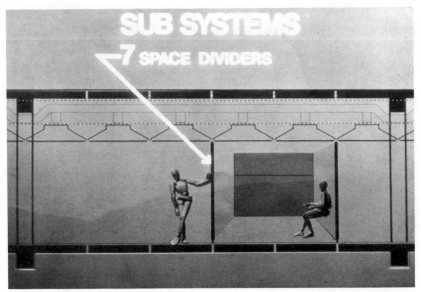

CS 6.15

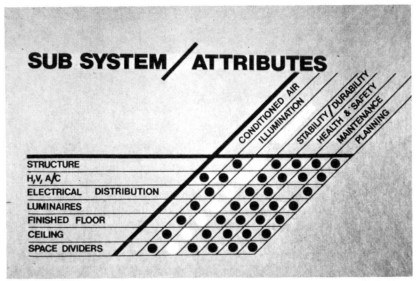

CS 6.16

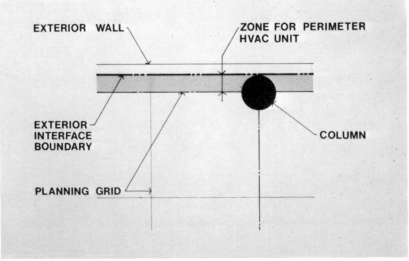

CS 6.17

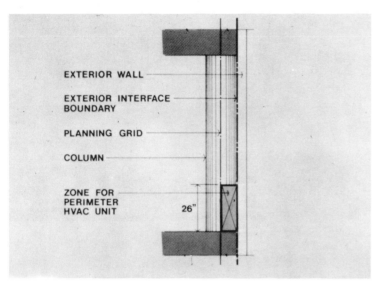

EXTERIOR WALL

EXTERIOR INTERFACE
BOUNDARY

PLANNING GRID

COLUMN

ZONE FOR
PERIMETER
HVAC UNIT   26"

CS 6.18

CS 6.18 Coordination drawing for
exterior interface boundary vertical
section.

CS 6.19 Mock-up for system component
testing.

CS 6.19

CS 6.20

CS 6.21

CS 6.20 Completed SSA Office Building of over a million square feet which bridges an interstate highway.

CS 6.21 The 700,000 square foot computer center just prior to completion.

CASE STUDY 7

Canaday Hall _____

The six previous case studies described how certain programs were organized and developed to provide new components to meet the specific needs of different building types and client situations. In each case, a specific need was defined in such a way that new technologies could be organized to respond specifically to that need. This type of opportunity is not the norm in architectural practice, which deals with projects on a one-at-a-time basis. Typically, a client looks for an architect to design a building in response to a particular need. In this situation, the market is not substantial enough and the time and dollar context is inappropriate for considering the development of new processes or components. Rather, the design of the individual building must use the information and technologies at hand. Thus, development of an internal database within the context of the architect's own office and practice provides an essential resource with which to approach any new project.

In Chapter 7, procedures were described by which a design office can develop its own database on cost and performance. This is of particular importance now when changes within the building industry, in terms of the character and cost of new products, continue to create a new and evolving design keyboard. The architect is invariably asked to meet specific client requirements within a constantly changing budgetary and technological context. The ability to do this effectively calls for the capacity to either normalize the otherwise fluid cost situation or commit to a design and then revise it in response to information supplied by cost estimators when the drawings are sufficiently completed to obtain a price. Even worse is the task of revising the design after overbud-

get bids are received. It is obvious that the latter response is not really acceptable, and it is therefore necessary within a practice to develop a process that allows for meeting client's needs within the prevailing dynamic situation.

The development of any database calls for careful records of past work so that this information can provide guidance for the future. To do this effectively, you have to organize the information along component lines so that exterior walls, interior partitions, or roof systems can be considered not as groups of different trades, but rather as component systems that can be compared in terms of performance. The critical point at which costs should be related to budget is the time when the design process actually begins.

You should be certain that the budget is sufficient before starting to design the building. The techniques for doing this have been described earlier in the book. It is of considerable importance to not begin serious design efforts if the budget and program are not in harmony.

Once the design of the building begins, the client will invariably assume that the budget is adequate: "If not, why is the architect spending my money?" Because the design must proceed to fairly substantial levels of detail before conventional estimating can check the cost, the client often builds up expectations which cannot be satisfied. This in turn leads to a variety of compromises which invariably reduce quality, performance, and services. Now that life-cycle costs are part of the planning and design process on every job, projects which meet the budget through the device of reducing quality are not acceptable.

So far, this book has concentrated on a series of programs and experiences which

played key roles in the formulation of the concepts expressed herein. Conventional design projects have not been discussed because of my belief that the systems process should not be evaluated in terms of a specific design with which the reader might, or might not, agree. Thus you should not think that a system approach is applicable only in those cases where a large program makes it procedurally and economically possible. This is not true and for this reason, the last case study will focus on a relatively small but significant design project.

Our architectural practice is based on the traditional design of buildings using a system approach to design work which has varied from projects ranging in size from the design of six staff housing units for the U.S. Embassy in Gabon to office buildings of a million square feet. In all cases, the understanding of the design context, the balance of needs and resources, and the thinking which underlies the systems approach are prerequisites to realistic design efforts. To translate the ideas and methods derived through work on specialized projects, we need an example of their application to a typical design project. Canaday Hall at Harvard was such a project.

One of our earliest jobs after the establishment of our office in New York City was to design a new residence hall for Harvard University in an extremely short period of time, working with a budget derived from FHA housing standards, which was obviously very tight for a building appropriate for Harvard Yard. The new commitments for the integration of Harvard and Radcliffe students called for a mingling of the two student bodies within the Yard, where all first-year students were hopefully to be lodged. Thus we had to obtain maximum density on the site. It was necessary to accommodate as many students as possible and to open the building as quickly as possible.

The program itself called for a living pattern which had three or four students sharing a suite of rooms, each with its own living room, and two such suites sharing bathroom facilities. These suites were organized vertically on each side of a central stairway. A student advisor was to be housed in each vertical unit.

Although the pattern was simple, given a tight site and the desire to house a maximum number of students, it became necessary to develop building configurations that would give as much perimeter as possible and yet work within the aesthetic and organizational framework of the Yard. Moreover, because of cost limitations Harvard suggested that we think in terms of wood-frame buildings, which limited building height to four stories because of code requirements. In order to accommodate the minimum number of students to be housed, the sight lines for all significant views in and out of that portion of the yard would have been interrupted.

While studies were being undertaken to analyze the capacity of the site to hold greater or lesser numbers of students, we ran a basic cost performance study on residence halls built with a variety of different materials. The database developed during the earlier URBS program provided a significant portion of the cost information for the analysis of different configurations and numbers of students that could be housed on the site within the budget. Wood, steel, and concrete construction were analyzed and costed; much to our surprise, we found that given the number of partitions that would be required as fire separations, the cost of concrete construction would be as cheap as wood construction. This enabled us to begin to plan on the basis of five-story construction for some of the buildings, rather than the four allowed by code for wood-frame construction.

This change opened up the design possibilities on the site, with regard to views on and off campus, so that the feeling engendered by the new building could conform with the established traditions of the Yard. Once this was done, it was possible to proceed with the design and meet the program. The ability to run a series of cost-performance trade-offs on a conceptional basis was critical; otherwise, we would have been doomed to failure in our efforts to meet both the housing and visual requirements.

A number of other factors had to be considered at various times in the design of the project. First, there was considerable concern about the acoustic environment since a traffic tunnel ended right behind the site and a firehouse was also located nearby, which constituted noise sources of unusual magnitude. The firehouse was a particular problem with its unknown timing and frequency of disturbance. As a result, the buildings were designed so that the living rooms, bathrooms, and stair tower shielded the bed-sitting rooms from the unwanted sound, and these were always turned away from the source of the noise.

In addition to organizing the design so as to reduce the amount of unwanted sound that would intrude on the students' bed-sitting rooms, the highest obtainable level of performance was set for the windows. We used the type of window typically used in airport hotels to minimize the sound of flying planes. Obviously, an extremely large part of the budget was allocated for windows.

Economies were realized in other portions of the building, such as the interior partitions between adjacent rooms, where simple sheetrock walls were put in place. A much more desirable approach would have been to line the walls with rough-sawn wood that would have provided a perfect surface for tacking or for attaching posters and banners to the wall. Over time there will be a relatively high cost for repainting and refinishing the sheetrock walls. But limitations on the overall budget required that the high performance level required for some items within the building be compensated for by relatively low levels on others in order to bring the total project in within budget.

The development of any project demands such trade-offs. The proper organization of information is essential so that both clients and designers understand the implications of these decisions before they are made. The impact on user satisfaction once the buildings are put into use is hard enough to predict even with good information, so one cannot be arbitrary. Otherwise, high maintenance costs related to a particular aspect of the building's design will be blamed on the poor judgment of the designer rather than accepted as a result of a rational decision, made with the client's concurrence, as to how to use the available resources.

The establishment of a database provides any designer with a framework within which to relate to the client's requirements at the outset of a project and develop a basis for the trade-off process. We have worked in this way in a wide variety of different building situations.

Illustrated History

The project began with tight schedule requirements: from programming to occupancy in 19 months. Costs were to relate to FHA multifamily allowances. The density was to be the maximum possible on the site. The programming determined the basic pattern of student suites.

The interior planning and design are a continuation of existing student living patterns. Three or four students share each suite of private bedrooms and a living room; two suites on each floor share a communal bathroom. The four or five floors of suites are accessible by one of the seven entrances, creating a community group averaging thirty students and one proctor. The typical floor plan is shown in Figure CS 7.1. In order to meet density requirements within a five-story constraint, views in and out of the yard were closed off as shown in Figure CS 7.2.

An analysis of the project's costs using the database developed within our office showed us what we could afford (Figure CS 7.3). The analysis of alternate forms of construction showed that the project could be built in concrete, which opened up the views, and the final design was accepted (Figure CS 7.4).

Figure CS 7.5 provides a bird's-eye view of the relationship between Canaday Hall and the Yard. Figures CS 7.6 to CS 7.9 show various views of Canaday Hall. Note that Canaday Hall was planned to relate to the existing materials, proportions, scale, and spatial sequence of the Yard. The eave line and roof profiles match those of the adjacent buildings and other dormitories. The courtyard respectfully shifts off-center to avoid blocking the light entering the windows of Memorial Church. The siting and orientation of the complex also respond to the noise generated by the traffic underpass and the fire station across from the Yard. The buildings are designed with the living rooms, stairs, and bathrooms facing toward the source of the noise and screening the bedrooms, which are oriented into the Yard. Figure CS 7.10 shows the opportunity for individual student expression within two of the top floor bedrooms.

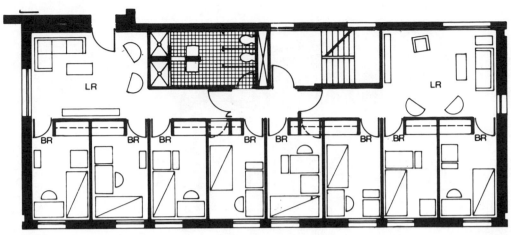

CS 7.1

CS7.1 Basic building block for dormitory, which was repeated 7 times to form the total building. The design also has all the bedrooms facing in toward the campus and away from the outside sources of noise, which are significant in this case.

CS 7.2 Site study model.

CS 7.3 Table of allowable costs from database. The budget was established for Canaday Hall based on typical FHA housing costs. Using our student housing cost database and escalating to the projected construction date for Canaday Hall, we saw the *Engineering News Record* cost index go from 988 to 1240. The cost of 26.65 was right at budget. This meant that we had approximately $2.33 per square foot to spend for structure, etc. By working with simple precast concrete planks, we were able to stay within our cost target with a fireproof structure of greater height and commensurately smaller footprint.

CS 7.2

Building Subsystem for Wood Frame Projects, Median Building	*Engineering News Record* Building Cost Index (Cost per outside gross square foot)	
	988 Database Project	1240 Canaday Hall
Below grade and ground floor	2.51	3.15
Roof system	1.58	1.98
Floor system	1.86	2.33
Partitions	2.49	3.13
Exterior skin	2.33	2.92
Heating, ventilating, and cooling	3.81	4.78
Electrical system	1.16	1.46
Plumbing	1.60	2.01
General furnishings	1.03	1.29
Total component cost	18.37	23.05
Installed cost including overhead and profit	$21.24	$26.65

CS 7.3

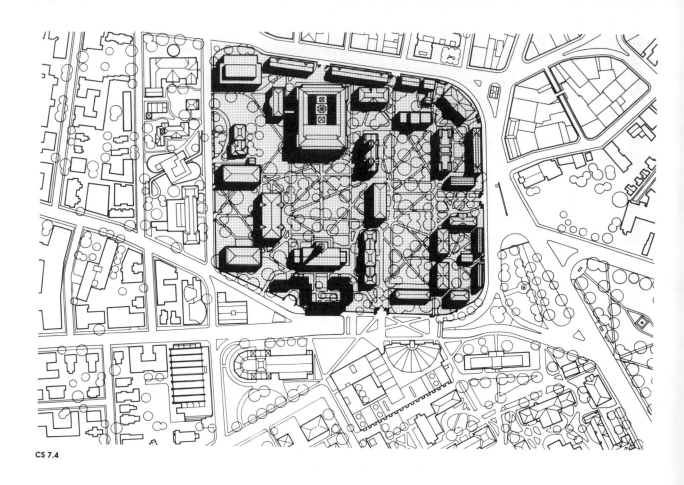

CS 7.4

CS 7.5

CS 7.6

CS 7.4 Site plan of Harvard Yard Canaday Hall was designed to tie into the scale of the Harvard yard buildings. As the site plan shows, the views in and out of the yard were kept.

CS 7.5 View into Harvard Yard from the air. Figures CS 7.6 and CS 7.7 show the entrance to the right of Canaday from the ground.

CS 7.6 Canaday Hall viewed from entrance to campus.

CS 7.7 Canaday Hall seen with its neighboring residential buildings.

CS 7.7

CS 7.8

CS 7.9

CS 7.10(a)

CS 7.8 Passageway between courtyards.

CS 7.9 Private courtyard.

CS 7.10 Interior views of students' rooms showing opportunity for individual treatment and expression. Student sleeping platform replaces bed on floor.

CS 7.10(b)

Part Four

Conclusion

Chapter Thirteen

Recent Applications of the Systems Approach

Overview _____

Since the time that many of the preceding case study projects were conceived and executed, the context within which a systems approach to a design might be exercised has changed considerably. The size and frequency of economic recessions, combined with changes in government support programs and tax policies, have succeeded in creating a volatile and uncertain market for the building industry. As a consequence, one of the main underpinnings of a systematic process to provide technical innovation and development — a large, aggregated, and *stable* market for the systems products — has become increasingly difficult to achieve. The result is that the adaptation of existing products, rather than the development of new ones, has become normal operating procedure for most building industry firms. The design of new products to meet basic and unmet needs, a natural and desired output of a successful systems approach, requires a level of continuity in the marketplace which our economy and public policies simply have not sustained.

At the time when many of our case study projects were being built, corporate vice presidents of research and development usually reported to the president of the typical major building industry manufacturing company. Today we find it more likely that the director of research reports to the vice president for marketing. The reasons for this change relate to the deterioration in our ability to project long-term building construction activity. A primary reason for this is that manipulation of interest rates and the money supply have become the medium by which the nation's economic balance is maintained. This type of manipulation directly affects the building industry and any other industry dependent on interest rates for long-term financing. When these rates are in a constant state of flux, long-term planning and, more important, long-term investment become increasingly risky. The result is a reduction in new product development and in overall technological advancement within the industry.

If economic corrections occurred once every 10 to 12 years, the building industry could probably handle it. Until approximately 1968, our experience was that escalation of building costs was something between 1 and 2 percent per year over the prior 10 to 12 years; interest rates were relatively constant and predictable. We had a very stable environment, much industry research and development, as well as considerable investment in manufacturing plant and equipment. Since that time, the environment in which we work has not been stable and these changes have had a major impact on our industry.

The development of a new building product, for example, typically takes 7 years from the decision to proceed until the product is developed, code tested, and ready for use. In an economic environment where a manufacturer has no guarantee that the market for his or her products will exist at the time they are ready for use, there is a clear disincentive for developing such products. How has our industry responded to these conditions? In essence, we have moved away from the development of new and more sophisticated building components and are increasing our use of commodity products. This requires far less capital investment in new plant and equipment, but also results in a lower level of productivity than might otherwise be possible. Additional labor at the site, in the factory, or both are needed to handcraft the less highly fabricated commodity products into a completed building, and our industry has exhibited considerable ingenuity in upgrading these products in terms of both design and process. Nonetheless, the implications of this approach with respect to cost and productivity are significant in that there is little opportunity for major gains from technological breakthroughs. This condition won't improve as long as our industry continues to act as a shock absorber for the national economy.

I am reminded of a story that I heard not long ago about the May Day Parade in Red Square, where the American ambassador was sitting with his associates watching the troops go by, followed by the armored personnel carriers, tanks, missiles, and foot soldiers. Finally there were 14 men carrying briefcases. The ambassador asked his aide, "See if you can find out who they are — is it the KGB?" And the question went all the way up to Gorbachev and the word came back, "No, those are our economists — you have no idea what trouble they can cause." In some respects I think it's unfortunate that *our* economists, the Federal Reserve, and the Office of Management and Budget have never had to submit an environmental impact statement with respect to the damage they do to our cities and to the built environment. It has been considerable.

Along with our economic planners, Congress has also conspired, albeit unwittingly, to destroy the building industry's research and development capacity with its lack of backing for any type of long-term planning for the built environment. Needs are discovered only when crisis conditions exist, and then programs are developed where what should be a test-bed prototype project actually becomes a full-scale, national program that has a prognosis for success based on wishes rather than knowledge. Within this context, our industry is put in a no-win situation. We are told: innovate, develop new housing technologies, energy conserving systems, etc.; the government will support the necessary markets and organize the finance and commitment

Figure 13.1 Dedication of the solar collectors on the White House by President Carter. These have since been removed.

Figure 13.2 View of Foxboro solar house. The project was successful but the products are no longer available and the company has withdrawn from the business.

because we need the innovation! Our industry then gears up and begins the work to create new products, only to have the market and finance commitment rug pulled out from under it again and again.

Given this type of environment it is hard to expect the building industry to maintain effective research and development activities. Creative people gravitate to aerospace, computers, electronics, or any other field where, if you succeed in your work, you have a chance of seeing it implemented.

Clearly, we do not currently have the proper framework in the building industry for innovation. In addition to market continuity to spur development, we need appropriate test beds to try and evaluate new concepts before they are promulgated. One of the problems with so many of the incentive programs that are legislated by Congress is that they don't follow an appropriate sequence of research, development, testing, evaluation, and improvement before full-scale implementation. We have tended rather to move very quickly to large-scale implementation because Congress doesn't really understand the need for long-term planning with respect to the built environment. They usually wait until instant solutions are needed to respond to major problems, and at that point an ordered developmental process, with appropriate opportunities for success, is no longer possible. The same congresspeople who would not consider legislating for the purchase of 1000 new airplanes before a successful prototype had been built and tested must recognize that our cities need similar attention.

Within a context that currently puts severe limits on responding to user needs through technical innovation, our firm, like the industry as a whole, has looked to design projects using existing components in the most effective way possible. Innovations have been and are likely to continue to be in the areas of programming, design, restoration, and environmental planning. Work done in solar energy (see Figures 13.1 and 13.2) has not been supported on a continuing basis. The three projects described in the following pages are representative of work we have pursued within this new context. Although they do not focus on the technical development of new products, they apply the same thought processes to the design of individual projects. This has always been important as the overwhelming majority of design projects are not and will never be vehicles for the design of new products.

CASE STUDY 1

Adaptive Reuse:
CUNY Law School
at Queens College, New York

This project was initiated by the City University of New York to build a new law school devoted to social interest. The funds that were made available were limited, and these budgetary constraints required the adaptive reuse of a 1950s middle school.

The program called for the design of an urban law school which would educate students to deal with a wide variety of social and urban problems. The project was designed and built at a point when major changes in the handling of information were taking place in the legal profession; there was an increasing emphasis on computer programs and the use of national information service systems. The very nature of the law library with its traditional dependence on hard copy was in flux. This situation, coupled with the fact that this would be a commuter institution requiring a workstation for each student on campus to integrate the students into the law school's culture, provided a unique design opportunity. In addition, the emphasis on social issues called for a higher than normal level of team work and interaction on the part of the students. The challenge was to create an appropriate learning environment for cooperative efforts at an institution that would be peopled completely by commuter students.

Dean Halpern and I toured many law schools and found that existing precedents would not fit his image of what was needed to forge a commuter student body into a dedicated and coherent entity. His organizational vision and that of a significant number of dedicated faculty members called for the creation of a home base for student interaction at the college, together with multiple opportunities for individual access to computerized sources of information. Close student and faculty relationships and being able to get groups of students to focus on critical problems were also required. The more traditional law school, with its emphasis on large lecture halls, hard copy libraries, and a campus-based student population with separate precincts for faculty members and their offices, did not provide a useful precedent.

The architectural design, as well as the academic program, emphasizes small group instruction in units known as "houses," which function as minilaw offices, each with its own conference space, working library, and computer facilities. This approach responds well to the physical opportunities and constraints imposed by the configuration of the 1950s middle school.

Students are assigned individual work and study spaces within a house, and each house, which consists of approximately 20 students, is supervised by a faculty member whose role is similar to that of a senior attorney in a law office. The houses are arranged in pairs, with support staff, research facilities, and office equipment analogous to that found in a small dynamic law office. Each house with its faculty leader may specialize in a variety of different subject areas in addition to the more traditional forms of legal education provided in the school.

Paul Goldberger of *The New York Times* in his review of the project wrote

What is most interesting about the houses from an architectural standpoint, however, is not their physical form, which is appealing but hardly exceptional esthetically. It is the statement the houses make about the relationship of a functional program to architectural form. Here, innovation came not out of an architect's predetermined ideas, but out of a genuine partnership between a client who thought and an architect who listened. Mr. Halpern and his colleagues were attempting to create a new kind of legal education and sought an architectural form that would be appropriate to it; Mr. Ehrenkrantz thought along with them, and together a form was arrived at that made sense. The rest of the building consists of a three-story library that was created out of the former gymnasium and a locker room below; a large lecture hall made out of the original auditorium; and central administrative offices, lounges, and a cafeteria. There is a relatively consistent degree of architectural expression to most of it. Here and there aspects of the original building, such as the glazed tile on the central corridor walls, peek through but the softly colored Ehrenkrantz interventions, far gentler in tone, predominate.

The plan of a typical student section is shown in Figure 13 CS 1.1 and a photograph is shown of the computer terminals in a house library in Figure 13 CS 1.2. Figure 13 CS 1.3 provides two views of the main library created within the old middle school gymnasium.

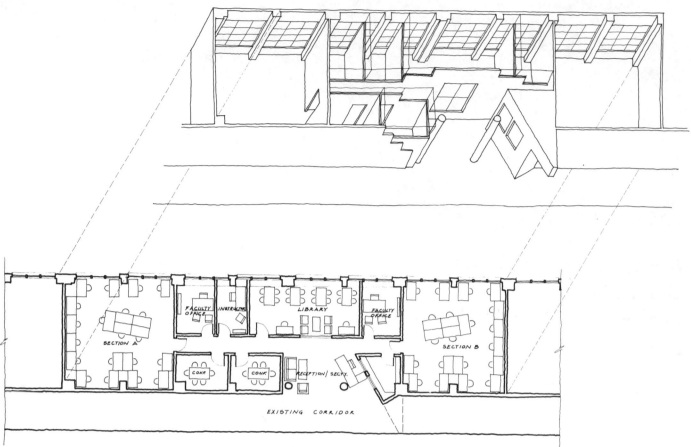

13 CS 1.1

13 CS 1.1 Plan of typical section providing a work-study environment with a dedicated place for each student.

13 CS 1.2 View of computer facilities contained in each of nine house libraries.

13 CS 1.2

13 CS 1.3(a)

13 CS 1.3(b)

CASE STUDY 2

Restoration:
The Woolworth Building

When completed in 1913, the Woolworth Building was the tallest building in the world and held that title for some 21 years (see Figure 13.CS 2.1). During this period of time the deterioration of the terra cotta skin reached a point where a program of continuous maintenance was necessary. By the 1970s the level of distress in the terra cotta made it obvious that new and more radical procedures were necessary to safeguard the public, the building, and the Woolworth Corporation.

The continued utilization of the building was dependent on either removing the terra cotta and reskinning the building or finding a way to reduce the deterioration of the existing skin and bring it back to a level of stability commensurate with existing norms for building safety. To remove the skin and replace it was expensive and would involve the displacement of all the inhabitants while the existing material was stripped off and replaced with some type of curtain wall. To keep the terra cotta, the deterioration would have to be stemmed and the cost would have to be less than replacement, as the requirements for continued maintenance would be greater than with a new curtain wall. The removal of the terra cotta from a historic building of such significant landmark quality obviously would have negative implications for the Woolworth Corporation which provided additional incentives for restoration. The company was dedicated to the preservation of the building and its own corporate history if it could be done safely and economically. Therefore, our initial task was to determine what was causing the terra cotta to fail and what could be done about it. Could it be stabilized and provide for a safe and continuing future within the cost context of replacement? Therefore we began with an analytic process to determine the feasibility and methodology for restoration.

Work began with the construction of a sidewalk bridge around the building and the cleaning of the facade to facilitate the visual inspection of the terra cotta. There were a variety of defects ranging from large cracks many stories high to pitting, hairline cracks in the glaze, bowed sections of the wall due to the rusting and related expansion of structural steel members, and numerous other types of deterioration (see Figures 13.CS 2.2 and 13.CS 2.3). The first stage of the work involved plotting the symptoms of distress in the hope of finding a pattern which would aid in the diagnosis of the building's distress (see Figure 13.CS 2.4). The possible causes included: rusting of structural steel and anchors, differential movements, wind pressure, water intrusion, thermal movement, expansion and contraction of the terra cotta, freeze thaw damage, and a variety of other possible causes of material failure.

There was no single pattern that could be identified by looking at the different facades to see which side or area had undergone the greatest number of freeze-thaw cycles and the greatest variations of expansion and contraction. We did find that the masonry backup for the terra cotta was wet, and that water was getting into the building over its entire face. The steel frame and many anchors showed signs of rusting which caused the skin to bow out and blocks to split. The maintenance activity which had been ongoing for some 60 years had not been able to stem the tide of deterioration. Reports of blocks which exploded outward during maintenance activities were further indications that major stresses had built up in the skin of the building.

Stress-relieving tests were designed for the project, and when run they showed stresses over 10 times higher than expected in a large number of cases. Later, material testing of the terra cotta showed that the glaze had a higher coefficient of expansion and contraction than the clay bisque of the terra cotta block itself. It was determined that after the blocks had been fired, the glaze had contracted more than the clay when the block cooled. This caused hairline cracks in the glaze, permitting the facade to absorb water. Masonry typically expands when it gets wet and contracts when it dries. The analysis showed the clay to be of poor quality, and the terra cotta, which expanded when it got wet, didn't contract completely when it dried. Then it expanded again the next time it got wet. Because the Woolworth Building was constructed before the invention of the expansion joint, and is, in fact, the largest building ever built without one, this continued expansion stressed the entire building skin, creating a particularly unique situation.

Once the apparent cause of the distress became evident we had to find a remedy which would have an acceptable prognosis for the future, even though there were few (or no) precedents to draw upon. First a series of repair techniques were tried over a winter in a nonvisible portion of the building to see how they worked over a period of time. Then we tried cutting the terra cotta blocks horizontally at every other course to relieve the stresses in each block on a portion of the building three bays wide and three stories high (see Figures 13.CS 2.5 and 13.CS 2.6). The results were monitored for a period of a year. The building did not restress itself during the year, and the technique was accepted as the basis for the facade restoration.

After the stress cutting, the distressed blocks were refinished, reanchored, or replaced. Then the horizontal joints were repointed. Some 500 different types and sizes of concrete blocks had to be fabricated and finished so they would match the terra cotta when it was both wet and dry. Many concrete blocks were required to replace ornamental terra cotta at various places throughout the building, and they were cast in latex molds (see Figure 13.CS 2.7). At the top of the building, the tourelles were so completely deteriorated that they had to be replaced. The cost of replicating the tourelles was so high that it affected the economic viability of the project. The replacement was, therefore, done with aluminum panels designed to provide appropriate profiles at the top of the building, as shown in Figure 13.CS 2.8.

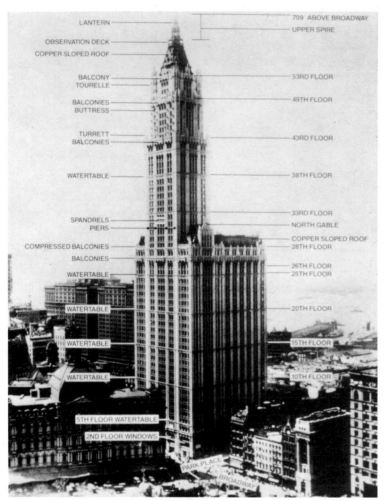

LANTERN — 709 ABOVE BROADWAY
— UPPER SPIRE
OBSERVATION DECK
COPPER SLOPED ROOF
BALCONY — 53RD FLOOR
TOURELLE
BALCONIES — 49TH FLOOR
BUTTRESS
TURRETT — 43RD FLOOR
BALCONIES
WATERTABLE — 38TH FLOOR
— 33RD FLOOR
SPANDRELS — NORTH GABLE
PIERS — COPPER SLOPED ROOF
COMPRESSED BALCONIES — 28TH FLOOR
BALCONIES — 26TH FLOOR
— 25TH FLOOR
WATERTABLE
— 20TH FLOOR
WATERTABLE
— 15TH FLOOR
WATERTABLE — 10TH FLOOR

5TH FLOOR WATERTABLE
2ND FLOOR WINDOWS
PARK PLACE
BROADWAY

13 CS 2.1

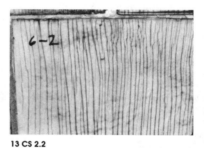

13 CS 2.2

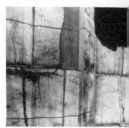

13 CS 2.3

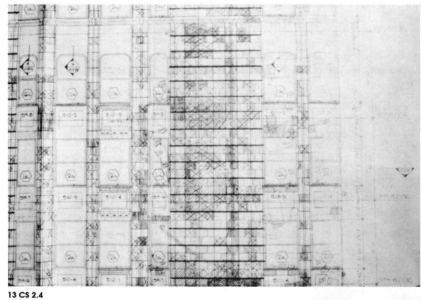

13 CS 2.4

13 CS 2.5

13 CS 2.6

13 CS 2.7(a)

13 CS 2.7(b)

13 CS 2.1 Woolworth Building.

13 CS 2.2 Extensive cracks in terra cotta.

13 CS 2.3 Bulge in terra cotta facing over steel beam.

13 CS 2.4 Documentation of facade conditions.

13 CS 2.5 Stress cutting of terra cotta block.

13 CS 2.6 Test section of building to validate stress-cutting methodology.

13 CS 2.8(a)

13 CS 2.8(b)

13 CS 2.7 Latex mold ready for concrete casting (a) and one of many such castings made to replace decorative terra cotta blocks (b).

13 CS 2.8 Woolworth Building with the new tourelles at the top (a) and a close-up view of one tourelle (b).

New Construction:
Port Liberté

Port Liberté was designed as a water-oriented community on the banks of the Hudson. The design approach was based on Francois Spoerry's work at Port Grimaud on the French Riviera. With that project in mind, the client wanted the housing to appear as if it had been built by many different people and not necessarily all at one time. On the other hand, the overall appearance was to relate stylistically to what New York harbor looked like at the time when small boats were common on the Hudson.

This program called for the design of a master plan based on the development of a network of waterways through the residential community. The site in Jersey City below Liberty State Park was flat and long neglected. Its pier had been used for loading ammunition on Liberty ships during World War II, and the site itself had the remains of trackage for the many trains which brought the ammunition. The site was in large part created in the early 1940s by dredging the main channel of the Hudson River for material to create the necessary surface area for the ammunition trains. Just to the west of the site below Liberty State Park is a shallow area of water that was designated as a Natural Area because it is a favorite resting point for migratory birds and was not to be disturbed.

The project was initiated at the same time as the environmental battles over the approval of Westway were being waged in New York City. There was concern over any project that might have an adverse effect on the striped bass fingerlings wintering over in the river. In addition, none of the projected New Jersey waterfront projects along the Hudson River had yet been environmentally approved even though some had been in process for over 5 years. It was against this background that we wanted to design a water-based community with some 2 miles of new canals to be carved out of the upland area of the site. The previous precedents in New Jersey for the design of projects based on the use of canals was very bad. Poor water circulation frequently led to the deteriora-

tion of the water quality in the canals, and the Department of Environmental Protection viewed prospective canal projects with a jaundiced eye.

Working with the developer and appropriate consultants, we saw our first task to be the development of a master plan and an environmental plan in concert with one another to ensure that the required approvals could be obtained. Critical to this effort was the development of an environmental design approach that called for us to view the site within its regional context. The key issues were not what we would do on site with respect to resident pheasants or Norway rats, but rather what could be done to enhance the viability of the weak links in the region's environmental chains.

As people displace nature in any region of the country environmental chains and linkages will be affected — some only slightly and others to a critical degree. We felt our responsibility was to be sensitive to the latter condition and to make a contribution by identifying and improving the situation where the distress was greatest. A design was developed in which the canal system ties together the two dead-end channels that bordered the site on the north and south. This will improve the water circulation and therefore the water quality within those channels. The canals themselves are designed to be nurseries for striped bass fingerlings, with the depth of water appropriate to preventing stratification and the resultant lack of oxygen at the lower levels. In addition, the canals are designed with riprap at their base so there are places for small fish to hide when larger fish come by to feed. The canal width is designed to promote a regular and consistent flow of fresh water into the canal system in order to keep it viable and in fact to improve the water quality of the entire area.

The establishment of the Natural Area adjacent to the site and the importance of the nearby areas as a resting place for migratory birds required that we study this aspect of the project in some detail. Our consultant on

birds was Joanna Burger from Rutgers University. She indicated that there was one species found in the area, The Least Tern, that is on the endangered species list. One of the main concerns with respect to the survival of the Least Tern is the availability of appropriate locations to establish a rookery. The Least Tern nests on the ground and is unable to protect its eggs and young from many predators. As a result of Dr. Burger's findings and recommendations, we provided an appropriate rookery location for the Least Terns. Dr. Burger, along with her students, determined the criteria for this "tern island" which we designed as part of the master plan. As an island it will be possible to keep it rodent free, and it is designed to discourage predatory water birds from wading ashore. It is purposefully too small for large birds to land on and no perches will be located nearby as further discouragement to predatory birds. We are hopeful that the Least Terns will take up residence.

In less dramatic ways we looked to improve the quality of soils at the water's edge around the project and to make appropriate plantings of vegetation to enhance the existing food chains within the area to support normal fish and bird life. This work included the development of an area which would contain brackish water and would be highly productive of nutrients to strengthen the food chain. Simultaneously, we looked at the environmental issues relating to traffic, pedestrian walkways, etc., as part of the total environmental program. We and our client believed that anything done to enhance the environment for flora and fauna would also be good for people. Being able to catch fish in one's backyard canal or to have access to controlled bird-watching locations enhances the environment for all. However, in certain areas we limited or made human access difficult in order to reduce the pressure on bird and aquatic life.

The master plan design shown in Figure 13.CS 3.1 indicates the scope of the total project. The outer ring of buildings encloses the community and gives it a waterfront focus. Canal condominiums predominate along the water's edge with townhouses on the islands. The town center, which is accessible to all, has a variety of housing units above the shops to provide the community with many different types of neighborhoods. Phase I is now under construction.

The plan was designed to take advantage of the view with the town center placed directly on axis with the Statue of Liberty. The outer ring was designed to enclose the project with the housing facing primarily inward to the new community and to the river. This also provides visual protection and separation from neighboring industrial areas and less desirable views. The neighborhoods are defined by the lower rise canal condominium units along the canals and the town houses which are located primarily on the islands. The canals curve and bend providing ever changing internal views as well as responding to the issues of water circulation and quality.

The buildings have been designed to provide a variety of appearances within a limited period vocabulary. The objective was to reduce the feeling of being part of a project and to emulate the way communities are more naturally built over a period of time. Considerable complexity is also built into the project as our client called for a level of plan variety which required different floor plans for the base, the middle, and the top of the multifamily buildings. This variety obviously enables the project to respond to the needs of many different buyers and helped to create visual interest. The result required a flexible structural frame which would support the differing plan layouts. The exterior walls were panelized for quality control and speed of erection, with conventional building components used throughout the project. Some typical plans and elevations are shown in Figures 13.CS 3.2 to 13.CS 3.4. A perspective view of the project is shown in Figure 13.CS 3.5, and construction photos are shown in Figures 13.CS 3.6 to 13.CS 3.9.

The thinking involved in the design of this project and in resolving the environmental and planning issues has much in common with the process used in the design of the CUNY Law School Building and the restoration of the Woolworth Building. The design process must always be capable of responding to the goals and objectives for any project. As a result, each project goes through a period of analysis to determine what is needed and what are the opportunities and areas of emphasis for creativity. The designer then seeks to provide appropriate solutions in line with the stated priorities.

13 CS 3.1 Site plan — Port Liberté.

13 CS 3.2

13 CS 3.3

13 CS 3.4

13 CS 3.2 Elevation of canal condominium residences.

13 CS 3.3 Elevation of town houses.

13 CS 3.4 Elevation of yacht club.

13 CS 3.5 Perspective showing Port Liberté at canal entrance from Hudson River.

13 CS 3.6

13 CS 3.6 Phase 1 construction photo at entry to canal system.

13 CS 3.7 Typical town house designs on entry side.

13 CS 3.8 View of phase 1 construction looking south.

13 CS 3.9 Town house and yacht club from across the canal. View towards the Statue of Liberty from Port Liberté.

13 CS 3.7

13 CS 3.8

13 CS 3.9

The R&D capacity in our industry has been severely diminished. Our ability to develop unique components to meet specific requirements has been greatly reduced and, in fact, many components previously available can no longer be obtained. The designer must now concentrate on orchestrating the use of a higher percentage of commodity products to meet the program of a specific project. It is a tremendous loss that these responsibilities are not being appropriately shared with industrial designers and industry.

A commitment to a sufficiently stable business environment and a protected framework for innovation are critical if we desire to redirect current trends to generate greater design freedom and economy. We desperately need more effective test beds and opportunities to develop prototypes with which we can experiment, make some mistakes, learn from those mistakes, and have a better chance of responding to significant problems, both functionally and economically.

Such current problems as homelessness and lack of affordable housing will not be solved simply through better design. They require a broader approach and much more substantial resources. Our inability to maintain market continuity for spurring capital investment by industry as well as the liability issues related to product development all militate against a sustained and effective effort to solve these specific problems. We do not plan, legislate, or prepare development strategies which would increase our ability to meet national goals and objectives with respect to the built environment. When an issue comes up we are more likely to address the symptoms or a part of the problem out of context.

If we are to compete effectively in a world economy, we must plan in terms of the requirements for the total system and not simply optimize on components of that system to the detriment of the end product. We must be willing to make commitments and devote the necessary resources to create opportunities for industrial development and increase the vocabulary which is available to us as designers. We must recognize that we need a national resolve and appropriate policies to provide a context for enlisting industrial research and development activity to meet housing needs as well as the needs of all the other building types and those of our cities' infrastructure. Designers can create civilized places with commodity products as we are doing today, but the percentage of the population that can afford them is too small for the health of our communities.

The filter-down process by which new buildings are acquired by the wealthy while the less wealthy move into previously owned housing and so on down the line will not work if enough people cannot afford the new buildings. Today a smaller percentage of the population can afford to buy a new house than was the case 20 years ago. If the level of productivity and capital investment in the building industry does not keep pace with the rest of the economy, the situation will not improve.

The assiduous support of research and development in the building industry together with capital investment in technology is not going to solve the problem by enabling everyone to afford a new home. Everyone can't afford a new car. But enough people can, so used cars are available to anyone who can afford to operate them. The differential reduction in cost that technology can help to provide is important. It will not do the whole job.

The systems approach to design is basic to any optimization process. We must seek to orchestrate the use of all our resources — land, finance, management, technology, and labor — to provide responsive buildings in appropriate settings within which civilized life can take place.

Index

About the Author

Ezra D. Ehrenkrantz, FAIA, gained his B.Architecture from MIT and subsequently received successive Fulbright Fellowships to work at Britain's Building Research Station researching the modular coordination of building components. Returning to the U.S. to teach and practice, he initiated the U.S. School Contruction Systems Development (SCSD) project that resulted in the components from which thousands of America's schools are contructed. For this effort he received the *Engineering News-Record* magazine's Man of the Year award. Since 1971, Mr. Ehrenkrantz has headed his own 100-member consulting firm, The Ehrenkrantz Group and Eckstut.

Credits